# Business Management

## for the IB Diploma
## Exam Preparation Guide

### Alex Smith

Cambridge University Press's mission is to advance learning, knowledge and research worldwide.

Our IB Diploma resources aim to;

- encourage learners to explore concepts, ideas and topics that have local and global significance

- help students develop a positive attitude to learning in preparation for higher education

- assist students in approaching complex questions, applying critical-thinking skills and forming reasoned answers.

CAMBRIDGE
UNIVERSITY PRESS

# CAMBRIDGE
## UNIVERSITY PRESS

University Printing House, Cambridge CB2 8BS, United Kingdom

One Liberty Plaza, 20th Florr, New york, NY 10006, USA

477 Williamstown Road, Port Melbourne, VIC 3207, Australia

4843/24, 2nd Floor, Ansari Road, Daryaganj, Delhi - 110002, India

79 Anson Raod, #06-04/06, Singapore 079906

Cambridge University press is part of the University of Cambridge.

It furthers the University's mission by disseminating knowledge in the pursuit of education, learning and research at the highest international levels of excellence.

www.cambridge.org
Information on this title: www.cambridge.org/9781316635735(Paperback)

First published 2017
20  19  18  17  16  15  14  13  12  11  10  9  8  7  6  5  4  3  2  1

Printed in the United Kingdom by Latimer Trend

*A catalogue record for this publication is available from the British Library*

ISBN 978-1-316-63573-5 Paperback

# Contents

Contents

# How to use this book

## Aims of the IB Business management exam preparation guide

This is an IB exam preparation book for Higher and Standard Level Business Management. The aims of the book are to provide you with effective support when preparing for the Business Management examination in the following ways:

- To set out clearly all the learning outcomes from the IB Business Management guide you can be tested on.

- To provide revision notes that cover all the learning outcomes you will need to know, understand, apply and evaluate when you are answering examination questions.

- To give you specific case study, illustrative and worked examples to illustrate the learning outcomes covered in the guide.

- To use progress questions and exam-style questions to develop your question answering technique.

- To develop your exam question answering technique by giving exam tips based on the assessment criteria used by the IB.

Using the exam preparation guide should give you a better understanding of the material in the IB Business Management course and help you to answer questions in a way that will give you the highest possible grade in the final examination. It should also help you understand Business Management as a subject in a real-world context and to think critically about the issues raised by the subject.

## Learning outcomes and assessment objectives

### Learning outcomes

A learning outcome sets out what you should know, understand, apply and evaluate when you cover each section of the Business Management Subject Guide. Only material set out as a learning outcome in the guide can be covered by the questions in the Business Management guide. If it is not a learning outcome, it cannot be in the exam.

The learning outcomes for each chapter are set out at the start of the chapter in the 'What you should know by the end of this chapter' section.

### Assessment objectives (AOs)

The assessment objectives specify the level of knowledge, understanding, application and evaluation students will need to show when they answer questions on the different learning outcomes. In the exam preparation guide, the assessment objectives (AOs) for each learning outcome are set out at the start of each chapter. The assessment objectives are set out in Table 0.1.

**Table 0.1**

| Assessment objective | From the learning outcomes students have to demonstrate: | Command terms | Example |
|---|---|---|---|
| AO1 | Knowledge and understanding | Describe, state, outline and define | Define the term 'short-term finance'. |
| AO2 | Application and analysis | Explain, analyse and suggest | Explain why an organisation's labour turnover might increase. |
| AO3 | Synthesis and evaluation | Discuss, evaluate and examine | Discuss the benefits and limitations of break-even analysis. |
| AO4 | Appropriate skills related to diagrams, charts and calculations | Construct, calculate and draw | Calculate a business's net profit margin. |

# Questions and case studies

## Emphasis on case study examples

Each chapter has business case study examples to illustrate the business theory covered. The illustrative examples are also developed into worked examples in the technical parts of the course. This particularly applies to learning outcomes involving (AO4) questions such as calculations and charts used in, for example, break-even analysis.

Case study examples are used in each chapter to develop the learning outcomes into real-world situations. The case study examples are used to give contextual case material that shows how business theory is used and applied by real organisations.

## Progress test questions

The case study examples are used with progress questions that test you on the learning outcomes covered in each chapter. The progress questions are all in IB Business Management format so that you are continuously practising writing answers used to test the different learning outcomes and in the way students are tested in the final exam.

## Exam practice questions

Each chapter finishes with exam-style questions based on the Paper 1 and Paper 2 Higher and Standard Level questions students will face in the final examination.

- **Paper 1** – Each section of the Business Management guide has a Paper 1 style case study used to test the learning outcomes in that section.

- **Paper 2** – These questions are based on individual case study organisations written in the same style as they would be in Business Management SL and HL Paper 2.

# Exam tips

Each chapter has two exam tips linked to progress questions and exam practice questions. The key theme of the exam tips is the way to answer questions in response to the assessment objective (AO) command terms used in the question. This is a key focus for practising questions to achieve the highest marks related to the assessment objective. An 'evaluative' command term, for example, is examined to AO3 level and requires you to write an answer that shows knowledge, understanding, application and evaluation to achieve full marks.

# Key terms

An important aspect of producing good examination answers is using precise business management terminology based on accurately defined key terms. Definitions of key terms are highlighted in each chapter by underlining the term and highlighting its definition.

# Business Organisation and Environment

# Introduction to business management

**What you should know by the end of this chapter:**

- How businesses combine human, physical and financial resources to create goods and services (AO2)

- The role of the business functions: human resources, finance and accounts, marketing and operations (AO2)

- The nature of the primary, secondary, tertiary and quaternary sectors of the economy (AO2)

- The impact of changes in the primary, secondary, tertiary and quaternary sectors on business activity (AO2)

- The role of entrepreneurship and intrapreneurship in overall business activity (AO3)

- Reasons why entrepreneurs start up a business or an enterprise (AO2)

- Problems that a new business or enterprise may face (AO2)

- The elements of a business plan (AO2).

**Chapter illustrative example**
A business that runs a chain of pizza restaurants

# Combining resources to create goods and services

## Human resources

**Key term**
**Businesses** are organisations that bring together resources to produce goods and services that are sold to customers.

Human resources are the people aspect of a **business**. This is the:

- direct labour that is involved in producing the good or service, such as the people who serve in the pizza restaurant in the example

- indirect labour that supports the running of the organisation like the pizza business's accountants

- managers that direct the organisation, such as the finance director of the pizza business who oversees its use of financial resources.

## Financial resources

Financial resources are the funds a business has to facilitate its organisation. Finance involves the:

- day-to-day funds used by a business to pay wages and buy raw materials

- long-term finance needed for investment in plant and machinery, such as opening a new pizza restaurant outlet

- recording of business profits and asset value.

## Physical resources

Physical resources are the capital of the business in the form of:

- buildings, such the outlets in the pizza business example

- equipment, such as the cookers used by the pizza business

- fixtures and fittings in the pizza restaurant outlets.

# The role of the main business functions

Business functions are the different aspects of business operations and they can be put into four different areas:

## Human resources

Human resource management (HRM) is the way in which a business manages the people in its organisation. This involves things such as how a business's employees are recruited, trained, motivated and promoted.

## Finance

The finance department in an organisation has to make sure the business has the funds to operate on a day-to-day basis as well as having the finance to invest in its future operations. This area of the organisation is also responsible for producing the business accounts and for budgeting.

## Marketing

The marketing department of an organisation is responsible for discovering, predicting and satisfying the needs and desires of consumers in a profitable way. It involves managing market research, product development, pricing, distribution and promotion.

## Operations

Operations management is the way that organisations manage physical resources. Businesses want to manage their stock, equipment, machinery and buildings in the most efficient way they can.

# 1.1

## CASE STUDY

**Apple**
Successful businesses manage their resources to produce goods and services that provide the income and profits allowing it to function. Apple exists as one of the biggest private organisations in the world, valued at $700 billion. It achieved a profit of $53 billion in 2015 because it manages its resources successfully to produce goods and services that so many people want to buy.

**Progress questions**

1 Define the term 'business'. [2 marks]

2 Outline two resources involved in Apple's production of goods and services. [4 marks]

3 Describe two of Apple's business functions. [4 marks]

# Different business sectors

## Primary

Businesses that operate in the primary sector of the economy are involved in agriculture, forestry, fishing and mining. The goods produced by primary sector businesses are sold to manufacturing firms in the secondary sector to produce goods sold to consumers. An example of a firm in the primary sector is a mining company.

## Secondary

The secondary sector of the economy is made up of manufacturing organisations that make goods to sell to other businesses and final consumers. Secondary sector organisations range from car manufacturers to makers of computer software.

## Tertiary

Firms in the tertiary sector provide services to consumers and other businesses. This involves organisations such as restaurants, retailers, insurance companies and banks. The pizza business example is part of the tertiary sector.

## Quaternary

Organisations involved in the quaternary sector of the economy are businesses focused on information technology. A social media business, for example, is part of the quaternary sector.

## Impact of sectoral change on business activity

Over time, the balance of industrial structure in an economy changes as that economy develops. Economic development generally means that there is shift in the balance of business operations from the primary sector to the secondary sector and from the secondary sector to the service sector.

The success of the example fast food restaurant in the service sector is one such business that might flourish as sectoral change takes place.

# Role of entrepreneurship and intrapreneurship in business activity

## Entrepreneurship

**Key term**
**An entrepreneur** is an individual that sees a business opportunity in the form of consumer want and then brings together human, physical and financial resources to produce a product to satisfy that want.

The founder of the pizza chain restaurant example is an **entrepreneur**.

## Intrapreneurship

**Key term**
**An intrapreneur** is someone who works within a business in an entrepreneurial way to develop a firm's products to attract new consumers.

**Gmail**

Google is a US-based multinational technology business that specialises in internet-related services including its search engine, cloud computing and software. The business was founded by entrepreneurs Larry Page and Sergey Brin in 1996. Gmail is the free email facility provided by Google. It was developed by Paul Buchheit in 2001 when he was working for Google and is an example of successful intrapreneurship.

**Progress questions**

1 Define the term 'intrapreneur'. [2 marks]

2 Describe the business sector Google operates in. [2 marks]

3 Explain two roles of the entrepreneurs who started Google. [4 marks]

**Exam tip**

For 'definition' command term questions, give a precise meaning of the term.

# Reasons for starting up a business or an enterprise

These are some of the reasons entrepreneurs might start a business:

• **Redundancy** – People frequently start businesses after losing a job and see running a start-up business as an opportunity for employment.

• **Independence** – New businesses are often started by individuals who want to control their own destiny and not be constrained by an employer.

• **Business opportunity** – Entrepreneurs often spot a market that is potentially profitable and then start a business to reach that market.

• **Greater income** – Starting your own business is often a way to earn more money than would be possible working for a company.

The pizza business example was started by two people who worked for another restaurant chain and wanted to be independent.

# Problems that a new business or enterprise may face

Any new business will face challenges when it enters a market. Some problems faced may include:

• **Competition** – Established businesses in a market will work hard to keep their existing customers and competitors will always try to attract any new buyers in a market.

• **Access to finance** – Because so many new businesses fail, banks and other lenders are reluctant to lend to new firms. This can mean they struggle to get finance for investment in capital and funds for working capital in order to support the day-to-day running of the business such as paying wages and suppliers.

• **Regulation** – Markets always have rules and regulations that new firms have to follow when they start up. The pizza business, for example, had to deal with licences, product standards, health and safety and employment law.

• **Information** – New businesses often lack essential data and records when they enter a market. Information systems have to be set up to generate information, for example, about consumers in the market, finance data for tax and industry regulations.

• **Management experience** – Starting a new business is often very difficult and requires considerable management skills. The process of setting up and then guiding a firm through the early part of its life can be a very complex one.

- **Changing markets** – The business environment is constantly changing: new competitors, tastes of consumers, regulations and the macroeconomic environment can move against a new enterprise.

---

## CASE STUDY

### CliniCloud

CliniCloud is an Australian health technology business that was started by physicians Hon Weng Chong and Andrew Lin. The firm's product is technology-based medical kits to manage and monitor people's health from home. Putting together a business plan was a key part of raising the $5 million needed to start their business.

### Progress questions

1  Outline two reasons why the owners of CliniCloud might have started the business. [4 marks]

2  Analyse two problems the owners of CliniCloud might have faced when starting their business. [6 marks]

---

## The elements of a business plan

**Business plans** are a very important planning tool for the successful management of a new business as well as providing important information for different stakeholders. An effective business plan was, for example, a crucial part of the pizza business securing a bank loan.

---

### Key term

**A business plan** is a formal document that describes the business, sets out its objectives and strategy, identifies its market and provides its financial forecasts.

## Elements

- **Business description** – Sets out the nature of the business in terms of size, product, target market and mission.

- **Competitive analysis** – Looks at the competing businesses in the market and alternative products available.

- **Business objectives** – These are the overall mission of the business and the strategic goals the firm needs to achieve to reach its mission.

- **Marketing strategy** – This sets out the market research the business has done and ways the marketing mix is going to be successfully set to sell the product to its target consumers.

- **Design and development plan** – This part of the business plan gives specific information on the processes involved in designing and developing the product.

- **Operations and management plan** – This is about how the product is going to be produced or manufactured and delivered or provided to the consumer.

- **Financial forecasts** – This section is critical for funding a new business. This involves setting out funds needed to cover both set-up and operating costs as well as forecasting the funds generated through selling the product.

---

# Exam practice questions

## Paper 1 question (HL and SL)

### Fine Olive Company

The Fine Olive Company is a Greek olive-grower that produces and markets its own high-quality olives and olive oil. The business was started by Mimis Manolas in 2009 after he was made redundant from his job working as a civil servant. He was able to buy the small farm and the equipment required from money loaned to him by his parents. He also needed to obtain a bank loan, which required a detailed business plan.

**a**  Define the following terms:

   **i**  Business plan [2 marks]

   **ii**  Entrepreneur [2 marks]

**b** Analyse two difficulties Mimis Manolas might have encountered when he started the Fine Olive Company. [6 marks]

[Total 10 marks]

## Paper 2 question (HL and SL)

### A business opportunity in Rome

Luca Abatangelo works for a national chain of estate agents in Rome. He is looking to open his own estate agency selling and renting residential property in the city.

The property market in Rome is beginning to grow after a period of stagnation. There is strong demand for properties to buy and rent. This has led to an increase in new businesses entering the market particularly at the top (luxury) end of the market.

There is a considerable amount of regulation in the Italian property market and this is something Luca will have to deal with. However, this is also a market where being well known is a distinct advantage and this will work to Luca's benefit.

**a** Identify two business functions that might be part of Luca's new estate agency business. [2 marks]

**b** Explain two reasons why Luca might want to start his own estate agency business. [4 marks]

**c** Explain two problems Luca might encounter as he enters Rome's property market. [4 marks]

**d** Discuss the usefulness to Luca of producing a business plan when starting his new estate agency business. [10 marks]

[Total 20 marks]

**Exam tip**
The 'discuss' command term means offering a considered and balanced review that includes a range of arguments of the factors associated with producing a business plan.

# Types of organisations

**What you should know by the end of this chapter:**

- Distinction between the private and the public sectors (AO2)

- Main features of the following types of for-profit (commercial) organisations: sole traders, partnerships, companies and corporations (AO3)

- Main features of the following types of not-for-profit social enterprises: cooperatives, microfinance providers, public–private partnerships (PPPs) (AO3)

- Main features of the following types of non-profit social enterprises: non-governmental organisations (NGOs), charities (AO3).

**Chapter illustrative example**
A state funded and managed hospital

# The private and the public sectors

## The private sector

**Key term**

**The private sector** is made of businesses and organisations owned and controlled by individuals or groups of individuals that are not under state control.

The private sector is made up of:

- **For-profit (commercial) organisations** that range from the largest multinational companies down to the smallest sole traders. The profit the business makes goes to its owners or shareholders.

- **Not-for-profit organisations** use their surplus revenue over cost to finance their objectives or mission. Examples might be housing charities, environmental organisations and sporting organisations.

## The public sector

**Key term**

**The public sector** is made up of organisations that are primarily financed and controlled by a country's government.

The public sector is made up of:

- **National organisations** where central government appoints managers and directors to run the organisation. They are often funded through government tax revenue and from revenue generated by the organisation. The hospital example is part of the public sector.

- **Local organisations** often controlled and funded by regional governments. These tend to be locally-based services such as waste disposal, schools and leisure centres. The hospital example is a locally-based organisation.

## CASE STUDY

**British Airways**

British Airways was formed by the UK government in 1974 as a public sector organisation owned and managed by the state. Any surplus revenue over cost that BA made was either returned to the UK government or reinvested in the airline itself. In 1987, the UK government privatised BA and it became a private sector business. Shares in BA were sold by the government to private individuals.

**Progress questions**

1. Define the term 'private sector business'. [2 marks]

2. Outline two characteristics of public sector businesses. [4 marks]

3. Analyse two benefits to British Airways of becoming a private sector business. [6 marks]

**Exam tip**

This 'outline' command term means giving a brief account or summary of the characteristics of public sector businesses.

# Features of different for-profit organisations

## Sole traders

**Key term**

**A sole trader** is an organisation owned and controlled by a single person.

**Sole traders' strengths:**

- small flexible organisations that can quickly react to change

- single owner means quick decision-making

- owner keeps and has access to all the profits and funds generated if the business is partly or wholly sold.

**Sole traders' weaknesses:**

- limited access to finance

- do not have the benefit of expertise from partners or joint owners

- as small businesses they miss out on economies of scale.

## Partnerships

**Key term**
**A partnership** is a business where two or more individuals jointly own and take responsibility for the enterprise.

Partners share the decision-making process and the profits made by the organisation.

**Partnerships' strengths:**

- organisations are often small enough for flexible decision-making

- partners bring different expertise to the organisation to help decision-making

- finance from partners increases the funds available to the organisation.

**Partnerships' weaknesses:**

- having more people involved in strategy can slow down the decision-making process

- there can be conflicts between partners

- profits have to be shared between partners.

## Private companies

**Key term**
**A private company** is a business that has shareholders who are invited to buy shares in the business by the existing owners.

The shares of a private company are not traded on a stock market. They have limited liability where shareholders are not personally required to pay any outstanding debts of the company if it goes bankrupt.

**Private company strengths:**

- access to additional finance through shareholders

- as the business increases in size, it gains economies of scale

- wide access to expertise through more shareholders.

**Private company weaknesses:**

- as more shareholders join the business, the control of existing shareholders is reduced

- with more shareholders, there is more opportunity for conflict between them

- profits need to be shared out between more shareholders.

## Public limited companies

**Key term**
**Public limited companies (PLCs)** are private sector businesses that sell their shares on a stock exchange to private investors.

Anyone is able to buy shares in a **Public limited company** and the shares are traded freely on a stock exchange.

**PLC strengths:**

- selling shares on a stock exchange can generate large amounts of funds for the business

- PLCs are often large businesses that have access to significant economies of scale

- there is limited liability for shareholders.

**PLC weaknesses:**

- new shareholders can affect strategic decision-making of the business

- there is the threat of an unwanted takeover if shares are freely traded

- profits are shared among a larger group of shareholders.

## CASE STUDY

### Twitter

Twitter was started in July 2006 by a partnership between Jack Dorsey, Evan Williams, Biz Stone and Noah Glass. By May 2015, Twitter had more than 500 million users and a revenue of $2.21 billion. It is rumoured that the Twitter concept came out of a day-long brainstorming session led by Jack Dorsey. In 2013, Twitter sold shares on the New York stock exchange and became a PLC.

### Progress questions

1 Define the term 'partnership'. [2 marks]

2 Explain two advantages to Twitter of being a partnership. [4 marks]

3 Evaluate Twitter's decision to become a PLC. [10 marks]

# Features of not-for-profit social enterprises

## Cooperatives

**Key term**

A **cooperative** is an organisation jointly owned by a group of people (members) who democratically run the organisation to meet the needs and aspirations of its members.

Each member of the **cooperative** has an equal vote on how the cooperative is managed.

**Strengths of cooperatives:**

- the democratic decision-making model motivates the employees of the enterprise

- income generated by the organisation goes to the members and motivates them

- income can be reinvested in the enterprise guided by its members.

**Weaknesses of cooperatives:**

- one member, one vote can make the decision-making process slow

- each member having equal control might limit the opportunity to raise funds from a big investor

- cooperatives struggle to attract the best managers because managers do not have the control they might want.

# Microfinance providers

**Key term**

**Microfinance** is providing financial services to poor and low-income customers who do not have access to normal banking services.

**Microfinance** providers offer loans, overdrafts and financial advice. Nobel Prize winner Dr Muhammad Yunus started microfinance by making loans to poor women in the village of Jobra, Bangladesh and went on to start the microfinance Grameen Bank in 1983.

**Strengths of microfinance:**

- low cost, accessible loans to people on low incomes

- business advice to borrowers

- empowerment of small business owners to control their working lives.

**Weaknesses of microfinance:**

- interest costs can be quite high because of the relatively high administrative costs of small loans

- some low-income people may not be able to repay the loans

- larger businesses need bigger loans than those offered by microfinance.

## Public–private partnerships

**Key term**
**Public–private partnerships (PPPs)** are where a public sector organisation has a contract with a private sector business to support the provision of a public service.

The hospital example has received private funds and support towards the redevelopment of part of the hospital.

There are three types of **public–private partnerships (PPP)** arrangements:

1 **Government funded** – Where the state provides the finance to set up the organisation and it is managed by a private sector firm.
2 **Private sector funded** – Where a private sector organisation provides the funds to set up and fund the public sector organisation but it is then managed by the government.
3 **Government directed but with private sector finance and management** – Where the government facilitates private businesses to set up and run public sector projects.

**Strengths of PPPs:**

- provides private funding for projects that may not otherwise happen and avoids higher rates of taxation

- private expertise means projects and services are run more efficiently

- government involvement in projects and services means they are run in the public interest.

**Weaknesses of PPPs:**

- private business will look to make a profit on a project or service that may be at the expense of public service

- conflict of cultures between government employees and private sector employees, particularly in management

- private businesses might fail during a project and leave it unfinished.

# Features of the non-profit social enterprises

## Non-governmental organisations

**Key term**
**Non-governmental organisations (NGOs)** are legally constituted, not-for-profit organisations that support issues in the public good.

**Non-governmental organisations (NGOs)** do not have government involvement in their operations and management although they are often supported by governments. An NGO's mission is often focused on social or humanitarian objectives related to the most vulnerable members of society. Many NGOs operate in developing countries. Amnesty International is an international campaigning organisation that promotes internationally recognised human rights for all.

**Strengths of NGOs:**

- provision of support to the people who can least afford necessary goods and services

- free from political influence by government

- trusted image because of the not-for-profit nature of the organisation.

Weaknesses of NGOs:

- access to funding because they often rely on charitable giving

- can conflict with governments because they sometimes highlight government mismanagement

- often have to work in very difficult conditions that make day-to-day management challenging.

## CASE STUDY

### Wikimedia

The Wikimedia Foundation has been around for just over a decade and has become famous for its freely available online encyclopaedia Wikipedia. It has about 100 000 volunteers who freely give their time to produce and update around 39 million pages. A central theme of Wikimedia's mission is to 'empower and engage people around the world to collect and develop educational content under a free license'. They are trying to provide low-cost education to everyone on a global level.

### Progress questions

1 Define the term 'non-governmental organisation'. [2 marks]

2 Outline two characteristics of non-governmental organisations. [4 marks]

3 Discuss the benefits of Wikimedia as an NGO to the education of a developing country. [10 marks]

## Charities

### Key term

A **charity** is a not-for-profit organisation set up to provide money and support to people in need.

**Charities** tend to focus on a particular area of need, often based on the philanthropic objectives of the person or people who founded the charity. The hospital example is supported by a number of local charities that provide funding and expertise.

The purpose of the charity can be to fund and support areas such as education, arts, health and the environment.

Strengths of charities:

- provide funds and support to people in need

- philanthropic nature gives them a positive image

- cover areas of support that governments have not provided for.

Weaknesses of charities:

- difficulty in attracting enough funds to provide effective support to those in need

- low wages mean they struggle to attract the best employees

- legal status often involves regulations that limit activities such as attracting investment finance.

# Exam practice questions

## Paper 1 question (HL and SL)

### Fine Olive Company

The Fine Olive Company was started by Mimis Manolas in 2009 after he was made redundant from his job working as a civil servant. Mimis is a sole trader and he faces all the challenges sole traders have to deal with as new businesses. He has approached a relative and invited her to become a partner in the business.

a Outline two characteristics of sole trader businesses. [4 marks]

b Analyse two benefits to the Fine Olive Company of becoming a partnership. [6 marks]

[Total 10 marks]

## Paper 2 question (HL and SL)

TED (Technology, Entertainment, Design) is a non-governmental organisation that provides conferences that are freely available on the internet. The TED organisation is run by the Sapling Foundation, whose aim is to 'to foster the spread of great ideas'.

As a non-profit organisation, its wider philosophy is education and making it globally available through an online media platform. The organisation is funded by a combination of revenue streams that include: conference attendance fees, corporate sponsorship (sponsors include Coca-Cola, Google and AOL), donations, merchandise sales and licensing fees.

**a** Define the term 'non-governmental organisation'. [2 marks]

**b** Outline two characteristics TED has as a non-governmental organisation. [4 marks]

**c** Explain one problem TED might face by funding its organisation through corporate sponsorship. [4 marks]

**d** Evaluate the view that non-governmental organisations are an effective way of providing global education programmes though the internet. [10 marks]

[Total 20 marks]

### Exam tip

The 'analyse' command term in this question means breaking down the benefits to the Fine Olive Company of becoming a partnership into their essential elements.

# 1.3 | Organisational objectives

**What you should know by the end of this chapter:**

- Vision statements (AO2)

- Mission statements (AO2)

- Aims, objectives, strategies and tactics (AO3)

- The need for organisations to change objectives and innovate in response to changes in internal and external environments (AO3)

- Ethical objectives (AO1)

- Corporate social responsibility (CSR) (AO1)

- The reasons why organisations set ethical objectives and the impact of implementing them (AO3)

- The evolving role and nature of CSR (AO3)

- SWOT analysis (AO3), (AO4)

- Ansoff's matrix (AO3), (AO4).

**Chapter illustrative example**
A consumer electronics business that specialises in high-specification headphones

# Vision statement and mission statement

## Mission statement

**Key term**
A **mission statement** is where an organisation formally sets out and publicises its core objectives.

The **mission statement** tries to capture a business's objectives in a short paragraph by setting out general themes rather than specific, quantifiable aims. The mission statement of the consumer electronics manufacturer is to think of better ways to do things and create better products to do this.

## Vision statement

**Key term**
A **vision statement** is where an organisation sets out where it would like to be in the long term based on its values.

A mission statement sets out the aims of a business and the vision statement adds why it would like to achieve those aims. The **vision statement** of the consumer electronics manufacturer is that every employee is united through a common belief in making better products.

**The aims of vision and mission statements are to:**

- give strategic decision-making an overall sense of direction

- provide employees and managers with a sense of the strategic direction of the business

- motivate employees and managers within the business and provide them with a reference point for their own aims and values

- attract outside stakeholders such as customers, banks and investors to the organisation.

# Aims, objectives, strategies and tactics

## Corporate Aims

**Key term**
**Corporate aims** are the long-term goals that a business wants to achieve in the future.

They are based on the mission and vision statements of the organisation but carry more specific, measureable outcomes. Business aims might include:

- increase market share above 10% next year

- start selling in South America within two years

- reduce costs by 5% in the next six months.

It is important for a business to set corporate aims because it gives the organisation a set of specific targets to:

- give a sense of purpose and direction for the whole organisation

- provide some measure to judge its performance against

- develop objectives and strategy for different parts of the organisation.

## Objectives

**Key term**
An **objective** is a target set by an organisation to achieve its corporate aims.

Business objectives are often set using **SMART criteria**:

- **S – Specific** objectives need to focus precisely on what the business does and what needs to be achieved.

- **M – Measurable** objectives are quantifiable. By putting a value on what needs to be achieved, the business can assess whether it has been successful in achieving the objective.

- A – **Achievable** objectives are important to make a meaningful assessment of the success or failure in achieving the objectives.

- R – **Relevant** objectives are important for different people in the organisation.

- T – **Time**-specific objectives are important because they make the measureable element of an objective meaningful.

The consumer electronics business example has the strategic aim to increase its market share by 10% next year and it has set departmental objectives to achieve this. This is based on the SMART criteria.

## CASE STUDY

### Nike

Nike has set the corporate aim of achieving $50 billion in annual revenue by 2020. As part of this, it is aiming to double its women's business over the same period. Nike is currently the world's largest sportswear brand with a revenue of $30 billion and 62 000 employees. Its mission statement is 'To bring inspiration and innovation to every athlete in the world'.

### Progress questions

1 Define the term 'corporate aim'. [2 marks]

2 Explain two differences between Nike's corporate objectives and its mission statement. [4 marks]

3 Evaluate the extent to which Nike's objective of achieving a revenue of $50 billion is a SMART objective. [10 marks]

## Strategy

### Key term

**Strategy** is the long-term plan that sets out the ways a business is going to achieve its corporate aims.

Developing **strategy** is based on the following elements:

- Aim – Strategy is focused on achieving the corporate aim of the organisation.

- Market – The business's market is in and consumers.

- Resources – This is the capital, employees, and managers the business has.

- Stakeholders – This is how different stakeholders will influence the strategy.

The business strategy of the consumer electronics business example might be:

- Aim – Increase market share by 10 per cent next year in the headphones market.

- Market – The market is changing with consumers looking for higher quality headphones.

- Resources – Improving the quality of the headphones means investing in new machinery.

- Stakeholders – Shareholders are happy with the strategy because it should increase profits and the security of the business in the long term.

## Tactics

### Key term

**Tactics** are the specific techniques used by a business to achieve its objectives.

When managers set the corporate aims and objectives, they then develop a strategy to achieve them, and **tactics** are the techniques part of the strategy used to achieve the aims and objectives.

To increase its market share in the headphones market, the consumer electronics business example will improve the quality of its product as a tactic.

# Changes in objectives due to changes in internal and external environments

Businesses constantly need to review, adjust and change their objectives as the internal and external business environment changes. The change in objectives is closely linked to innovation where an organisation changes its approach to do something in a new way.

# 1.3

## Changes in the internal environment

This is where a business changes its objectives because of changes within the business. This type of change is normally based on changes in ownership and management.

## Changes in the external environment

Organisations constantly face changes in the business environment which can make them change their objectives. External environment changes might come from:

- **Political change** – As government policy and the laws change, businesses might have to react and adjust their objectives. The consumer electronics business example has had to adjust the volume settings on its headphones in response to changes in the law.

- **Economic change** – The macroeconomy is constantly changing and this will affect nearly all businesses in some way and can lead to a change in their objectives.

- **Social change** – Consumer taste and preferences might change, which could increase or reduce the demand for a firm's product, and if this happens its objectives might change. The consumer electronics business example has responded to consumers wanting on-ear rather than in-ear headphones.

- **Technological change** – As technology advances, organisations might have to change their objectives.

## CASE STUDY

### Netflix

Netflix is the leading provider of streamed movies and television series in the world. The business began as a DVD-by-mail service in 1998 and developed into streaming in 2007. Its on-demand service has been made possible by technological advances and is also a reflection of the way people want to watch films and TV series. Netflix has had to continuously change its corporate aims, objectives and strategy as the market it operates in has changed.

### Progress questions

1 Define the term 'business strategy'. [2 marks]
2 Outline two changes in the market in which Netflix operates that might have led to a change in its business strategy. [4 marks]
3 Analyse two problems Netflix might encounter when it tries to change its business strategy. [6 marks]

# Ethical objectives and corporate social responsibility (CSR)

## Ethical objectives

Ethical objectives are business objectives influenced by moral values. These values often come from different stakeholders in the organisation and reflect their ethical position on moral issues.

# Corporate social responsibility (CSR)

There is a close link between **corporate social responsibility (CSR)** and a business's ethical objectives because the principle of social responsibility is closely allied to the ethical approach adopted by a business. Many businesses formalise CSR through a CSR report that sets out their approach to CSR issues.

## The reasons organisations set ethical objectives and adopt CSR

Businesses exist as part of a community. There may be no wider advantage to the business of being an ethical organisation. It may purely be a socially responsible approach.

The advantages to businesses setting ethical objectives and adopting CSR might be:

* drives innovation as businesses develop products and system to be socially responsible
* attracts consumers to buy products and increases sales
* strengthens a business's brand image
* attracts employees and investors
* has favourable tax advantages and government grants are available
* helps to avoid some government regulations and investigation.

Setting an ethical approach and adopting CSR can have the following disadvantages:

* it can increase business costs
* if businesses fall short of their ethical standards, it is damaging to brand image

* it can lead to a conflict with stakeholders who might see profits reduced by ethical objectives.

## The evolving role and nature of CSR

Corporate social responsibility is constantly changing as the internal and external business environment changes. As these changes take place, businesses will change their CSR as the values of different stakeholders change and organisational decision-making needs to reflect this. Some examples of changes might be increases in:

* awareness of the LGBT community as stakeholders
* need for religious tolerance
* concern over income inequality
* challenge of migration.

# SWOT analysis

Managers can use a **SWOT analysis** as a starting point for business decision-making. It looks at the current situation facing a business through its strengths and weaknesses, which are internal to the business. Opportunities and threats relate to future prospects that are external influences on the organisation. Opportunities and threats can be developed through a STEEPLE analysis (see Chapter 1.5). Examples of some typical considerations of a SWOT analysis are given in Table 1.3.1.

**Table 1.3.1**

| Internal and current | |
|---|---|
| **Strengths** | **Weaknesses** |
| Strengths of an organisation are competitive advantages and the focus is from an internal perspective. The analysis would consider things such as: | Weaknesses of a business come from an internal perspective and involve the competitive disadvantages. The analysis would consider things such as: |
| • Quality of the goods or services produced<br>• Skills of the workforce<br>• Investment in the latest technology<br>• Efficiency of production methods<br>• Strength of an organisation's leadership. | • Manufacturing problems with the product<br>• Difficulties in motivating employees<br>• Outdated machinery<br>• Inefficient production methods<br>• Conflict within management. |
| **External and future** | |
| **Opportunities** | **Threats** |
| The opportunities a firm faces come from the external business environment and are things an organisation can develop its strategy to take advantage of. The analysis would consider factors that affect the business such as: | The threats an organisation faces come from the external business environment and are factors it will have to plan to manage as it develops its business strategy. The analysis may consider factors such as: |
| • Growth in the economy and market<br>• Technological advance in the product it sells<br>• Reduced regulations in the market<br>• Change in the taste of consumers that favours its product<br>• Positive media reports about the market the product is sold in. | • An economic recession and declining market<br>• Political instability<br>• Technological advance from its competitors<br>• Increased regulation in the market<br>• Bad publicity relating to the market where the product is sold. |

# Evaluation of SWOT

The advantages of SWOT analysis are that it:

• identifies important factors that might affect a business now and in the future

• creates a clear framework to develop business strategy

• generates new ideas that have not been considered before

• is relatively low-cost and easy to produce.

The disadvantages of SWOT analysis are that it:

• is simplistic and does not develop the relative importance of factors

• does not provide solutions and strategy will still need to be developed

• can generate ideas that are not relevant to the strategic decision

• some factors considered may not fit easily into the SWOT framework.

# Ansoff's matrix

**Key term**
**Ansoff's matrix** is a tool used by management to develop a marketing plan by considering strategies related to the products the business sells and the markets it operates in.

**Ansoff's matrix** is forward-looking and focuses on a firm's existing and potentially new products as well at its existing and potentially new markets (Table 1.3.2). It also builds some assessment of risk into marketing strategy.

**Table 1.3.2**

| | | Products | |
| | | Existing | New |
|---|---|---|---|
| Markets | Existing | Market penetration *Lowest risk* | Product development *Medium risk* |
| | New | Market development *Medium risk* | Diversification *Highest risk* |

## Market penetration

Market penetration is where the business focuses on selling an existing product in an existing market. The consumer electronics business, for example, tries to increase the sales of existing brand by:

- using a competitive pricing strategy
- increasing advertising expenditure
- developing new promotional methods.

Market penetration represents the least change for the firm and is therefore seen as the lowest-risk decision.

## Market development

Market development involves marketing an existing product in a new market. The consumer electronics business may, for example, look to market its headphones in a new market such as Brazil. To do this, the business may:

- use new distribution channels
- change their pricing strategy
- develop a new promotional mix.

Market development does mean more change for the organisation than market penetration so it is a medium-risk option.

## Product development

The product development approach means launching a new product in an existing market. The consumer electronics business could, for example, launch a new speaker system into its existing market. To do this the firm may:

- research and develop a new product
- use significant research to see what the customer wants
- develop a new pricing, distribution and promotional strategy.

Product development means more change for the organisation than market penetration so it is a medium-risk option.

## Diversification

Diversification means marketing a new product in a new market. The consumer electronics firm may diversify into electronics products for hospitals and would need to:

- research and develop a new product
- conduct market research into a new market
- develop a new pricing, distribution and promotional strategy.

This is the riskiest marketing strategy because it represents the greatest change for the organisation and involves the areas where it will have the least experience.

## Evaluation of Ansoff's Matrix

**Strengths of Ansoff's matrix:**

- clearly sets out different growth strategies

- sets out the different approaches needed for different strategic directions

- gives some assessment of risk associated with a strategy

- can be presented in an understandable way to different stakeholders.

**Weaknesses of Ansoff's matrix:**

- difficult to apply the model to complex strategic decisions

- judgements about risk are difficult to forecast accurately

- static model that does not adjust for changes in business environment.

## CASE STUDY

### Virgin Galactic

The UK conglomerate Virgin is one of the world's most diversified organisations. It is a large business with a turnover of more than $20 billion and it employs over 50 000 people. In 2012 it launched Virgin Galactic, the world's first commercial Spaceline that will take ordinary citizens into space. It will also launch large numbers of small satellites. The cost of trips will be expensive, at $250 000.

### Progress questions

1 Define the term 'SWOT analysis'. [2 marks]

2 Explain two ways a SWOT analysis might have helped Virgin develop its business strategy for the development of Virgin Galactic. [4 marks]

3 Analyse two strengths of Ansoff's matrix in helping to develop Virgin's decision to launch Virgin Galactic. [6 marks]

### Exam tip

The 'explain' command term in this question means giving a detailed account of how SWOT analysis could help Virgin Galactic.

# Exam practice questions

## Paper 1 question (HL and SL)

### Fine Olive Company

The Fine Olive Company was started by Mimis Manolas in 2009 after he was made redundant from his job working as a civil servant. One of Mimis's important business principles is using sustainable farming and production methods for the firm's olives. He is a very strong believer in CSR.

a Describe two reasons the Fine Olive Company business might adopt a CSR approach to its operations. [4 marks]

b Analyse two benefits the Fine Olive Company might receive from Mimis Manolas's approach to CSR. [6 marks]

[Total 10 marks]

## Paper 2 question (HL and SL)

### Aeron Green Gardens

Aeron Green Gardens is a family-run organisation that prides itself on the very best customer service. The owners have been concerned by increased competition in the market from lower-cost firms that are taking away its market share and reducing its sales. A new operations director has been appointed from outside the business to try to develop a new business strategy. One of the new operations director's plans is for Aeron Green Gardens to move into landscape gardening. The business has a number of experienced garden specialists that could help support this new service, although an experienced landscape gardener would need to be appointed to head up the landscape gardening section.

**a** Define the term 'business strategy'. [2 marks]

**b** Outline two strengths Aeron Green Gardens might have as a business. [4 marks]

**c** Increased competition is one threat the Aeron Green Gardens faces; explain two other threats that the business might potentially face. [4 marks]

**d** To what extent is Ansoff's matrix useful to Aeron Green Gardens as it decides whether to develop a landscape gardening business. [10 marks]

[Total 20 Marks]

**Exam tip**

The 'to what extent' command term in this question means considering the relative merits of Ansoff's matrix.

# Stakeholders

**What you should know by the end of this chapter:**

- Different types and interests of internal stakeholders (AO2)

- Different types and interests of external stakeholders (AO2)

- Areas of mutual benefit shared by stakeholders (AO3)

- Areas of conflict affecting different stakeholders (AO3).

**Chapter illustrative example**
A large advertising agency

# The nature of different stakeholders

**Key term**
**Stakeholders** are any people, groups or organisations that have an interest in a particular organisation.

**Stakeholder** interests are crucial to an organisation because of the impact stakeholders have on their decision-making. The advertising agency example will make decisions that are influenced by the reaction of stakeholders such as customers, employees and investors.

# Internal stakeholders

**Key term**
**Internal stakeholders** are people or groups who are part of the organisation.

The main **internal stakeholders** are employees and **shareholders**.

**Key term**
**Shareholders** are the individuals who own the shares in a business, which makes them part owners of the organisation.

## Shareholders

Shareholders appoint the directors of the business to run it on a day-to-day basis.

As shareholders are owners of the business, their interests are crucial and they will be particularly concerned with:

- any profit made because as investors they put money into the organisation and are paid part of the profit in the form of a dividend paid on each share they own

- receiving a good dividend payment or yield from the shares they own because it increases their income

- seeing the value of the shares they own rise. Both dividend and value will be affected by the performance of the business and the better the performance of the organisation, the higher the dividend and share value are likely to be

- other non-profit related factors such as the ethical position of the business and its social responsibility.

The advertising agency example is a public company where shareholders are able to express their views at the business's AGM.

## Employees

The people who work for an organisation can be senior managers or directors and more regular employees. As stakeholders, their key interest is likely to be:

- the pay they receive from the organisation

- their job security

- how good an employer the organisation is in terms of working conditions and the way workers are treated by management

- the job prospects offered by the organisation.

## Trade unions

Where employees belong to trade unions, the union is a stakeholder in the business and is interested in making the situation of their members as good as it can be in terms of:

- pay

- job security

- working conditions

- employment prospects.

# 1.4

**Lidl**

Lidl is a German-owned supermarket chain that has been very successful over the last few years. Started in 1930 by Dieter Schwarz, the business has grown to be one of the most successful discount retailers in the world. It now has 10 000 stores in 28 different countries and it employs 315 000 people.

**Progress questions**

1  Define the term 'stakeholder'. [2 marks]

2  State two internal stakeholders. [2 marks

3  Explain two reasons why Lidl's employees would be interested in the business's performance. [4 marks]

**Exam tip**

The 'state' command term in this question means to identify internal stakeholders specifically.

# External stakeholders

**External stakeholders** are also crucial to an organisation's success.

**Key term**

**External stakeholders** in a business are people, groups and organisations that are outside the organisation but are affected by its decisions.

## Customers

The people and organisations that buy a business's products will be interested in things such as:

- guaranteed supply

- the quality of the product

- future price changes.

## Suppliers

The businesses that supply an organisation will be concerned with the security of the business they are selling to in terms of:

- the security of long-term sales

- getting paid by the business being supplied.

## Local community

Individuals and groups who live and work near a business will be affected by its activity in the following ways:

- pollution and traffic congestion that result from the organisation

- custom from the organisation's employees, such as in restaurants and shops

- work the organisation does supporting the local community.

## Government

Local and national governments will be interested in the decisions made by business because they:

- are a source of local and national tax revenue

- are employers at a local and national level

- produce output that contributes to the local and national economy.

## Competitors

Businesses operate within markets and will face direct competition from other firms in those markets. They will also face competition from businesses in other markets. Any competitor will be interested in the following details of an organisation:

- financial data to make comparisons on performance

- development of new competition

- workforce issues

- technological developments.

## Lenders

Banks and other institutions that provide finance for a business will be interested in its:

- ability to make repayments
- ability to cover interest costs
- cash flow position
- general financial security.

### CASE STUDY

**Prada**

The luxury brand Prada is one of the most successful fashion businesses in the world. It specialises in clothing, handbags, shoes, watches, perfumes and other fashion accessories. The business was started in 1913 by Mario Prada. Its sales are over $3 billion and it employs more than 12 000 people.

**Progress questions**

1  Identify two external stakeholders in Prada. [2 marks]

2  Explain why suppliers and the government would have an interest in the success of Prada. [4 marks]

# Areas of mutual benefit between stakeholders

Different stakeholders will share mutual benefits that result from the activities of an organisation. If an organisation is successful then different stakeholders will share many of the benefits of this success. The advertising business example is experiencing rising sales revenues, profits and increasing share price. Table 1.4.1 shows the resulting likely benefits to stakeholders:

**Table 1.4.1**

| Stakeholder | Benefit |
| --- | --- |
| Shareholders | • Rising dividends<br>• Rising share price increases the value of their shareholding. |
| Employees | • Greater job security<br>• Increasing wages<br>• More job opportunities within the business. |
| Customers | • Security of the business as a supplier<br>• Better products because the business has funds to reinvest<br>• Economies of scale that lead to lower prices. |
| Suppliers | • Continuity of supply and sales<br>• Increased future sales<br>• Easier to get paid. |
| Local community | • Job security from local employer<br>• More job opportunities are created<br>• More funds spent in the local community. |
| Government | • More tax revenue from increased profits<br>• Increased output adds to national output<br>• Increased employment reduces unemployment. |
| Competitors | • More customers are attracted to the market by a successful organisation<br>• More finance is attracted to a successful market. |
| Lenders | • Greater likelihood of repayment<br>• Opportunity for increased lending. |

# Possible areas of conflict between stakeholders' interests

Some decisions made by organisations can lead to a conflict between different stakeholders because the effects of a decision made by an organisation affect different stakeholders positively and negatively.

Here are three decisions that can lead to a conflict between different stakeholders:

## The takeover

When the advertising agency example was nearly taken over by another company, the stakeholders in the advertising agency may have been affected in the following ways:

- Shareholders might benefit because of a potential rise in sales and profits, which leads to an increase in dividends and rise in share price.

- Employees might react negatively to the takeover because when companies are taken over this may lead to workers being made redundant and/or changes to working conditions.

## New environmental policies

When a business decides to implement new environmental policies that reduce negative impacts on the environment, it could affect stakeholders in the following ways:

- The costs of the business might rise due to the new environmental policies. This could lead to a fall in profits and a fall in the shareholders' dividends.

- The local community and government might benefit because the new environmental policies improve the environment in the local area.

## The decision to outsource

If a business decides to outsource part of its manufacturing process to an overseas producer, it could affect stakeholders in the following ways:

- If it leads to a rise in sales and profits, shareholders will be pleased with a possible rise in dividends.

- The local community and the government may not support the decision to outsource because it may lead to redundancies and the closure of a local production plant.

## CASE STUDY

### American Airlines
In 2013, American Airlines merged with US Airways to form the American Airlines Group. This created the largest airline in the world, employing 118 000 people, with sales revenue of over $40 billion and a profit of $7 billion. They called it a 'mega' merger.

### Progress questions

1 Explain the difference between internal and external stakeholders. [4 marks]

2 Evaluate the impact of the merger on shareholders and employees of US Airways. [10 marks]

# Exam practice questions

## Paper 1 question (HL and SL)

### Fine Olive Company
The Fine Olive Company was started by Mimis Manolas in 2009 after he was made redundant from his job working as a civil servant. Mimis Manolas is committed to the local community where the business is located. He is particularly keen to make the Fine Olive Company a sustainable organisation.

a Outline two reasons why the local community as a stakeholder would be interested in the performance of the Fine Olive Company. [4 marks]

**b** Analyse how Mimis Manolas's decision to make Fine Olive a sustainable business which is committed to the local community might affect two stakeholders in the business. [6 marks]

[Total 10 marks]

## Paper 2 Questions (HL and SL)

## Filgo Aztec

Filgo Aztec is a medium-sized bank. It is an important organisation in the economy where it is based because it employs large numbers of people and it accounts for a small but significant number of customers. It is a 'trusted' organisation that markets itself on good customer service and as an ethical organisation. But the pressure is building at Filgo Aztec. Its profits have fallen by 35% over the past three years and it is struggling to control its costs. The workforce is strongly protected by a main banking trade union. This has forced up wage costs for Filgo Aztec and made it difficult for management to bring about change. The Chief Executive Officer (CEO) Helena Maara wants strategic change to make the bank more dynamic and to reduce its costs. She would like to outsource a number of administrative functions to India to reduce labour costs.

**a** Identify two external stakeholders in Filgo Aztec. [2 marks]

**b** Explain why Filgo Aztec's shareholders might be interested in the fall in the bank's profits. [4 marks]

**c** Outline the two roles of the trade union as a stakeholder representing Filgo Aztec's employees. [4 marks]

**d** Evaluate the impact on three of Filgo Aztec's stakeholders of its decision to outsource some of its administrative functions. [10 marks]

[Total 20 marks]

**Exam tip**
The 'evaluate' command term in this question means making a judgement by weighing up the strengths and limitations of the merger for shareholders and employees.

# External Environment

## 1.5

### What you should know by the end of this chapter:

- STEEPLE analysis of a given organisation: social, technological, environmental, economic, political, legal, ethical (AO2, AO4)

- Consequences of changes in STEEPLE factors for a business's objectives and strategy.

**Chapter illustrative example**
A car manufacturer

# Importance to business of the external environment

All organisations exist in an external environment that has important effects on their decision-making. The external environment can be taken to mean where the business is in terms of the:

- local city or area it is located in

- country where it operates

- international/global environment.

An organisation needs to consider how its decisions and strategies will impact on the external environment and how it should react to changes in that environment. This is important when an organisation is developing strategy using SWOT analysis. The example car manufacturer might develop an electric car in response to more environmentally conscious consumers, and use the opportunity to receive financial support from a government that wants to improve the environment.

# STEEPLE analysis

**Key term**
**STEEPLE analysis** is a strategic planning tool used by organisations to focus on the different aspects of the external environment that affect businesses when they are developing strategy and making decisions.

**STEEPLE analysis** sets out the external environment as:

Social, Technological, Environmental, Economic, Political, Legal, Ethical

## Social factors

**Key term**
**Social factors** consider how culture, demography and attitudes of the people in the external environment all need to be accounted for in a business decision.

The growth in ethnic diversity, for example, in many countries has affected the way the example car manufacturer advertises its products.

### Social factors might include:

- **Ageing population** – In many developed countries an older population is more likely to suffer from ill-health, which increases the demand for medicines and health facilities.

- **Ethnic diversity** – Many societies have become more multicultural, which changes the demand for products sold by, for example, food retailers.

- **Empowerment of women** – As more women take leading roles, this is often being reflected in the way organisations promote and hire staff.

- **Health consciousness** – A growing desire for a heathy lifestyle has created new leisure markets such as fitness apps and physical activity trackers.

- **Sexual orientation** – The increased acceptance of the LGBT community in many countries has increased the need for equality in the workplace in those countries.

## Technological factors

**Key term**
**Technological factors** relate to the way equipment, machinery, communications and IT affect business.

As technology advances, it constantly forces businesses to react in terms of the way they operate. The car manufacturer, for example, has had to embrace the growth of online car-buying.

**Technological factors might include:**

- **Research and development** – As competing firms in a market spend money and use resources to develop new products and systems, an organisation will need to spend its own money and resources in order to compete.

- **Innovation of new products** – The introduction of new products in a market forces an organisation to introduce its own products to compete.

- **Production techniques** – As more advanced manufacturing machines become available, businesses would look to invest in them.

- **Communication technology** – Mobile phones have become increasingly more advanced and have opened up huge operational and marketing opportunities for businesses.

- **Information technology** – New IT systems and the development of the internet provide significant operational and marketing opportunities for organisations.

## Environmental factors

**Key term**
**Environmental factors** are based on the land, atmosphere and living things alongside which society exists.

Businesses will affect the environment within which they operate. The development of the production site of the car manufacturer, for example, has had an effect on the local environment because of traffic congestion and industrial waste.

**Environmental factors might include:**

- **Government policy and regulation** – This often involves laws relating to production and also to the goods that firms sell.

- **Consumer reaction** – Social change has occurred in recent years in many countries as consumers become increasingly environmentally conscious in their buying decisions.

- **Technological changes** – Advances in technology can lead to environmental challenges such as improvements in renewable energy.

- **Environmental incidents and problems** – Many argue that climate change makes weather more unstable and this has a major effect on agricultural businesses.

- **Recruitment** – Potentially environmentally conscious workers may be attracted to firms with a positive reputation on environmental issues, and be put off by businesses with a poor environmental record.

## Economic factors

**Key term**
**Economic factors** relate to the operation of markets and industries at a local, national and global level.

**Economic factors might include:**

- **Economic growth** – Rising economic growth often increases demand in the economy and firms experience a rise in sales. A recession, where economic growth is negative, often leads to a fall in business sales revenue. The example car manufacturer is particularly affected by this.

- **Inflation** – When the overall price level of the economy is rising, this can often lead to rising business costs. Workers, for example, may demand higher wages when prices rise and their cost of living increases.

- **Unemployment** – If unemployment rises in a country it can have a depressing effect on consumer demand, which leads to falling sales, but it can also make it easier for organisations to recruit staff.

- **Interest rates** – If interest rates rise then businesses will be affected by higher borrowing costs and a possible fall in sales as consumers pay more interest themselves and have less money to spend on goods and services. If interest rates fall then a business's borrowing costs fall and there may be a rise in demand for their products.

- **Exchange rates** – If a country's exchange rate falls, then business costs rise because imported raw materials and components become more expensive. A lower exchange rate will make the price of goods exported by domestic firms cheaper, which may lead to a rise in sales. If the exchange rate rises, then import costs fall and the price of goods exported increases. The example car manufacturer is affected by this when it imports components and exports its cars.

## CASE STUDY

### Luxottica Group

The world's largest producer of eyewear is the Italy-based Luxottica Group. It is a global organisation involved in the design, manufacture, distribution and retail of eyewear. Luxottica's important brands include Sunglass Hut, Sears Optical, Glasses.com, Ray-Ban and Oakley. The business also manufactures frames for designer brands such as Chanel, Prada, Giorgio Armani and Versace. As a global organisation, it is affected by changes in the world economy, particularly economic growth and exchange rates.

### Progress questions

1. Outline two social factors that might affect the Luxottica Group. [4 marks]

2. Explain how changes in communication technology and product innovation by competitors might affect the Luxottica Group. [4 marks]

3. Analyse how rising economic growth in India might affect the premium bands sold by Luxottica. [6 marks]

### Exam tip

The 'explain' command term in this question means give a detailed account of how changes in communication technology and product innovation by competitors might affect the Luxottica Group.

## Political factors

### Key term

**Political factors** are how governments influence organisations at local, national and international levels.

National and local government affect the political environment within which businesses operate. When, for example, the government decided to increase income tax, it adversely affected the demand for the example car manufacturer's cars.

### Political factors might include:

- **Tax** – If tax rates increase in a country, then businesses may have to pay more tax on their profits or on the goods they sell, which reduces their profits.

- **Government spending** – Expenditure by governments on infrastructure projects, state benefits and public services can benefit firms directly if, for example, they get a government contract and indirectly if government spending increases incomes in the economy and households have more money to spend.

- **Regulations** – Government puts regulations on the way that businesses produce goods and services, employ their workforce and sell their products. Government regulations on recycling cars has had a big impact on the example car manufacturer.

## Legal factors

### Key term

**Legal factors** are the laws, rules and regulations that organisations have to follow.

### Legal activities might include:

- **Contracts** – Organisations are constantly involved in contracts relating to employment, sale of goods, buying from suppliers and with lenders. Any change in contract law will affect a business's operations and costs.

- **Employment regulations** – Changes in regulations on operations and employment will affect business. The car manufacturer has, for example, been affected by the maximum hours its employees can work.

- **Health and safety** – If a government introduces new legislation on health and safety, this often drives up business costs.

- **Product standards** – Most countries set standards for the products businesses sell to make products safe. For example, there are safety rules on the cars produced by the example car manufacturer.

- **Competition rules** – Many countries have rules to try to ensure fair competition between firms. Businesses, for example, sometimes try to agree to fix their prices with other firms in the market and this disadvantages the consumer. Competition rules are used to stop this happening.

## Ethical factors

### Key term

**Ethical factors** are the moral principles and values held by people in society.

For example, the car manufacturer may want to produce cars at the lowest possible cost but doing this means paying very low wages, which could be seen as unethical.

### Ethical factors might include:

- **Nature of products marketed** – Some goods and services raise controversial ethical issues that can make different stakeholders uncomfortable. Examples include online gambling, tobacco and alcohol.

- **Pay and working conditions of employees** – Businesses that fail to meet acceptable standards on pay and conditions of their employees often attract considerable amounts of negative publicity.

- **The way products are promoted** – Advertising campaigns that involve issues such as over-thin models or racial stereotyping frequently attract bad publicity or regulatory control.

- **Treatment of suppliers and creditors** – Some businesses delay payment for goods and services to improve their own cash flow positions.

- **Treatment of customers** – Unethical behaviour of businesses towards customers might involve poor customer service or misleading customers about the nature of a good they sell or the full price that will be charged.

### CASE STUDY

#### Bet365

One of the world's largest online gambling organisations is the UK-based Bet365 Group. Bet365 has 19 million customers in almost 200 countries. It is a private company that employs more than 3 000 people with a turnover of £1.5 billion. One of the important threats to Bet365 is government regulation and laws that will control the way the business operates and markets its services. Many stakeholders are also concerned by ethical considerations of their involvement with a gambling business.

#### Progress questions

1. Explain one legal factor and one technological factor that might affect Bet365. [4 marks]

2. Analyse how ethical factors might affect two of Bet365's stakeholders. [6 marks]

3. Examine how social, technological and political factors might affect Bet 365's strategy of entering a market in another country. [10 marks]

## Consequences of a change in any of the STEEPLE factors

Changes in the external environment can have significant effects on the objectives, strategy and decision-making of businesses. Changes in the external environment create opportunities and threats for business which means the STEEPLE analysis is used with a SWOT analysis in developing business strategy. Table 1.5.1 sets out how the example car manufacturer is affected by changes in the external environment.

**Table 1.5.1**

| STEEPLE factor | Change in STEEPLE factor | Impact on the business | Strategic decision |
|---|---|---|---|
| Social | An ageing population. | Rise in demand for smaller cars. | Plan to develop cars targeted at older consumers. |
| Technological | Development of driverless cars. | Opportunity to develop driverless cars. | Develop partnerships with businesses that produce the driverless car technology. |
| Environmental | Climate change leads to higher temperatures. | Cars have to be developed that can function at higher temperatures. | Introduce new engine cooling technology. |
| Economic | Economic recession. | Reduced demand for new cars. | Discount the price of new cars to attract consumers. |
| Political | Government policy to reduce car emissions. | Tax is increased on cars with emissions above a certain level. | Develop low-emission engine technology. |
| Legal | New safety standards introduced on cars. | Car designs and production methods need to be changed. | Market upgraded safety standards on all new cars. |
| Ethical | Media reports that emission testing data on its cars is misreported. | Bad publicity for the business. | Public relations campaign to show how emission testing procedures have been changed. |

# Exam practice questions

## Paper 1 question (HL and SL)

### Fine Olive Company

The Fine Olive Company was started by Mimis Manolas in 2009 after he was made redundant from his job working as a civil servant. Economic recession in Greece has had a huge impact on the Fine Olive Company and made trading conditions very challenging.

a Describe two types of social change that might affect the business environment the Fine Olive Company operates in. [4 marks]

b Analyse two ways the economic recession in Greece might affect the Fine Olive Company. [6 marks]

[Total 10 marks]

## Paper 2 question (HL and SL)

### Salem Magazines

Salem Magazines is a medium-sized publisher based in New Zealand.

The last few years have brought significant threats. The development of downloadable magazines, fewer people reading magazines and slow economic growth in New Zealand have all led to falling sales and profits at Salem. The CEO wants a strategy to increase sales.

a Define the term 'STEEPLE analysis'. [2 marks]

b Outline how technological and social change might affect Salem Magazines. [4 marks]

c Analyse two strategies Salem Magazines could use in reaction to technological and social challenges. [4 marks]

# 1.5

**d** Recommend a strategy to the CEO on how to increase magazine sales to young readers. [10 marks]

[Total 20 marks]

## Key Concept question

With reference to one or two organisation(s) that you have studied, discuss how changes in culture and innovation affect the business environment. [20 marks]

**Exam tip**

The 'recommend' command term in this question means presenting an advisable course of action on how to increase magazine sales to young readers.

# 1.6 | Growth and evolution

**What you should know by the end of this chapter:**

- Economies and diseconomies of scale (AO2)

- The merits of small versus large organisations (AO3)

- The difference between internal and external growth (AO2)

- The following external growth methods: mergers and acquisitions (M&As) and takeovers, joint ventures, strategic alliances, franchising (AO3)

- The role and impact of globalisation on the growth and evolution of businesses (A03)

- Reasons for the growth of multinational companies (MNCs) (AO3)

- The impact of MNCs on the host countries (AO3).

**Chapter illustrative example**
A department store retailer

# Economies and diseconomies of scale

Economies and diseconomies of scale represent part of the advantages and disadvantages of an organisation increasing in size.

## Economies of scale

**Key term**
**Economies of scale** are the cost advantages firms benefit from as their scale of production increases.

As a business increases in size and production, it may benefit from the following types of **economy of scale**:

- **Commercial economies (or marketing economies)** – The ability of large firms to buy and sell in bulk. The department store, for example, has huge buying power and can negotiate very low purchase prices from its suppliers.

- **Technical economies** – Large firms are able to use large-scale machinery that reduces unit costs. For example, the department store example can move its goods in large lorries, which are cheaper per unit shipped than moving goods in small vans.

- **Financial economies** – Banks are willing to offer large firms low rates of interest as they represent a lower risk than smaller businesses.

- **Labour or managerial economies (specialisation economies)** – Workers in large firms are able to specialise in particular tasks. They can be employed in specific functions like marketing which is more efficient than working across functions as happens in smaller firms.

## Diseconomies of scale

**Key term**
**Diseconomies of scale** are the cost disadvantages that result from the increase in the size of an organisation.

As a business increases in size and produces more, it may experience the following types of **diseconomy of scale**:

- **Communication** – When a business expands, communication diseconomies occur because it becomes more difficult for managers to communicate with workers as the number of employees, departments and offices increases.

- **Motivation** – Large firms often find it more difficult to manage workers because employees can feel more distant from the senior management of the business.

- **Administration** – Increased costs of administration are more likely in large organisations where the level of bureaucracy increases, which can hinder the decision-making process.

## CASE STUDY

**Tesco**
Tesco is one of the largest supermarket retailers in the world. It has always had a competitive edge because of the economies of scale it has enjoyed. It has struggled in recent years with falling sales, profits and share price. Many critics think it has got too big and unwieldy and has found it difficult to compete with smaller more flexible competitors.

### Progress questions

1 Define the term 'economies of scale'. [2 marks]

2 Explain two types of economy of scale Tesco might benefit from. [4 marks]

3 Analyse how communication and staff motivation may have become more difficult for Tesco as it increases in size. [6 marks]

**Exam tip**
The 'analyse' command term in this question means breaking down into its essential reasons how communication and staff motivation may have become more difficult for Tesco as it increases in size.

# The merits of small versus large organisations

Most industries are made up of large national and multinational businesses and also small and medium-sized enterprises. The reality of different industries is that a place exists for organisations of different sizes. The department store example exists in the retailing industry where there is a huge range in the size of businesses.

## Advantages of large businesses

- **Economies of scale** – These can lead to lower unit costs that can give a competitive price advantage and increase profit margins.

- **Reduced risk** – In big organisations, risk can be spread across different markets, which protects them from adverse conditions in one market. They are also more likely to have the financial resources to withstand a downturn in demand in poor market conditions.

- **Barriers to entry** – Large businesses are often able to control entry into their markets, which reduces the threat of competition.

- **Brand recognition** – The most recognisable brand names are often those of big companies because of the resources they have for marketing and the media coverage they receive.

- **Resource availability** – The human, financial and capital resources available to large firms enables them to do things small businesses often struggle to do. Big businesses, for example, can attract the best talent with high wages and have the funds to embark on the most innovative research and development.

## Advantages of small businesses

- **Diseconomies of scale** – The management and communication difficulties large firms often face can drive up their unit costs, reducing price competitiveness and profit margins.

- **Flexibility** – Small firms are often able to change quickly to deal with changes in the business environment. Decisions can be made quickly without the bureaucracy that faces larger businesses.

- **Marketing image** – Large businesses can sometimes attract bad publicity because of their wealth and power.

- **Niche markets** – Small, specialised markets are often served more effectively by small businesses. This is particularly true where there are limited economies of scale in an industry.

- **Attractive to workers** – Many people like the idea of working in small businesses because they feel more attached to an organisation where they are more in touch with the owners, other employees and customers.

# The difference between internal and external growth

## Internal growth

Internal growth, sometimes called organic growth, is where an organisation increases in scale using its own resources. This often means financing growth using retained profits and borrowing. The business retains its original legal identity as an organisation.

It often involves the business:

- increasing the range of products it sells
- operating in more locations
- developing new products
- investment in new production capacity
- penetrating markets by increasing sales volume.

The example department store was founded over 50 years ago and has increased through internal growth, continuously opening new stores in different locations.

# 1.6

## External growth

External growth is when a business grows by joining together with other organisations through mergers, takeovers, joint ventures and strategic alliances. This often means that the legal status of the organisation changes.

## Types of external growth

**Key term**
**Merger** Where two firms agree to join together under a single legal identity.

**A merger** is a consensual relationship between two businesses to form a new, normally larger, organisation.

**Key term**
**Takeover** When one firm acquires more than a certain of number shares in another firm and effectively takes control of that business then a takeover has taken place.

**Takeovers** can be 'friendly' when the business being taken over decides to accept the offer by another business to take control of it. A 'hostile' takeover occurs when the business being taken over does not agree to the takeover bid.

**Key term**
**Joint venture** Where two businesses enter into an agreement to create a separate entity to manage a particular project.

**Joint venture** normally involves shared ownership, profits, risks and governance. This might be, for example, opening a new production plant, a research and development project or investment in a piece of infrastructure.

**Key term**
**Strategic alliance** is an agreement between two businesses to manage a project but it is a less formal arrangement than a joint venture and does not involve creating a separate legal identity.

A drug company may, for example, enter into a **strategic alliance** with a research laboratory to develop a new drug.

**Key term**
**Franchising** is where a business (a franchiser) sells the rights to produce a good or service under its brand name to another business (a franchisee).

The **franchise** agreement normally involves an initial purchase cost to the franchisee along with an annual royalty fee.

### CASE STUDY

**Jaguar Land Rover**
Britain's leading luxury car maker Jaguar Land Rover has a contract with Chinese company Chery Automobile to form a joint venture with a £1.1 billion of investment in a manufacturing plant in Shanghai. The investment included a research and development centre and an engine production facility. Models produced by the plant will be specifically tailored for the Chinese market.

**Progress questions**

1 Define the term 'joint venture'. [2 marks]

2 Explain the difference between a joint venture, a strategic alliance and a merger. [4 marks]

3 Analyse two reasons why Jaguar might have chosen a joint venture rather than opening its own production facility. [6 marks]

# Globalisation and the growth and evolution of businesses

## Key term

**Globalisation** is the increasing international influence in the business environment in terms of growth in international trade, movement of labour and influence of multinational organisations.

Table 1.6.1 details some of the opportunities and threats of globalisation.

**Table 1.6.1**

| | Opportunity | Threat |
|---|---|---|
| International trade | • Increased number of consumers to sell to<br>• Spreads risk across different markets<br>• More choice of overseas suppliers to access<br>• Lower cost of imported inputs. | • Increased competition from overseas business<br>• Exchange rate movements can adversely affect costs and revenues<br>• Imports and exports can be subject to trade restrictions like tariffs<br>• Overseas markets may require specialist knowledge. |
| Movement of labour | • Access to more skilled labour<br>• Access to lower-cost labour<br>• Domestic workers learn new skills from migrants<br>• Migrants increase demand for domestically produced goods and services. | • Existing workers react badly to lower wages and increased competition in the labour market<br>• Language and cultural differences among workers have to be managed<br>• Overseas workers can be more transient which increases labour turnover. |
| Influence of multinationals | • Creates demand for local goods and services<br>• Domestic firms learn from multinational's technology and operating systems<br>• Provides goods and services for local firms to access<br>• Can improve local infrastructure. | • Increased competition for domestic firms<br>• More competition for domestic resources particularly labour<br>• Local suppliers to the multinational become dependent on its existence which is a problem if it withdraws. |

The impact on **globalisation** on the growth and evolution of businesses can be looked at in terms of the opportunities and threats it presents to organisations.

The department store retailer has been affected by globalisation through foreign competition in the retail market, the number of immigrant workers it employs, and the number of imported products it buys.

# The growth of multinational companies (MNCs)

## Key term

**A multinational company (MNC)** is a business that has an operational base in more than one country.

The growing influence of **multinational companies (MNCs)** in the world economy has been a key feature of globalisation.

The growth of multinationals can be explained by the following factors:

• desire for business to grow and increase their scale of production means by expanding into overseas markets because there are more consumers to sell to

- increasing scale of production allows multinational organisations to achieve economies of scale

- organisations can spread their risks across different countries, which means a decline in one market can be covered by growth in another

- businesses often looking to reduce costs and production in another country can mean reduced labour, raw material and land costs

- in an increasingly globalised world, large firms need to have a position in international markets to keep their brands competitive.

# The impact of MNCs

## Advantages to countries of multinationals

The growth of multinational organisations brings the following benefits to the countries where they set up:

- **Employment** – Multinational firms often provide significant numbers of job opportunities to the countries and communities where they set up.

- **Infrastructure** – When large manufacturing companies set up, they sometimes develop transport links and other forms of infrastructure that domestic businesses and people can benefit from.

- **Economic output** – The production of goods and services by multinationals adds to the host country's Gross Domestic Product (GDP), which contributes to its economic growth.

- **Exports** – Many multinationals use the country where they locate as a production base to export from. The exports they sell add to the export revenue of the domestic economy.

- **Consumer and business choice** – The products marketed by the multinational add to the buying choices of domestic firms and consumers. This is particularly true in services such as retailing.

- **Knowledge economy** – Multinationals often introduce operational techniques and systems that domestic businesses can learn from.

- **Linked suppliers** – The size and scale of multinationals often provides significant marketing opportunities to domestic businesses that provide inputs and services to the multinational.

## Disadvantages to countries of multinationals

There can also be disadvantages to the country where the multinational sets up:

- **Competition** – Competition increases for domestic firms who come up against a large powerful foreign business.

- **Loss of local culture** – Globalised organisations can dominate local markets and create a homogenous international feel to a market, which reduces the feeling of domestic culture.

- **Exploitation of labour** – Many critics of multinationals accuse them of paying low wages and offering poor working conditions to their employees. Sometimes the highest paid managerial roles and skilled work is offered to people from the multinational's home country.

- **Repatriation of profits** – Some multinational organisations send their profits back to their base country, which is an outflow of funds from the domestic economy.

- **Dependency** – Where a domestic economy becomes dependent on multinationals for output, employment and exports, there is a risk to that economy if the multinationals reduce their involvement or withdraw from the domestic market.

# Exam practice questions

## Paper 1 question (HL and SL)

### Fine Olive Company

The Fine Olive Company was started by Mimis Manolas in 2009 after he was made redundant from his job working as a civil servant. Mimis believes part of the business's success is that it is a small business, which makes it attractive to consumers and means it does not experience diseconomies of scale.

**a** Describe two types of diseconomy of scale. [4 marks]

**b** Analyse two reasons why the Fine Olive Company's size has helped its performance. [6 marks]

[Total 10 marks]

### Exam tip

The 'describe' command term in this question means giving a detailed account of diseconomies of scale.

## Paper 2 question (HL and SL)

### McDonald's

One of the world's most famous multinationals is McDonald's. As the world's largest fast food retailer, it has nearly 70 million customers a day served by 37 000 outlets. It operates in 119 countries and its famous golden arch logo is difficult to avoid wherever you go in the world. It is a multinational organisation based on franchising, which has allowed it to expand very quickly without huge initial capital costs. It employs 420 000 people and in 2015 it had a revenue of $25 billion with a net profit of $4 billion.

**a** Define the term 'multinational'. [2 marks]

**b** Suggest two reasons why McDonald's would want to expand into many different countries as a multinational. [4 marks]

**c** Explain two challenges that local fast retailers might face as McDonald's restaurants enter their market. [4 marks]

**d** Evaluate the benefits to a country of the presence of McDonald's restaurants operating in their fast food market. [10 marks]

[Total 20 marks]

# Organisational planning tools (HL only)

# 1.7

**What you should know by the end of this chapter:**

- How to explain, construct, interpret and evaluate the following organisational planning tools:

    - Fishbone diagram

    - Decision tree

    - Force field analysis

    - Gantt chart.

**Chapter illustrative examples**
A clock manufacturer, restaurant chain, food and clothing retailer, and conference organising business

# The use of organisational planning tools

In order to make effective decisions, businesses need to have the best understanding they can of where their decision might take them. Businesses can use the following techniques to help them plan decisions:

- **fishbone diagrams**

- decision trees

- force field analysis

- Gantt charts.

# Fishbone diagram

## Analysing an organisational problem

**Key term**
**A fishbone diagram** is a diagram used to set out the different causes and effects of a business issue or problem.

**Fishbone diagrams** are often used by management as part of a brainstorming meeting to organise ideas into specific categories.

**WORKED EXAMPLE**

The process for producing a fishbone diagram:

1 **Identify the problem** – poor product quality.

2 **Establish the major factors** that affect the problem and use these to form the structure of the fishbone diagram – components, employees, capital equipment, production systems and other factors.

3 **Identify the causes of the problem** by brainstorming around the major factors – these are drawn as 'bones' branching off the major factors. The clock business, for example, could look at motivation levels, the quality of management and training.

4 **Analysis of diagram** – managers can focus on the areas of the diagram that highlight significant causes of the problem. In the clock manufacturers example, the focus of the factors causing the problem might be poorly motivated staff and lack of training.

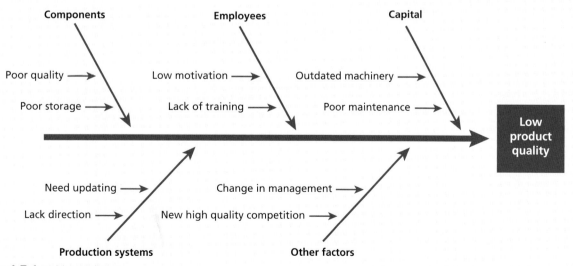

**Figure 1.7.1** Fishbone diagram.

## Fishbone method

The worked example in Figure 1.7.1 is for a clock manufacturer that is receiving customer complaints about the reliability of its clocks and high product returns.

## Evaluating the fishbone diagram

### Strengths

Fishbone diagrams help the decision-making process by:

- Using a scientific approach to look at a problem-solving situation that faces an organisation. By clearly defining cause and effect within a problem, decision-makers are more likely to develop solutions that are effective.

- Supporting an innovative method to problem-solving by considering the causes of a problem that managers have not considered.

- Being an effective visual aid that can be used to present a problem-solving approach to different stakeholders.

### Weaknesses

The weaknesses of the fishbone diagram are:

- The brainstorming approach gives too many factors and causes that can make a problem look too daunting.

- The process produces irrelevant factors and causes that could side-track management and are time consuming to deal with.

- The method is often based on opinions rather than evidence which can make the causes unreliable.

### The Instant Mug Company

The Instant Mug Company was founded three years ago by two business graduates from the Netherlands, Johnny De Boor and Francis Van Der Hoek. The business specialises in selling online mugs that can be designed by their buyers. Customers can add pictures, messages and individual designs to the mugs by uploading them to the company's website. The mugs are then dispatched to the customers. The company has received a large number of returned products in the last six months due to mistakes in design and poor quality printing on the mugs.

### Progress questions

1  Outline two possible causes of the Instant Mug Company's problem under the areas of capital and employees. [4 marks]

2  Explain how a fishbone diagram might be used to contribute to the solution of the Instant Mug Company's problem. [4 marks]

# Decision tree

## Financial assessment of a decision

**Key term**

A **decision tree** is a tool used by organisations to assess the different possible financial outcomes of a particular decision.

A **decision tree** is a valuable tool because it clearly sets out for each possible decision:

- different outcomes that might occur

- costs and revenues associated with an outcome

- the probability of an outcome occurring.

## Producing a decision tree diagram: worked example

Table 1.7.1 sets out:

- the decision the restaurant needs to make – refurbishing its restaurants, buying new outlets, doing nothing

- financial outcomes of each option

- probabilities of those outcomes occurring based on the prevailing market conditions

- expected values (probability × net income)

- total expected value of each option

- net gain of each option (total expect value – set-up cost)

**Table 1.7.1**

| Decision | Set-up cost ($000s) | Market conditions | Probability | Net income ($000s) | Expected value ($000s) | Total expected values ($000s) | Net gain ($000s) |
|---|---|---|---|---|---|---|---|
| Refurbishing existing restaurants | 2,600 | Strong | 0.6 | 3,100 | 1,860 | 3,020 | 420 |
| | | Weak | 0.4 | 2,900 | 1,160 | | |
| Buying new outlets | 3,400 | Strong | 0.6 | 4,200 | 2,520 | 4,080 | 680 |
| | | Weak | 0.4 | 3,900 | 1,560 | | |
| Do nothing | 0 | Strong | 0.6 | 700 | 420 | 460 | 460 |
| | | Weak | 0.4 | 100 | 40 | | |

The values from Table 1.7.1 can be used to build the decision tree diagram:

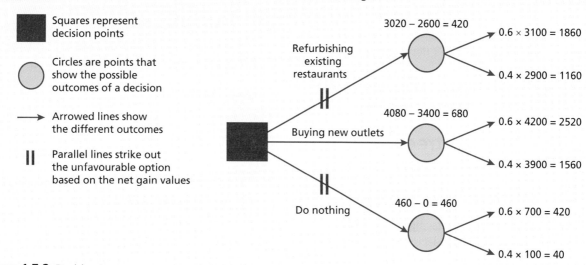

**Figure 1.7.2** Decision tree.

# Decision tree method

Figure 1.7.2 shows a case example of be a restaurant chain deciding between refurbishing its existing restaurants or buying new outlets to try to increase its sales and profits.

A decision tree is set up by:

1   Setting out the different possible decisions a business might face. In this example, these are refurbishing or buying new outlets or doing nothing. On the decision tree diagram, these are shown as squares.
2   Assigning the monetary costs of setting up the alternative decision – see Table 1.7.1. Outcomes are shown as circles on the decision tree diagram.
3   Forecasting the revenue, costs and/or profits associated with the outcomes of a decision – see Table 1.7.1.
4   Forecasting the probabilities of the outcomes of the different decision being considered – see Table 1.7.1.
5   Calculating the expected values of the decision's financial outcomes by multiplying its probability and financial value.
6   For each decision, the sum of the expected values is calculated.
7   The set up cost of each cost is subtracted from the total excepted value to give a net gain for the decision.
8   The decision whose outcome gives the greatest net gain is the most desirable decision on this basis.

# Evaluating decision trees

## Strengths

Decision trees help the decision-making process by:

- clearly setting out the decision(s) facing an organisation and the possible outcomes of the decision(s)

- setting out the possible monetary consequences of a decision(s)

- building in the chances and risk associated with different consequences by using probabilities

- being an effective visual aid that can be used by management when presenting decisions.

## Weaknesses

The weaknesses of decision trees for decision-making are:

- the problem of forecasting future costs and revenues

- the difficulty of assessing the probabilities of different outcomes

- the complexity of the decision tree, which makes decisions difficult to produce and interpret

- the model is static and does not allow for changes in variables over time.

## CASE STUDY

**Espirit Camping**

Espirit Camping is a French business that operates five campsites in south-west France. It has experienced various changes in the camping market over the last few years. People are looking for a higher-quality experience from their sites and want to hire lodges and fixed camping units rather than using their own tents and caravans. Espirit has the choice between investing in lodges, fixed camping units or upgrading and leaving the current space on their campsites for customers to use their own caravans and tents. The costs revenues and probabilities of different outcomes are set out in Table 1.7.2.

**Progress questions**

1   Construct a fully labelled decision tree to show the different options open to Espirit including the costs, revenues and probabilities of each option. [6 marks]

2   For each option, calculate the expected value less the initial cost and state which option should be chosen on a financial basis. [4 marks]

3   Evaluate the usefulness of the decision tree approach to Espirit in making its decision. [10 marks]

**Exam tip**

The 'calculate' command term in this question means obtaining a numerical answer for the expected values, making sure you show the relevant stages through your workings.

**Table 1.7.2**

| Option | Initial cost (€000 000s) | Net income with favourable economy (€000 000s) Probability 0.3 | Net income without favourable economy (€000 000s) Probability 0.7 |
|---|---|---|---|
| **1** Invest in new lodges | 1.9 | 5.1 | 2.2 |
| **2** Invest in fixed camping unit | 1.1 | 1.8 | 1.6 |
| **3** Leave current space for campers | 0.2 | 0.6 | 0.5 |

# Force field analysis

## Management of change

**Key term**
**Force field analysis** is a model that assesses the relative importance of different environmental factors that impact on business strategy when managing change. **The force field analysis model** divides the environmental factors into driving forces and restraining forces.

## Driving forces

### Internal forces

These come from within the business and might include the desire to:

- improve revenues, profits and cash flow
- increase efficiency and reduce costs
- respond to deteriorating performance
- raise motivation among the workforce.

### External forces

These come from outside the business and might include the desire to respond to:

- challenging market and economic conditions
- changes in input costs and wages

- technological advances
- political change.

## Restraining forces

### Internal forces

- corporate culture that is resistant to change
- constraints on finance
- limited access to resources
- poor leadership.

### External forces

- conservative customers
- poor trading conditions
- legal and political constraints
- banks and other lenders resistant to change.

## Producing a force field analysis

A major retailer that sells food and clothing has seen a significant fall in its clothing sales over the last few years. The senior management of the retailer are looking to withdraw from the clothing sector and concentrate on food.

## WORKED EXAMPLE

**The steps for a force field analysis are shown in Table 1.7.3:**

1 **Brainstorming internal and external driving and restraining force.** For the retailer's management this included the following driving forces for discontinuing its clothing stores:

- consumer tastes moving away from its old-fashioned brand image

- growth in the market for low-price clothing

- growth in online shopping for clothing where the retailer has a limited presence

- increased competition for the retailer's target market segment because of new entrants

- poor reaction to the retailers most recent clothing collections

- success of the food section of the business through rising sales and market share.

The retailer's restraining forces for discontinuing its clothing stores included:

- loss of significant revenue stream for the business

- as a smaller business, it would lose economies of scale

- damage to the company's brand image, which could adversely affect its food business

- job losses in the clothing stores have redundancy costs and might damage staff morale

- loyal clothing customers might stop buying its food

- conflict among senior managers about the decision.

2 **Make an assessment of the relative strength of the driving and restraining forces** and give them a numerical value. In the force field diagram below, the driving and restraining forces are given a rating of 1–5 based on their relative strength, with 1 being weakest and 5 being strongest.

3 **Put the forces into a force field diagram** showing the relative strength of each force. The arrows in the diagram show the driving and restraining forces with the size of the arrows illustrating the strength of the forces.

4 **Make a judgement on the change decision** based on the balance between driving and restraining forces. In this retailer example, the restraining forces are greater than the driving forces so the decision to withdraw from the clothing sector is not justified on the basis of this analysis.

**Table 1.7.3**

| Decision to withdraw from the clothing sector and concentrate on food | | | | |
|---|---|---|---|---|
| **Driving forces** | **Rating 1–5** | | **Rating 1–5** | **Restraining forces** |
| Consumer tastes moving away | 4 | | 5 | Loss of revenue stream |
| Growth in low price clothing | 2 | | 2 | Loss of economies of scale |
| Growth in online shopping for clothing | 2 | | 5 | Damage to brand image |
| Increased competition from new entrants | 3 | | 3 | Job losses damage staff morale |
| Poor reaction to clothing collections | 3 | | 1 | Clothing customers stop buying its food |
| Success of the food section | 4 | | 3 | Conflict among senior managers on decision |
| Total | 18 | | 19 | |

# Evaluating the force field analysis

## Strengths

Force field analysis helps the decision-making process by:

- setting out clearly the different opposing factors that affect a decision

- introducing relative numbers to value the strengths of different forces which gives some objectivity

- looking at qualitative factors (employee motivation, conflict between management) as well as quantitative factors

- being an effective visual aid that can be used by management when presenting decisions.

## Weaknesses

Weaknesses of force field analysis for decision-making are:

- the complexity of some decisions, which are difficult to apply force field analysis to because there are so many forces

- the values put on the forces are subjective

- the views of people involved in the analysis are judgement and may not be accurate.

# Gantt chart

## Project management

---

**Key term**

A **Gantt chart** is a planning tool used to make the management of activities during business projects as effective as possible.

Effective project management means organising each activity of a project by maximising the efficiency of the organisation's systems and the skills and knowledge of its work force.

For a business project, a **Gantt chart** sets out the:

- activities involved

- start time and end of each activity

- duration of each activity

- activities that might overlap with each other

- start and end time of the entire project.

Gantt charts help the project management process by:

- setting out a complex set of activities in a clear, organised way

- making it clear when to take undertake certain activities to make the project run efficiently

- providing targets to managers and employees on starting and completing activities and the entire project

- being an effective visual aid that can be used by management when managing projects.

Weaknesses of Gantt charts for project management are:

- activity timings based on forecasts that may not be accurate

- charts can be overly complex for large projects and lose their clarity for presentation

- bars reflect time for an activity but do not represent how much work an activity might involve

- the need to update the chart as the project progresses as start and end times change.

Table 1.7.4 shows an example of the activities an events management business needs to do to set up a conference

**Table 1.7.4**

| Activity | Start time | End time | Duration |
|---|---|---|---|
| Organise presenters | 1.7.16 | 30.9.16 | 92 days |
| Choose and book venue | 1.8.16 | 31.10.16 | 92 days |
| Advertise event | 1.11.16 | 31.1.17 | 92 days |
| Send out customer invitations and take bookings | 15.11.16 | 31.1.17 | 77 days |
| Hire event staff | 15.1.17 | 31.1.17 | 16 days |
| Set up the event | 15.2.17 | 28.2.17 | 13 days |

Figure 1.7.3 represents this as a Gantt chart:

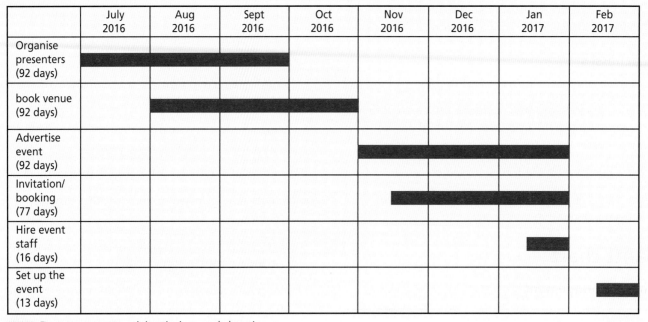

■■■ Bars represent activity timing and duration

**Figure 1.7.3** Gantt chart for setting up a conference.

## CASE STUDY

### Solar Solutions

Solar Solutions is a medium-sized Morocco-based renewable energy company. The key to the company's success is the fast, efficient development of new products. A project team has been put together to produce and market a new lightweight solar panel that can be easily put up and taken down on smaller dwellings. The 'Bit Solar' product is seen to have massive growth potential in developing countries. Table 1.7.5 sets out the different activities and timings involved in the project to set up production of 'Bit Solar'

### Table 1.7.5

| Activity | Start date | Duration (months) |
|---|---|---|
| Market research | 1.09.16 | 1 |
| Preliminary product design | 2.09.16 | 3 |
| Manufacturing assessment | 1.09.16 | 1 |
| Choose best product design | 1.12.16 | 1 |
| Design manufacturing process | 1.01.17 | 4 |
| Develop detailed product design | 1.01.17 | 4 |
| Test prototype | 1.05.17 | 1 |
| Finalise product design | 1.06.17 | 1 |
| Order components | 1.07.17 | 2 |
| Order production equipment | 1.07.17 | 4 |
| Install production equipment | 1.11.17 | 2 |

### Progress questions

1 Explain how the use of a Gantt chart might be useful to Solar Solutions. [4 marks]

2 Construct a fully-labelled Gantt Chart for setting up production of the 'Bit Solar' product. [8 marks]

### Exam tip

The 'construct' command term used in this question means displaying Gantt Chart information in a clearly set out diagrammatic form.

# Exam practice questions

## Paper 1 question (HL only)

### Fine Olive Company

The Fine Olive Company was started by Mimis Manolas in 2009 after he was made redundant from his job working as a civil servant. Mimis would like to grow and develop the business. He is also looking to improve the firm's project management.

Evaluate the effectiveness of two different organisational planning tools to support decision-making at Fine Olive Company. [20 marks]

## Paper 2 question (HL only)

### Ansom PLC

The European-based Ansom PLC manufactures consumer electronic products focusing on so-called 'white goods': fridges, washing machines, tumble dryers and dishwashers. Ansom's directors are looking to open a plant in India to take advantage of the opportunity to market its products in this growing market. An Indian base would also give it the opportunity to reduce costs through cheap labour and low set-up costs for the new factory. The new plant also offers Ansom the opportunity to export to other countries in the region. There is some opposition to the change. A large number of workers from its major centre in Germany have been asked to relocate to India and many are reluctant to go. To release funds for the Indian project, Ansom will have to sell off a loss-making plant in the UK which has led to opposition from the UK government and trade unions. Some directors of Ansom are also concerned about the firm's lack of understanding of the Indian market and the cultural challenges of operating in Asia.

A project team has been set up by Ansom to write a detailed report on the India project. Part of the process has been to conduct a force field analysis.

**a** Define the term 'force field analysis'. [2 marks]

**b** Outline two driving forces that face Ansom's decision to open a plant in India. [4 marks]

**c** Explain why 'the cultural challenges of operating in Asia' might be considered a restraining force in Ansom's decision to open a plant in India. [4 marks]

**d** Discuss the usefulness of force field analysis as part of the decision-making process as Ansom PLC considers whether to open a plant in India. [10 marks]

[Total 20 marks]

# Human Resource Management

# Functions and evolution of human resource management

**What you should know by the end of this chapter:**

- Human resource planning (workforce planning) (AO1)

- Labour turnover (AO2)

- Internal and external factors that influence human resource planning such as demographic change, change in labour mobility, new communication technologies (AO3)

- Common steps in the process of recruitment (AO2)

- The following types of training: on-the-job (including induction and mentoring), off-the-job, cognitive and behavioural (AO2).

**Chapter illustrative example**
A bicycle manufacturer

# Human resource planning

## Aim of a human resource plan

When an organisation sets a workforce plan, the key objective is to have the right number of employees with the appropriate skills to achieve the businesses's corporate aims. This could be, for example, a bicycle manufacturer planning a workforce to produce and sell a certain number of bicycles.

## Steps to produce a human resource plan

- **Work from the corporate objectives** – This provides managers with HR needs to achieve the overall aims for the coming year.

- **Human resources audit** – This is an assessment of the business's current HR situation in terms of the numbers of employees they have and their skill levels.

- **Forecast the numbers of employees required** – This is based on the number of products the firm aims to produce, how productive the workers are and the regulations affecting workforce such as maximum hours worked.

- **Forecast the skills required** – This will be determined by the nature of the products to be produced and the skill level of the current workforce.

# Labour turnover

## Measuring labour turnover

**Key term**

**Annual labour turnover** in an organisation measures the rate at which employees are leaving an organisation in one year. It is measured by number of employees leaving in 1 year / average number of people employed × 100

If the average number of staff a business employs is 60 people and 12 people left the business in the past year then the **annual labour turnover** would be:

$$12/60 \times 100 = 20\%$$

## Causes of labour turnover

- **Nature of the industry** – Fast food retailers will generally have high staff turnover because they employ lots of temporary workers such as students.

- **Morale of the workforce** – If the overall feeling of staff in a business is unhappy and morale is low then they are more likely to leave and this increases turnover.

- **Levels of unemployment** – When unemployment is low, staff turnover tends to increase because workers find it easier to get a new job.

**Table 2.1.1**

| Advantages | Disadvantages |
|---|---|
| • Less productive and skilled staff might be replaced by more effective workers. | • Increases costs because of the need to recruit and train new staff. |
| • Businesses that need to reduce labour costs find it easier when workers are more likely to leave. | • Customer service and business efficiency might fall because workers are constantly changing. |
| • New workers can make the organisation more dynamic by introducing innovative methods. | • Group morale is more difficult to establish. |

# 2.1

## Advantages and disadvantages of high labour turnover

**Tamdown Group**

The Tamdown Group, which produces infrastructure, groundwork and reinforced concrete frame services has been named Employer of the Year in the UK for 2016. The business is seen to have exceptional focus on its people and is viewed as an exceptional organisation to work for. Its key human resource initiatives include: effective management succession planning; outstanding health and safety standards; free health checks for staff; and generous financial remuneration. The results of its high standards as an employer have been high employee morale and low labour turnover.

**Progress questions**

1  Define the term 'labour turnover'. [2 marks]

2  State how labour turnover is calculated. [2 marks]

3  Analyse two benefits to Tamdown of having a low labour turnover. [6 marks]

**Exam tip**

The 'state' command term in this question means giving a specific equation for labour turnover.

# Factors that influence human resource planning

## Internal factors

Internal factors are within the business and affect human resource planning. To a large extent they can be controlled by the organisation:

- **Staffing needs** – These are jobs that need to be done for the organisation to achieve its corporate aims.

- **Finance available** – The recruitment of staff needs to done within budgetary constraints.

- **Skill levels** – The current skill levels of a business's employees will influence planning in terms of training needs and hiring policy.

- **Productivity** – How a business can improve its level of productivity to reduce unit costs and increase profits.

## External factors

External factors in the business environment affect workforce planning and are outside the firm's control:

- **Demographic change** – This is the how the population of a country changes over time in terms of its total number and its age structure. An organisation, for example in a country with a rising population of people between the ages of 20 and 35 due to migration, may have the opportunity to recruit highly-skilled staff at relatively low wages.

- **Labour mobility** – This is the ease with which workers can move between jobs on the basis of the skills they have (occupational mobility) and their ability to move to different locations to take work (geographical mobility). For example, an advertising agency will find it easy to recruit new staff in a region with high occupational and geographical mobility.

- **New communications technology** – As technology advances in this area it becomes increasingly possible for businesses to outsource certain types of work and to have employees work from home. An insurance company can, for example, use communication technology to move administrative tasks to workers located in another country.

# Common steps in the recruitment process

A crucial part of workforce planning is recruitment of the right people to meet the corporate aims of the organisation. Recruitment is the attraction, appraisal and selection of the right person to meet the employment needs of an organisation.

An example of the recruitment process can be applied to a lighting manufacturer that is looking for lighting engineers to be involved in the design of industrial lighting systems.

These are the common steps of the recruitment process:

1   **Identify the vacancy** – Establish the precise nature of the job the organisation requires doing.
2   **Write a job description** – This could include the job title, tasks to be performed, responsibilities involved and working conditions.
3   **Person specification** – This sets out what the organisation wants from its employee in terms of qualifications, experience, positions of responsibility held and also personal qualities.
4   **Advertise the position** – This can take the form of internal recruitment within the organisation or external recruitment outside the organisation.
5   **Shortlist applicants** – Once people have applied for the position, their details will be set out on an application form or curriculum vitae (CV). These will be screened to create a shortlist of the most suitable applicants.
6   **Conduct interviews** – The shortlisted candidates can now be interviewed for the job and they are judged on how they best fit against the job description. The best candidate(s) is then selected to do the job.

## CASE STUDY

### Accenture

Accenture is a multinational professional services company, providing services and solutions in strategy, consulting, digital and technology. It is a big organisation, with 336 000 people working in over 200 cities across 56 countries. It sees itself as one of the world's leading graduate employers 'offering challenging roles to talented individuals'. Accenture is currently recruiting software engineering graduates to design, build and support innovative technical solutions.

### Progress questions

1   Describe two parts of the recruitment process Accenture will use to recruit a software engineering graduate. [4 marks]

2   Analyse two external factors that might determine the number of software engineering graduates Accenture will be able to recruit. [6 marks]

# Types of training

Training refers to the process of improving the knowledge and skills of employees to give them the ability to do their work more effectively. Training is critical to the success of an organisation in terms of making sure all its employees have the right skills needed to do their jobs effectively. There are four main types of training and these are shown in Table 2.1.2

**Table 2.1.2**

| Type of training | Characteristics |
|---|---|
| **1** On-the-job training | • takes place within the workplace<br>• training given by training department and experienced workers<br>• involves induction training for new staff who are given guidance on a business's rules, procedures, culture, work colleagues and communication methods<br>• use of mentoring where an experienced member of staff guides and advises a new employee |
| **2** Off-the-job training | • takes place outside the workplace<br>• involves outside training using an agency such as a college, university or industry body<br>• used when a firm lacks expertise and resources to train staff itself<br>• brings new ideas and methods |
| **3** Cognitive training | • based on developing the way employees think at work<br>• general approach to improving the way people work rather than task-specific<br>• tries to develop in employees' things such as: self-confidence, creative thought, dealing with stress, and independent thought |
| **4** Behavioural training | • based on developing the way workers interact, relate and communicate with others<br>• sometimes called soft skills training<br>• includes training in skills such as communication, negotiation, conflict management, presentation and customer service |

# Appraisal of employees

Appraisal of employees is an assessment of an employee's performance at work against an agreed set of targets between a worker and their line manager. Employees will complete an appraisal form where they set out their job description and personal objectives for the coming year. Their performance at work will then be appraised against those targets along with their overall performance at work.

## Importance of appraisal

Appraisal is important for the effective management of employees because it can be used to:

• set clear objectives for employees to work towards

• give employees feedback on their current work

• make decisions on financial and non-financial rewards

• make decisions on promotion

• give guidance for further training

• make decisions about redundancy or dismissal.

## Types of appraisal

• **Formative** – The aim of formative appraisal is to develop an employee's performance at work by evaluating their work using a range of different methods of assessment. This can be through regular formal appraisal meetings or informal observations and discussion.

• **Summative** – Summative appraisal is to provide an objective measure of an employee's success at work set against certain standards. This is normally done after a set time period when the employee has completed a certain amount of work. In a sales job, for example, this could be achieving a particular level of target sales. Summative assessment is often used to set pay levels, bonuses and promotions.

- **360-degree feedback** – 360-degree feedback is summative appraisal based on judgements on an employee's performance made by all the people they come into contact with at work. As a sales manager, for example, this might be from the sales team they manage, other sales managers, the sales director they report to and the customers they deal with.

- **Self-appraisal** – Self-appraisal is where a worker is asked by their manager to complete a self-evaluation form to make judgements about their own performance at work. The manager will then go through the worker's self-evaluation with them to see whether the manager's appraisal of the employee's performance at work matches the employee's self-appraisal.

# Common steps in dismissal and redundancy

## Dismissal

A worker may be dismissed or 'sacked' from a job if they break their contract of employment. Their contract of employment sets out the terms and conditions of their employment including things like pay, hours of work, holiday entitlement and duties at work. A worker in a bank might be sacked if they are rude to customers or if they consistently make mistakes with the money they handle.

### The steps for dismissal are:

1 Establish the break of contract: poor conduct at work or not having the capability to do the job.
2 Investigate the breach of contract fully.
3 Consider other penalties rather than dismissing: warning letters or extra training.
4 Disciplinary hearing..

## Redundancy

Redundancy is where a worker leaves a business because their job is no longer required by the business. Redundancy can occur if a business closes down, an area of business the employee is working in shuts down,

and if new machinery replaces the work of an employee. The employees of a retail chain may be made redundant if the company decides to close a number of outlets.

### Steps for redundancy are:

1 Choose workers for redundancy because their work is no longer needed.
2 Consult with the worker on the need for redundancy.
3 Give formal notice of redundancy.
4 Look to offer alternative work if this is possible.
5 Agree terms of redundancy such as redundancy pay and time to find another job.

## CASE STUDY

### Goldman Sachs

The investment banking organisation Goldman Sachs uses a 360-degree appraisal system where the employees' superiors, peers and reports are all used to judge the employees' performance over the year. Goldman managing directors are 'reviewed by up to 15 people: 3 peers, 9 seniors, one junior, and 2 primary reviewers'.

A Goldman employee is rated on a scale of 1–5 by each of their reviewers. The final scores are analysed by a computer algorithm that adjusts for anomalies attributable to reviewer such as harshness or leniency. The employee is then ranked in the organisation according to the appropriate quartile.

### Progress questions

1 Explain two reasons why appraisal is important to Goldman Sachs. [4 marks]

2 If, as a result of their appraisal, a Goldman Sachs employee is going to be dismissed, state two elements of the dismissal process. [2 marks]

3 If a Goldman Sachs employee has a poor appraisal they might be asked to do cognitive training. Analyse how cognitive training might improve their performance at work. [6 marks]

# Changing working patterns, practices and preferences

## Changes in the working environment

Like all aspects of the business environment, the working environment is constantly subject to change. This could be because of things like social change with, for example, increasing numbers of women in management roles or technological change, such as allowing more employees the opportunity to work from home.

Table 2.1.3 presents three examples of how changing working patterns, practices and preferences affect employers and employees.

# Outsourcing, offshoring and re-shoring strategies

## Outsourcing

Outsourcing is a human resource strategy where a business contracts out an activity to another business. This is often done to a firm's non-core activities, which may be performed more effectively by a contractor and at a lower cost.

This can include activities such as catering, market research, cleaning, accounting and IT support.

An example might include an insurance company that has outsourced its catering.

**Strengths:**

* outsourcing catering activities to specialist employees in another company where catering can be performed more effectively

* can lead to lower costs because there are no staff salaries to providing the catering activity

* leaves the insurance company's employees to concentrate on their own core functions.

**Weaknesses:**

* buying-in cost to the insurance company of outsourced catering

* reduces control over the outsourced catering activity, particularly if there are concerns regarding quality.

## Offshoring

Offshoring is where a business relocates a human resource activity done in one country to another country. The business can do the activity itself or get another business to do the activity on its behalf.

Businesses normally offshore activities to reduce costs because the labour and operating costs are lower in another location. Moving activities does, however, mean that an activity is not as easy to manage and the quality of service may not be as good. Some banks, for example, have moved their IT services to lower-cost providers in other countries.

## Re-shoring

This is the reversal of offshoring. Re-shoring is where the human resource activities of a business are brought back to the country of origin because the business has found managing offshore providers challenging due to communication and management problems.

**Table 2.1.3**

| | | Employer | Employee |
|---|---|---|---|
| Teleworking | Working online from home | **Advantages** | **Advantages** |
| | | • draw on workers from a wider geographical area<br>• reduced cost of office space and worker facilities | • save on time and cost of transport<br>• easier to manage home life |
| | | **Disadvantages** | **Disadvantages** |
| | | • need to finance functional IT systems to facilitate working from home<br>• management is more difficult because there is less direct control over workers | • less direction from management<br>• less interaction with colleagues at work |
| Flexitime | A working schedule that allows workers to set their own start and finish times | **Advantages** | **Advantages** |
| | | • improves worker morale and increases productivity<br>• more working hours covered reduces the need for overtime | • easier to manage home life<br>• reduces transport costs if travelling at off-peak times |
| | | **Disadvantages** | **Disadvantages** |
| | | • can increase costs if the work place is open for longer<br>• management becomes more difficult if workers are not present at the same time | • social implications of working different times to co-workers<br>• reduce effectiveness if not present at important work times |
| Migration for work | Geographical movement of people to find jobs | **Advantages** | **Advantages** |
| | | • gives more choice of potential employees with particular skills<br>• increasing labour supply reduces wages | • more employment opportunities available<br>• chance to learn new skills and have new experiences |
| | | **Disadvantages** | **Disadvantages** |
| | | • cultural differences and language barriers foreign employees bring<br>• workers can be quite transient which increases labour turnover | • increased competition from migrant workers<br>• reduced wages because of increased labour supply |

# Influences on human resources

## Innovation

Innovation can affect human resource strategy in the way people are managed. Organisations have developed new ways of managing people that include team working, 360-degree appraisals, performance-related pay, quality circles, job enrichment and worker empowerment. By doing this, businesses have achieved the following benefits:

- improved staff motivation
- increased productivity
- better customer service
- reduced labour turnover
- reduced absenteeism rates
- human resource management.

## Ethical considerations

There are important ethical considerations that need to be considered in the way employees are managed. Many of these ethical considerations are covered by regulations and also by organisational policies. They include:

- **Discrimination** – All workers need to be treated in the same way by managers and by their co-workers regardless of their ethnicity, race, gender, sexuality or age.

- **Fairness** – Managers need to treat their subordinates in a fair and respectful way.

- **Complying with legal guidelines** – This could include paying the minimum wage, offering statutory sick leave and paid holidays.

- **Following a country's cultural expectations** – There are certain ways employees expect to be treated, which differ from country to country, and businesses need be respectful of this in human resource management.

## Cultural differences

Corporate culture is the behaviours, values and attitudes that are shared by people in an organisation. Cultural differences occur in organisations that draw their employees from different social and ethnic backgrounds. For example, a European bicycle manufacturer may relocate in China and have to deal with a different working culture to the one they have experienced in Europe.

Here are some of the cultural differences that might influence the way in which the European bicycle manufacturer manages in a production plant they open in China:

- **How people work and their working patterns** – The European bicycle manufacturer might find Chinese employees respond better to shift work than their European counterparts.

- **How employees relate to each other and to customers** – Chinese people may deal with each other differently in the workplace compared to European workers.

- **How managers lead their subordinates and how subordinates react to managers** – This would be important if European managers are used in the Chinese bicycle plant.

- **How employees deal with the policies, rules and regulations of the business** – A European bicycle manufacturer's policies, rules and regulations might need to be adapted for the Chinese production plan.

# Exam practice questions

## Paper 1 question (HL and SL)

### The Juice Truck

The Juice Truck is one of the leading mobile beverage businesses in India. It has more than 200 mobile units based in a variety of major cities in India. Specialising in fresh fruit, smoothies and health foods, it has benefited from a growth in health consciousness among the Indian population. The HR director, Surender Singh, has had the responsibility of overseeing the recruitment and training of many mobile unit managers. He is a strong believer in on-the-job training because he believes people need to be exposed to the day-to-day pressures of the job and that you learn best by dealing with the customer.

**a** Define the terms:

   **i** recruitment [2 marks]

   **ii** appraisal [2 marks]

**b** Analyse two benefits to The Juice Truck of using on-the-job training to increase the skill level of its employees. [6 marks]

[Total 10 marks]

**Exam tip**

The 'analyse' command term in this question means breaking down the benefits of on-the-job training to The Juice Truck to bring out their essential elements.

## Paper 2 question (HL and SL)

### Isao Technology

Isao Technology is a small Japan-based digital technology business that develops digital communications systems for multinational organisations. It is quickly growing. In the past four years, its workforce has grown from 20 to 250, many of whom are highly skilled software specialists. The firm's CEO believes recruiting the right staff is the key to the organisation's success.

The business faces two human resource challenges: one is whether to outsource some of its non-core activities, particularly in finance where a number of small companies would like to take on these activities; and the other is whether to start recruiting software specialists internationally. The senior management at Isao are split on both issues and worry that the business may lose some of its identity with the changes.

**a** Define the term 'human resource plan'. [2 marks]

**b** Describe two elements that might be part of Isao's human resources plan. [4 marks]

**c** Explain two reasons why Isao might be looking to outsource some of its non-core activities. [4 marks]

**d** Evaluate Isao's decision to recruit some of its software specialists internationally. [10 marks]

[Total 20 marks]

# Organisational structure

# 2.2

## What you should know by the end of this chapter:

- The following terminology to facilitate understanding of different types of organisational structures: delegation, span of control, levels of hierarchy, chain of command, bureaucracy, centralisation, decentralisation, delayering (AO1)

- The following types of organisation charts: flat/horizontal, tall/vertical, hierarchical, by product, by function, by region (AO2, AO4)

- Changes in organisational structures, such as project-based organisation, Handy's Shamrock organisation (AO2)

- How cultural differences and innovation in communication technologies may impact on communication in an organisation (AO3).

**Chapter illustrative example**
A major airline

# Organisational structure

**Key term**
**Organisational structure** is the formal human resource framework of a business, which sets out how managers and employees are linked together and the way authority is passed through an organisation.

The **organisational structure** of the airline example sets out how its people, such as directors, senior managers, pilots, cabin crew and ground staff, are interrelated throughout the organisation.

## Hierarchical organisation structure

**Key term**
A **hierarchical organisation structure** is based on different levels of authority that exist in the organisation.

As you move up the hierarchy, the level of seniority increases until you reach the CEO. At each level of hierarchy, employees share similar status and are managed by people in the next level of the hierarchy.

Figure 2.2.1 sets out a **hierarchical organisation structure** for a computer manufacturer.

## Different organisation charts

Organisation structures can be very different between different organisations. They can vary for cultural, historical, organisational and strategic reasons. Figure 2.2.2 shows four main examples of different organisation structures.

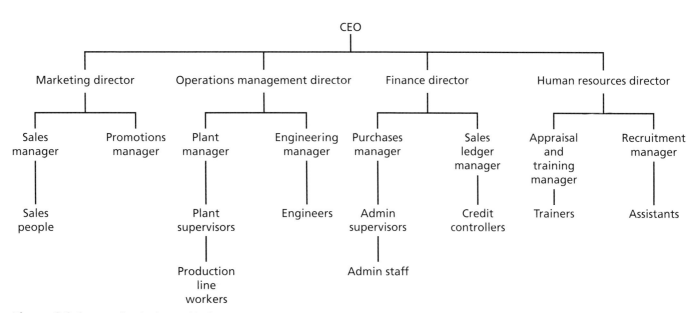

**Figure 2.2.1** Example of a hierarchical structure.

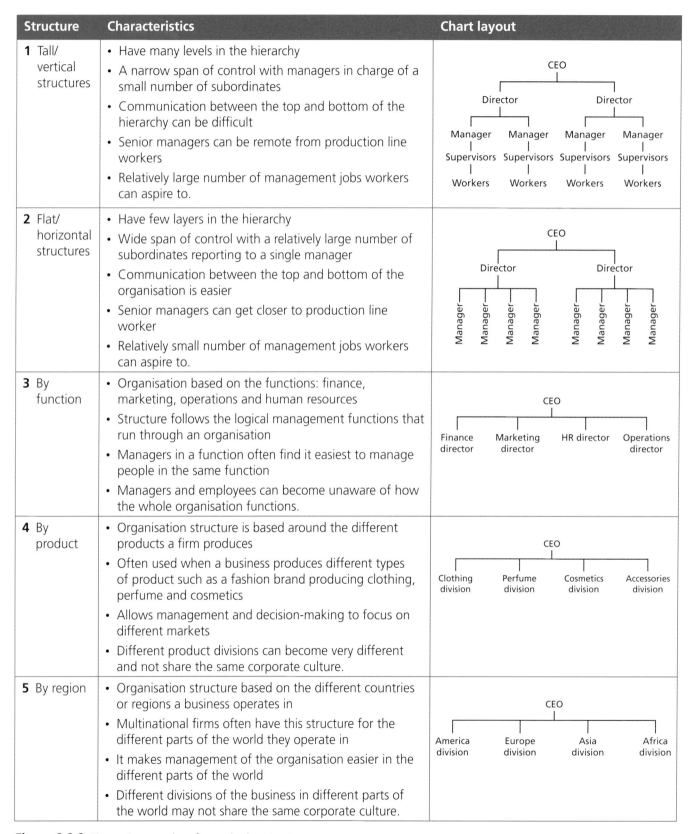

| Structure | Characteristics | Chart layout |
|---|---|---|
| **1** Tall/ vertical structures | • Have many levels in the hierarchy<br>• A narrow span of control with managers in charge of a small number of subordinates<br>• Communication between the top and bottom of the hierarchy can be difficult<br>• Senior managers can be remote from production line workers<br>• Relatively large number of management jobs workers can aspire to. | |
| **2** Flat/ horizontal structures | • Have few layers in the hierarchy<br>• Wide span of control with a relatively large number of subordinates reporting to a single manager<br>• Communication between the top and bottom of the organisation is easier<br>• Senior managers can get closer to production line worker<br>• Relatively small number of management jobs workers can aspire to. | |
| **3** By function | • Organisation based on the functions: finance, marketing, operations and human resources<br>• Structure follows the logical management functions that run through an organisation<br>• Managers in a function often find it easiest to manage people in the same function<br>• Managers and employees can become unaware of how the whole organisation functions. | |
| **4** By product | • Organisation structure is based around the different products a firm produces<br>• Often used when a business produces different types of product such as a fashion brand producing clothing, perfume and cosmetics<br>• Allows management and decision-making to focus on different markets<br>• Different product divisions can become very different and not share the same corporate culture. | |
| **5** By region | • Organisation structure based on the different countries or regions a business operates in<br>• Multinational firms often have this structure for the different parts of the world they operate in<br>• It makes management of the organisation easier in the different parts of the world<br>• Different divisions of the business in different parts of the world may not share the same corporate culture. | |

**Figure 2.2.2** Five main examples of organisation structure.

2.2 Organisational structure

## CASE STUDY

### Qantas

In 2014 the major Australian airline Qantas made significant changes to its senior executive team. In an attempt to improve management efficiency, Qantas has removed a number of its directors and adopted a flatter organisation structure. The airline has not stopped at senior management and has sought to reduce costs through redundancies and by removing many middle management positions.

### Progress questions

1 Define the term 'hierarchical organisation structure'. [2 marks]

2 Describe the process of Qantas adopting a flatter organisation structure. [4 marks]

3 Explain how a flatter organisation structure might reduce Qantas's costs. [4 marks]

# Characteristics of organisational structures

## Chain of command

### Key term

The **chain of command** is the link between the manager who has overall responsibility for making a decision and the employees who are responsible for carrying out the decision.

An example of a **chain of command** is the training manager who decides which employees are going to be trained by which trainer and the trainers who carry out the actual training.

## Delegation

### Key term

**Delegation** is decision-making responsibility being passed down the chain of command to someone with a lower level of seniority.

The marketing director in the computing firm might delegate the responsibility of employing a new sales person to the sales manager.

The amount of **delegation** that occurs in an organisation will depend on:

- The personality of manager – some managers want to keep control over decision-making so little delegation takes place.

- Whether employees are motivated and able—they are more likely to have decisions delegated to them.

- Whether there are challenging business conditions—managers are less likely to delegate because decisions can be more difficult to make.

## Span of control

### Key term

The **span of control** is the number of subordinates (workers) a manager is directly responsible for.

A manager in the example airline has seven sales people responsible to them so the span of control is seven. The wider the span of control a manager has, the more people they have to direct and the more challenging the management situation is.

### Factors affecting the span of control:

- In flat organisation structures, the span of control tends to be wider than tall structures.

- Able managers have the ability to manage a wider span of control.

69

- Employees who have high ability and are well motivated can be managed with a wider span of control.

- Difficult tasks in challenging situations often need a smaller span of control.

## Centralisation/decentralisation

**Key term**
**Centralisation** is where the senior management of an organisation maintains a high level of control over decision-making in the organisation.

Decentralisation is where the CEO and senior management delegate decision-making responsibility to managers in different areas of the business.

Factors affecting centralisation and decentralisation include:

- Centralisation often occurs because of the nature of the CEO and senior management who might want to keep tight control of the organisation.

- Corporate culture influences how centralised a business is. A more autocratic culture may mean more centralised control over decision-making.

- Quality of managers and employees in the organisation. An organisation with lots of talented managers with highly motivated employees is more likely to flourish as a decentralised organisation.

- When the organisation structure is regionalised or arranged by product, then the organisation becomes more decentralised because different decisions are needed by the different regions/products.

## Bureaucracy

**Key term**
**Bureaucracy** is the rules, policies and procedures that exist in an organisation.

When someone works in an organisation, **bureaucracy** are the principles they have to follow in their everyday activities and decision-making. As an organisation increases in size and complexity, the number of rules, policies and procedures become more complex.

The level of bureaucracy affects the way decision-making takes place in the organisation structure. The more bureaucratic an organisation, the more difficult it is to make decisions. The more complex an organisation structure is, the more bureaucratic it tends to be.

## Delayering

**Key term**
**Delayering** is where the senior managers of the organisation remove layers from the organisational hierarchy to make it 'flatter'.

**Delayering** can have the following effects on the organisation:

- removes management layers, which reduces costs

- makes decision-making between the top and bottom of the organisation easier

- increases the span of control of managers

- involves more delegated decisions

- reduces the number of management positions for employees to aspire to.

### Kentucky Fried Chicken

The huge Kentucky Fried Chicken (KFC) fast food restaurant chain is one of the biggest franchise operations in the world. Based in Louisville, Kentucky it has nearly 20000 outlets in 123 different countries. It is a subsidiary of the Yum! Restaurant brand that also owns the Pizza Hut and Taco Bell chains. Like so many franchise operations, it is seen as a decentralised business with the day-to-day decisions on the way the store is run delegated to store managers although control over major strategic decisions is still held centrally by senior managers.

### Progress questions

1 Define the term 'delegation'. [2 marks]

2 Outline two 'day-to-day' decisions that might be delegated to KFC store managers. [4 marks]

3 Explain two benefits to KFC of a decentralised organisation structure. [4 marks]

### Exam tip

In this 'outline' command term question, you need to give a brief account of two 'day-to-day' decisions that might be delegated to KFC store managers.

# Changes in organisational structures

Management theorists have tried to develop new ways to organise human resources and deliver greater efficiency, solve problems and innovate new products.

## Matrix-based structures

### Key term

**Matrix organisation structures** are used by businesses to manage projects they are working on by drawing on specialist employees from different parts of the business.

Projects that involve expertise from operations management, design, marketing and finance will draw specialists from these areas to work on the project.

The specialists used on the project teams are drawn from more formal parts of the organisation structure to work on the project. The matrix structure is shown by Figure 2.2.3.

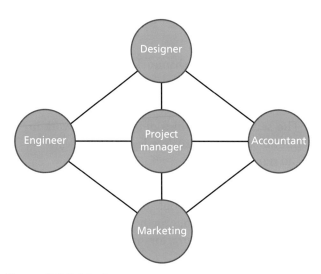

**Figure 2.2.3** Matrix structure.

## Shamrock Organisation

Thomas Handy developed the Shamrock Organisation structure in 1990 to reflect changes in the way human resources are organised. This is often used to explain the move to outsourcing non–core functions such as different elements of marketing and administration. Figure 2.2.4 shows the Shamrock Organisation.

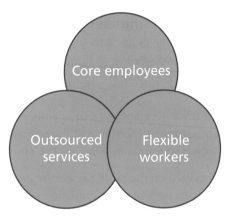

**Figure 2.2.4** Handy's Shamrock Organisation.

It is based on the three ways workers are employed by a business:

- **The top leaf** of the shamrock represents the valued core employees of the business such as senior managers and highly skilled workers.

- **The second leaf** consists of people who work in outsourced services such as legal services, catering and transport.

- **The third leaf** is made up of the flexible labour force. These are the people brought in to the organisation when they are needed. This is part-time workers, outside contractors and consultants.

## Communication in organisations

Effective communication between people in an organisation is an important part of its success. Effective communication occurs when information is transmitted by the sender and received and understood by the receiver.

## Impact of cultural differences

Cultural differences affect effective communication in an organisation because of the different ways employees that come from different countries and cultural backgrounds communicate with other. This is important for organisations that:

- locate operations overseas

- employ migrant labour

- outsource activities to foreign providers

- merge with or have joint ventures with organisations from another country.

The challenge of cultural differences means organisations need to manage:

- language differences by, for example, publishing messages in different languages

- different ways employees interpret messages, such as the use of certain words

- the speed at which employees respond to information.

## Impact of innovation

Advances in communication technology have a significant impact on the way people communicate with each other in businesses. Communication technology means information can now be sent by email, text, video messaging, social media, video conferencing and internet messaging. This can be from fixed units in the organisation, PCs and laptops or on mobile devices such as smartphones and tablets.

The advantages of innovation on communication on the example airline might be:

- Messages can be instantly delivered to its employees all over the world at relatively low cost.

- Multimedia messages can be sent on the airline's new advertising campaign.

- Feedback can be quick and easy through 'voting buttons' on, for example, the airline business's managers attending a meeting.

- Set-up and operating costs for the airline's intranet system.

- Video conferencing a meeting between airline's senior managers in different parts of the world.

The disadvantages of innovation on communication on the example airline might be:

- The volume of written communication has increased, which means people can miss messages.

- Employees get over-burdened with electronic information, which creates stress.

- Too many written communications can mean people spend more time dealing with, for example, emails than on their core activity.

- Employees spend less time talking to each other, which reduces team culture.

- Electronic communication replaces more effective communication like meetings.

# Exam practice questions

## Paper 1 question (HL and SL)

### The Juice Truck

The Juice Truck is one of the leading mobile beverage businesses in India. It has more than 200 mobile units based in a variety of major cities in India. For the first seven years Aarti Sen, the CEO, let the business develop in a traditional hierarchical structure. However, after working with a management consultancy firm she was advised to delayer the organisation although she was warned this would have a significant effect on the span of control of the organisation's management.

**a** Outline two factors that determine a manager's span of control. [4 marks]

**b** Analyse two consequences of the business's decision to delayer its organisation structure. [6 marks]

[Total 10 marks]

## Paper 2 question (HL and SL)

### Activation Plc

Activation Plc is a publishing company based in Mexico. It specialises in fashion, lifestyle, celebrity and entertainment magazines. The new CEO is concerned that Activation's hierarchical organisation structure slows down decision-making because it is too bureaucratic. The CEO wants to delayer the organisation, but this has brought significant resistance from many of Activation's employees who have looked for union advice on the changes. There is a genuine feeling of unease and morale among the staff of an already struggling business is low. The CEO is, however, right behind the changes and sees this as the only way to arrest the business's decline in performance.

**a** Define the term 'matrix organisation structure'. [2 marks]

**b** Explain two reasons why Activation's management structure might adversely affect the firm's performance. [4 marks]

**c** Outline the characteristics of the Shamrock Organisation structure. [4 marks]

**d** Evaluate the new CEO's decision to go ahead with the organisational changes suggested by the project team. [10 marks]

[Total 20 marks]

**Exam tip**

This question uses the 'evaluate' command term, which means making a judgement of the decision to go ahead with organisational changes by weighing up the strengths and limitations of the decision.

# Leadership and management

## 2.3

**What you should know by the end of this chapter:**

- The key functions of management (AO2)

- Management versus leadership (AO2)

- The following leadership styles: autocratic, paternalistic, democratic, laissez-faire, situational (AO3)

- How ethical considerations and cultural differences may influence leadership and management styles in an organisation (AO3).

**Chapter illustrative example**
A car rental business

# The difference between leadership and management

A **leader** in an organisation can be anyone who employees choose to follow even if they have not been formerly appointed to a leadership position.

---

**Key term**

A **leader** is someone in an organisation who employees choose to follow.

---

Effective **managers** are often good leaders because they can take a group of employees in a direction that successfully achieves the objective they have been set.

---

**Key term**

A **manager** is someone appointed by an organisation to be in charge of a group of employees to achieve a particular objective.

---

# The key functions of management

The management theorist Henri Fayol summarised the key functions of management as:

## Setting objectives and planning

The senior management of an organisation sets its corporate aims and develops the strategic objectives needed to achieve them. From there, tactical objectives are set for managers throughout the organisation. Planning how the business is going to achieve its objectives is another part of the manager's role.

## Organising resources to meet the objectives

To meet the organisation's objectives, its managers need to organise the business's raw materials and components, its workforce and its capital. To achieve the corporate aim of a certain level of output, a car manufacturer will, for example, need to set an appropriate amount of factory capacity, order in enough parts and components, and employ the right number of workers.

## Directing and motivating staff

This function focuses on the people aspect of a manager's role. Managers need to direct, lead and monitor the work of their subordinates. For example, the store manager in a fast food retailer will on a daily basis direct their staff to do set tasks, motivate them to do the task effectively and check that they are doing the task correctly.

## Coordinating activities

As an organisation increases in size and complexity, managers are responsible for coordinating activities so the organisation operates efficiently. In the example car rental business, it is important that health and safety systems developed in one division of the organisation are not replicated in another division.

## Controlling and measuring performance against objectives

Having created a hierarchy of objectives throughout the organisation, managers need to make sure the objectives are achieved. Managers can do this by setting precise performance targets and using their motivational skills to make sure the targets are achieved.

## Different leadership styles

---

**Key term**

**Leadership style** is the manner and approach a manager uses when carrying out their key management functions.

The different **leadership styles** have strengths and weaknesses that depend on:

- personality traits of the manager

- nature of the subordinates

- the management situation

- the task.

The different leadership styles are set out in Table 2.3.1.

**Table 2.3.1**

| Leadership style | Definition | Characteristics | Strengths | Weaknesses |
|---|---|---|---|---|
| Autocratic | Where a leader keeps strict centralised control over decision-making, communication, information and the workers they manage. | • Keep strict centralised control over decision-making<br>• One-way communication<br>• Tight control over information<br>• Authoritative management style<br>• Close control over workers. | • Works well for workers who want clear, precise direction<br>• Useful in crisis/difficult situations<br>• Useful when problems need to be solved quickly. | • Workers demotivated if they want some say in decisions<br>• Experienced, skilled workers can react badly<br>• Misses out on valuable worker input on decisions<br>• Not helpful for long-term strategic decision-making situations. |
| Paternalistic | An autocratic leader who has a controlling presence who 'cares' and looks after their employees. | • Acts like the leader of a 'large family'<br>• Dominant but controlling presence<br>• Leader 'cares' for employees<br>• Some consultation and two-way communication<br>• Employees not involved in the decision-making process. | • Encourages loyalty among workers<br>• Caring manner raises motivation<br>• Central control gives direction. | • Workers demotivated if they want some say in decisions<br>• Misses out on valuable worker input on decisions<br>• Lacks the drive needed for change in difficult situations. |

**(continued)**

**Table 2.3.1 (continued)**

| Leadership style | Definition | Characteristics | Strengths | Weaknesses |
|---|---|---|---|---|
| Democratic | Involves decentralised management where employees are given some role in decision-making through delegation. | • Involves wider employee participation in decision-making through delegation<br>• Decentralised management<br>• Two-way communication<br>• Workers fully informed on business direction<br>• Empowerment of workers. | • Involvement of employees increases motivation<br>• Valuable employee contribution to decision-making<br>• Two-way communication improves information flows<br>• Good for long-term strategic decisions. | • Worker involvement in decision-making slows the process<br>• Not as effective in difficult business situations<br>• Sharing information too widely can cause problems with sensitive situations<br>• Some employees just want clear direction. |
| Laissez-faire | An approach that involves the full delegation of most of the day-to-day decision-making to employees | • Delegation of most of the day-to-day decision making to employees<br>• Freedom for employees to work in the way they 'think is best'<br>• Can be used with experienced, highly skilled workers. | • Effective when workers need very little management and work independently<br>• Reduces time and cost of management. | • Businesses can lose control over employees<br>• Poor decisions can be made because of a lack of consultation<br>• Motivation falls if workers do not feel 'looked after'. |
| Situational | Where the leadership depends on the task, situation and the employees being managed | • No best leadership approach<br>• Leadership depends on the task, situation and employees<br>• Effective leaders need to be flexible. | • Managers adopt the most effective leadership approach to the situation that faces them at the time<br>• Reflects the dynamic nature of the business environment<br>• Useful in culturally diverse multinational businesses | • Requires highly skilled, flexible managers that may be in short supply<br>• Can lead to inconsistent approaches to management in the business<br>• Could be more difficult to develop a distinct corporate culture. |

## 2.3

## CASE STUDY

### Martha Stewart Living

Martha Stewart is the chairman of media business Martha Stewart Living. She is famous in the US for her achievement in business but also as a former model, author and broadcaster. She is considered by many to be an autocratic leader. She is described as someone who shows 'no compassion' for her subordinates and 'always has the final say' on everything she is involved in.

### Progress questions

1  Define the term 'autocratic leadership style'. [2 marks]

2  Explain two situations when Martha Stewart's leadership style might be effective. [4 marks]

3  Outline the situational approach to management. [4 marks]

# Ethical considerations

Ethical influences on leadership and management are based on the principles and moral values held by the different stakeholders in the organisation. The ethics of managers throughout an organisation have an important impact on the way, for example, it is viewed by customers and the wider community.

Ethical issues might influence the example car hire business in the following ways:

- The personal treatment of employees by the managers on an everyday basis. The extent to which the car hire staff are managed in a respectful way by their line manager.

- The systems set up by the senior management for the whole organisation are fair to its employees. This might involve things like rest breaks, shift patterns and holiday entitlements given to store employees.

- The working methods staff are expected to use. Should care hire staff be expected to promote highly profitable products that are not suitable to customers?

- Managers conduct themselves with honesty and integrity and expect the same conduct from their employees. In the car hire firm, managers would not take time off work that has not been sanctioned and they would not expect this from their subordinates.

# Cultural differences

## Cultural differences in the workplace

Increased globalisation has had a significant impact on the cultural mix of people in organisations. The growth in migration and multinational organisations has meant that managers of one ethnicity increasingly have to lead workers of a different ethnicity.

## The importance of managing cultural differences

Cultural differences can influence the different aspects of leadership and management in the following ways:

- **Achievement of a set goal or task** – The way a task is approached will vary between workers of different countries.

- **Leading a team of people** – Developing an effective group approach is important for managers trying to achieve an objective.

- **Managing the individual employee** – Part of a manager's role is to deal with workers individually and get the best out of them.

The example car hire business has offices all over Europe, Asia and the US and faces all these cultural factors.

## CASE STUDY

### Gap

The US-based clothing brand Gap was given the 'Public Eye' award for the most unethical business of the year in 2014. The award is backed by Greenpeace and its previous winners include Goldman Sachs and Barclays. Gap, along with many other multinational clothing businesses, has manufactured garments in developing countries like Bangladesh, benefiting from cheap labour and low operating costs. The background to the award is the 2013 Rana Plaza disaster in Bangladesh where 1100 people, mainly women making clothing, were killed when the building they were in collapsed. The main reason for the award was Gap's refusal to contribute to effective safety reforms in the textile industry.

### Progress questions

1 Analyse two cultural factors that might affect Gap's US managers when managing workers in Bangladesh. [6 marks]

2 Examine the ethical management issues Gap faces when operating in developing countries such as Bangladesh. [10 marks]

### Exam tip

For an 'examine' question you need to consider an argument or concept in a way that uncovers the assumptions and interrelationships of the issue.

# Exam practice questions

## Paper 1 (HL and SL)

### The Juice Truck

The Juice Truck is one of the leading mobile beverage businesses in India. The operations director, Roshan Shastri, is a manager who likes to be inclusive and get the workers who run the Juice Truck units fully involved in decision-making. Roshan constantly runs meetings with the Truck operators to get their views on current market conditions and get

their suggestions on new products. The truck operators feel empowered and their productivity levels are high.

a Outline two characteristics of a democratic management style. [4 marks]

b Analyse two benefits to The Juice Truck that may arise from Roshan Shastri's management style. [6 marks]

[Total 10 marks]

## Paper 2 (HL and SL)

### Mountain Key

Mountain Key is an outward bounds business based in New Zealand. It is run by one of New Zealand's leading mountaineers, David Fox. The organisation employs 22 outward bound specialists who run activities that include climbing, canoeing, rafting, cycling and hiking. The trips run by Mountain Key are for skilled and experienced people and they operate in a niche market. A climbing trip run by one of the firm's lead climbers Ash Adams might be a 14-day climb and she will have a lot of autonomy to run the trip as she wants. Indeed, David delegates almost complete control over decision-making to activity leaders because he 'only employs the best' and trusts them to do the right thing. He is a very laid-back character and cares more about choosing the right people and then letting them work.

The trips and activities themselves often involve very autocratic control for their leaders. Ash Adams has a particularly strict approach to her climbing trips. She quite an abrasive, direct management style because she argues that she has to get trip completed to a precise timescale and they have to be safe. There have, however, been complaints about her management style particularly from employees in her team who are not from New Zealand and are not used to her direct approach.

a Define the term 'laissez-faire management'. [2 marks]

b Explain why David Fox might be considered to be a laissez-faire manager. [4 marks]

c Explain why laissez-faire management might be an appropriate management style in this case. [4 marks]

d Discuss the ethical and cultural challenges Ash Adams might find in the way she manages her trips. [10 marks]

[Total 20 marks]

# Motivation

**What you should know by the end of this chapter:**

- The following motivation theories: Taylor, Maslow, Herzberg, Adams and Pink (AO3)

- The following types of financial rewards: salary, wages (time and piece rates), commission, profit-related pay, performance-related pay (PRP), employee share ownership, schemes and fringe payments (perks) (AO2)

- The following types of non-financial rewards: job enrichment, job rotation, job enlargement, empowerment, purpose/the opportunity to make a difference and teamwork (AO2)

- How financial and non-financial rewards may affect job satisfaction, motivation and productivity in different cultures (AO2).

**Chapter illustrative example**
A supermarket chain

# The importance of employee motivation

**Key term**

**Employee motivation** is a worker's desire to try and achieve a certain level of performance in their work.

An organisation's success in achieving its corporate aims is certainly going to be affected by how motivated its employees are throughout the organisation.

Well-motivated employees are likely to have the following effects on the organisation:

- high levels of productivity

- produce high-quality goods and services

- low staff turnover

- low absenteeism rates.

# Motivation theories

Different management theorists over time have developed ideas on what motivates workers and how businesses can manage their employees to increase their motivation at work.

## Frederick W. Taylor

The key focuses of Taylor's work focused on improving efficiency in manufacturing businesses using an approach called scientific management.

**The important principles of his work were:**

- Employees are not intrinsically motivated to work hard because they do not instinctively enjoy their jobs.

- Work needed to be broken down into small measureable tasks and employees given precise targets to achieve their production tasks.

- Workers should be trained to do the work task and financially rewarded for achieving the set production target.

- This involved an autocratic management style where workers were precisely directed and controlled by management.

### Application

Taylor's theory was seen by many managers as a relatively simple approach to management that could be applied to workers to increase productivity, reduce unit costs and increase profits. A supermarket chain may, for example, set clear sales targets with bonuses for their store managers to motivate them.

### Weaknesses

Workers were often demotivated by tasks that were boring and repetitive as well as the autocratic nature of management which gave employees little control over their work.

## Abraham Maslow

Abraham Maslow was part of the human relations school of theorists. He considered the importance of psychological reasons in motivating workers and his hierarchy of needs is set out in Figure 2.4.1.

| |
|---|
| **Self-actualisation needs** – Employees need to achieve their full potential |
| **Esteem needs** – How workers feel about the way others respect them and view their status |
| **Social needs** – The relationships workers have with others in the form of friendship and belonging |
| **Security needs** – A worker's sense of physical and emotional safety |
| **Physiological needs** – Workers need to satisfy things such as thirst, hunger, shelter and warmth. |

**Figure 2.4.1** Maslow's hierarchy of needs.

**The important principle of his work was:**

- Workers were seen to be motivated by the factors in a hierarchical way such that a worker would not move to the higher levels in the hierarchy until they had met their needs in the lower levels.

81

## Application

Maslow's human relations approach looks at workers as complex people who are not all the same and are motivated by a range of different factors. By understanding this, organisations are able to improve the motivation level of their workers. A supermarket chain might, for example, provide social activities for their staff to allow them to reach the social level of the hierarchy.

## Weaknesses

The complexity of Maslow's theory can make it difficult to apply. For some people the social aspect of work is important and for some it is not. This may mean creating an expensive social environment that only benefits a certain number of workers.

# Frederick Herzberg

Herzberg was an American psychologist whose view on employee motivation had similar roots to Maslow. He was most famous for his two-factor theory, which suggested that worker motivation was affected by hygiene factors and motivating factors.

**The important principles of his work were:**

- Hygiene factors were things in the workplace that did not directly motivate employees but if they were not present or were unsatisfactory then workers would be demotivated.

- Hygiene factors included company policy and administration, supervision, salary, relationships with others and working conditions. If, for example, workers are overburdened with administration and bureaucracy then they will be demotivated.

- Motivating factors can directly increase employee motivation if they are present in the working environment.

- Motivating factors include things such as responsibility, promotion, achievement and the quality of the work itself. A worker, for example, who directly saw a link between performance in their job and promotion would be motivated by this.

## Application

Herzberg's work was particularly useful for managing employee motivation through job design, their working environment, pay and conditions, and promotions offered to employees. The supermarket chain, for example, makes sure that the rules and regulations are not over-burdensome, that there are comfortable working conditions and a fair rate of pay as hygiene factors. It would then use a system of staff achievement rewards and promotions as motivating factors for staff.

## Weaknesses

Herzberg's work was based on interviewing employees about factors that affected their motivation at work. People sometimes give answers to interviewers that the interviewer wants to hear.

## CASE STUDY

### Google

Google employs 57 000 employees worldwide who seem to 'Love working for Google'. Employees enjoy free Wi-Fi-enabled shuttle transport to and from work, free healthy meals, laundry and fitness facilities, 18 weeks of fully paid maternity leave and on-site childcare, and competitive pay. The job satisfaction rates are incredibly high and in the US the average salary is $133 000 after five years. Google sees its success as having a workplace that is always bringing in new ideas and making work enjoyable.

### Progress questions

1 Outline Google's approach to Herzberg's hygiene factors. [4 marks]

2 Analyse two of Herzberg's motivating factors that could be used to motivate Google's employees. [4 marks]

3 Evaluate the usefulness of Maslow's human relations approach to managing employee motivation at Google. [10 marks]

### Exam tip

The command term 'outline' in this question means giving a brief account or summary Google's approach to Herzberg's hygiene factors.

# John Stacey Adams

Adams was a behavioural psychologist who put forward his theory of motivation at work through his equity theory model in 1963. The central theme of his work was how employees' motivation is affected by their perception of how fairly they feel they are treated at work compared to others.

**The important principles of his work were:**

- An employee's effort at work was called 'inputs' and their rewards 'outputs'. For a worker in a supermarket, for example, inputs would be their time, enthusiasm and energy given to the job and their outputs would be the pay and promotion they receive.

- Employees partly see fairness at work as the balance between their 'inputs' and 'outputs'. The pay they receive, for example, should be relative to their hours of work.

- Adams stressed the importance of how workers judge themselves against others in the organisation. In a supermarket chain, for example, a store manager might compare their pay and conditions against other managers in the chain.

- The theory can explain how an employee's motivation can change even if their own pay and conditions have not changed. If, for example, one supermarket worker sees another supermarket worker get a pay rise then there might be a drop in motivation for the worker who does not get the pay rise.

## Application

Equity theory helps business to understand how to manage workers in their organisation in a way that seems fair in terms of the relationship between their efforts and their rewards, not just on a personal level to an employee but also as it relates to others in the organisation.

## Weaknesses

Fairness is a difficult to thing to judge and employees can sometimes have an unrealistic view of how fairly they are being treated compared to others in the organisation. Managers can have a difficult task dealing with this. A manager in a supermarket chain may deserve a big pay rise even if this appears unfair to other managers.

# Dan Pink

Pink believed the more traditional models of motivation had become less effective in the modern workplace. With more and more people working in service sector jobs where creativity and problem-solving are important, he felt managers should focus on new approaches to motivation centred on autonomy, mastery and purpose.

**The important principles of his work were:**

- **Autonomy** – Where workers are given the opportunity to work independently and use their own ideas they tend to feel more motivated.

- **Mastery** – People feel motivated when they are developing in their work and getting better at what they do. It is important for organisations to give employees tasks that challenge them at the appropriate level.

- **Purpose** – People's motivation levels rise when they find meaning in their work and feel that what they do makes a difference. The principle of purpose means employers need to design work that is interesting, enjoyable and has meaningful outcomes.

## Application

Organisations that want to increase the motivation of their workers need to create a working environment where people have control over their own work, feel they are making progress in their ability to do their job and have a role that has meaning and purpose to them. A supermarket might, for example, allow their store staff to decide the order in which they perform their tasks, train them in the latest ordering technology and use communication technology to show how their work contributes to the performance of the organisation.

## Weaknesses

Creating a working environment that builds on the conditions that Pink's work suggests may be difficult and expensive. Giving the supermarket workers, for example, increased autonomy over their work might reduce the control managers have over the direction of the business.

# Types of financial rewards

Financial rewards can have a significant impact on the motivation of people at work. Different management theorists do, however, show the importance of money in motivating people is not necessarily a straightforward one.

Table 2.4.1 shows the different financial rewards available to organisations.

## CASE STUDY

### Morgan Stanley

Morgan Stanley is an American financial services company based in New York. It employees 60 000 people in 42 countries. While the base annual salary is $111 801, the total pay package jumps up to $233 446 after bonuses. These bonuses are based on the profits of Morgan Stanley and the performance of the individual employee. A financial analyst's basic earnings will be around $85 000, but a managing director earns nearly $800 000. With bonuses, the top earners at Morgan Stanley can earn several million dollars.

### Progress questions

1 Define the term 'profit-related pay'. [2 marks]

2 Outline how Morgan Stanley uses profit-related pay and performance-related pay to motivate its employees. [4 marks]

3 Using the work of two different management theorists, evaluate the view that financial incentives are the best way to motivate employees at Morgan Stanley. [10 marks]

# Types of non-financial rewards

The work of different theorists shows how important factors other than money are in motivating workers. Table 2.4.2 shows the different non-financial rewards available to organisations.

# The impact of financial and non-financial rewards in different cultures

In an increasingly globalised business environment, organisations need to be aware that people from different countries and cultural backgrounds will react differently to the financial and non-financial rewards offered to them by businesses.

## Cultural differences

Financial and non-financial rewards will have some of the following effects in different cultures:

- **Equality** – Some cultures allow for greater inequality among people in their organisation, which means businesses can use performance-related pay as a way of motivating workers. In more equality-based cultures, employees may be better motivated by profit-related pay, where workers share the financial rewards of the business.

- **Individual** – In individualistic cultures where people focus more on themselves, workers are more likely to want to have autonomy and control over their work. Workers in collective cultures may be motivated by group activity such as greater use of team working.

- **Gender** – The balance of men and women in the working environment can impact on the effectiveness of financial rewards like performance-related pay.

- **Risk** – People in some cultures want to avoid risk and like to have financial and non-financial rewards that are fixed and certain. Where cultures allow for greater risk-taking, employees may be motivated by financial rewards like performance-related pay.

- **Tradition** – Workers from traditional cultures are more comfortable with formal, established methods of financial and non-financial rewards such as a set salary and job promotions for good performance.

**Table 2.4.1**

| Reward | Definition | Advantages for motivation | Disadvantages for motivation |
| --- | --- | --- | --- |
| Salary | Fixed amount of pay made to permanent employees on a monthly or annual basis. | Security of income can have a positive effect on motivation. | Certainty can make workers complacent and reduce motivation. |
| Wage (time-based) | Payment to workers on a fixed time basis: hourly, daily and weekly. | Employees know how much they are doing to be paid and can focus on their work. | No incentive for workers to raise productivity to increase their pay. |
| Wage (piece-rates) | Workers are paid for each unit they produce. | Employees are motivated to work harder/faster to increase their pay. | Workers may substitute quality of work for quantity produced and there is a problem if workers cannot control how much work they do. |
| Commission | Payment to sales people based on the value or volume of sales they make. | People who choose to work in sales are often seen as financially orientated and motivated by this approach. | Uncertainty about pay may put pressure on employees, reducing their security and motivation. |
| Profit-related pay | Where employees receive a bonus payment on top of their basic pay related to the annual profit the business has made. | Motivates workers because they feel they are making an overall contribution to a firm's success. | Some workers may be demotivated if their co-workers get paid the bonus even if they do not work as hard. |
| Performance-related pay | A payment system where employees receive extra payment on top of their salary to reward them for good performance in their job. | Employees are financially motivated to improve their performance at work. | Difficult to apply to jobs where there are problems measuring an employee's performance. |
| Employee share ownership schemes | Employees receive a financial reward above their normal pay in the form of shares in the business. | Employees are motivated to work effectively because the success of the business drives up the share price and their financial reward. | Payment method can make some managers take decisions to drive up the share price rather than be effective in their jobs. |
| Fringe payments | Sometimes called 'perks' they involve non-money payments such as company cars, private healthcare, pension and discounts on the firm's products. | Can motivate workers because they feel valued and looked-after by the organisation. | May demotivate workers in the organisation who do not receive these often 'obvious' rewards. |

**Table 2.4.2**

| Reward | Definition | Advantages for motivation | Disadvantages for motivation |
|---|---|---|---|
| Job enrichment | Changes an employee's job to increase the range and complexity of tasks they have along with giving them greater responsibility and autonomy. | Develops the motivating factors Herzberg identified to increase worker motivation. | Not all workers would want to deal with the extra responsibility associated with a job. |
| Job enlargement | The work of an employee remains basically the same but the number and variety of tasks is increased so that the worker does not have to do the same task over and over again. | Reducing the monotony of work motivates workers because they have the opportunity to learn new skills and do more interesting work. | Unless pay is increased to account for a more challenging job, it may reduce motivation. |
| Job rotation | Where there are a number of similar tasks in a particular area of a business, workers are periodically moved between those tasks. | Reduces the monotony of work and increases employee motivation by giving them variety in their work. | Once a worker has had their work rotated a number of times it may only have a limited effect on motivation. |
| Empowerment | Workers are delegated a greater role in decision-making, which gives more autonomy and control over their work. | Greater autonomy is seen as an important motivating factor for workers in Dan Pink's theory. | Some workers may find the increased responsibility stressful, which reduces their motivation. |
| Purpose (opportunity to make a difference) | Designing work and giving information that provides employees the opportunity to see how their work affects the overall outcome of the business. | Giving work purpose is seen as an important motivating factor for workers by the theorist Dan Pink. | In large organisations, seeing the reality of an employee's work and the limited effect it might have on the organisation might be demotivating. |
| Team working | Where employees are organised into groups to work together to complete a particular job. | Working in teams is seen as an important part of the 'social' motivating factor identified by Maslow. | Team working can be demotivating if the people in the team do not work effectively together. |

# Exam practice questions

## Paper 1 question (HL and SL)

### The Juice Truck

The Juice Truck is one of the leading mobile beverage businesses in India. The company sees motivation of its employees as critical to the business's long-term success. HR director, Surender Singh was appointed because of success in her previous roles at getting the very best from the people that worked for her. She is someone who truly values people and trusts them to do their own jobs effectively. She believes in paying people well but more than that she sees that giving workers autonomy and a say in decision-making are important for a motivated workforce. She also believes very strongly in treating all workers in an equitable way where they believe they are valued.

a   Outline two ways in which John Stacey Adams's equity theory is being applied by Surender Singh. [4 marks]

b   Analyse two non-financial methods of employee motivation being applied by The Juice Truck. [6 marks]

[Total 10 marks]

### Exam tip

The command term 'analyse' in this question means breaking down two non-financial methods of employee motivation in order to bring out the essential elements or structure.

## Paper 2 question (HL and SL)

### Arc International

When the Arc International resorts took over the Caribbean Beach Hotel in October 2016, Arc management was shocked by the level of employee morale at the prestigious hotel on the waterfront in Barbados. The labour turnover and employee absenteeism rates were both unacceptably high. Customer service was friendly but extremely inefficient. Arc International's management held several meetings with the hotel's staff to see what the problems were. The main findings were:

1   low rates of pay relative to other comparable hotels

2   boring, repetitive work

3   poor leadership from the previous owner who never spoke to the staff but just dealt with the previous manager

4   the previous manager was autocratic, dealt very inconsistently with staff and certainly had his favourites.

Arc has appointed a new manager to improve the performance of the hotel with a major objective of increasing the hotel's employee motivation. He is considering a plan that includes job enrichment, job enlargement and job rotation.

a   Define the term 'labour turnover'. [2 marks]

b   Using two of Herzberg's hygiene factors, explain why motivation at the Caribbean Beach Hotel might have been so low. [4 marks]

c   Using Adams's equity theory, explain two reasons why the leadership style of the hotel's previous manager might have reduced its employees' motivation. [4 marks]

d   Evaluate the potential of job enrichment, job enlargement and job rotation to improve employee motivation at the hotel. [10 marks]

[Total 20 marks]

# Organisational (corporate) culture (HL only)

**What you should know by the end of this chapter:**

- Organisational culture (AO1)

- Elements of organisational culture (AO2)

- Types of organisational culture (AO2)

- The reasons for, and consequences of, cultural clashes within organisations when they grow, merge and when leadership styles change (AO3)

- How individuals influence organisational culture and how organisational culture influences individuals (AO3).

**Chapter illustrative example**
A social media company

# Organisational culture

**Key term**
**Organisational/corporate culture** is the values, philosophy and behaviour of the people who work in an organisation.

**Organisational/corporate culture** is important to organisations because of the impact it has on its stakeholders. A positive, strong culture that supports a well-motivated workforce is attractive to investors and customers. Therefore a business with a strong organisational culture is likely to be more successful than a business with a less favourable culture.

# Elements of organisational culture

## Formal elements

The formal elements of the corporate culture can be set out in the following ways:

- **Vision and mission statements** – A social media company may, for example, have the mission of 'giving a voice to the community'. This might suggest the firm believes in equality, opportunity and speaking out.

- **Policies, rules and regulations** – All organisations will set out how employees should act in particular circumstances. The nature and tone of these statements have a powerful influence over corporate culture.

- **Recruitment and training** – The type of employees recruited by the business and the way they are trained by the business gives it a powerful influence over organisational culture. If a social media organisation has a policy of hiring managers that are liberal, progressive, outgoing people and they are trained to manage in this way then it will create a culture that reflects this.

- **Corporate social responsibility** – An organisation sets out a statement about its attitude to the community and environment within which it operates.

## Informal elements

While a business might want to formally control its culture, it will also be affected by informal things it cannot control such as:

- **Business environment** – If the economy is in recession with social and political tension, then this will probably have a negative impact on culture. Growing diversity in society may have an effect of the corporate culture of, for example, a social media company.

- **Organisation performance** – Culture may be easy to manage when a business is performing well but if it is struggling then this can have a negative impact on culture.

- **Inter-employee dynamics** – Even with an effective recruitment policy, it is sometimes difficult for an organisation to achieve a mix of personalities that creates a particular culture.

- **Stakeholder conflict** – Sometimes the cultural aim of a business's management is different to that of other stakeholders in the organisation. This creates conflict and adversely affects the corporate culture. In a social media business, for example, there may be a clash between the high profits demanded by the shareholders and the ethical objectives of the management.

**SolarCity**

The US-based renewable energy business SolarCity was founded by brothers, Lyndon and Peter Rive in 2006. It has grown rapidly across 17 states in the US with headquarters in San Mateo, California. It has a very distinct corporate culture that, the owners say, comes from their recruitment policy. They like to appoint military veterans and graduates that strongly believe in reversing climate change. It has a strong belief in social and global responsibilities as part of its organisational culture. Its mission is focused on continuous innovation in the renewable energy section.

**Progress questions**

1 Define the term 'corporate culture'. [2 marks]

2 Describe two characteristics of SolarCity's corporate culture. [4 marks]

3 Explain two factors that might have contributed to SolarCity's corporate culture. [4 marks]

**Exam tip**

The 'describe' command term in this question means giving a detailed account of SolarCity's corporate culture.

# Types of organisational culture

The management theorist Charles Handy identified four types of organisation culture that can exist (see Table 2.5.1). The cultures are not formally designed by organisations but they evolve over time as a result of its organisation structure, the types of people in the business and the management style.

# Cultural clashes within organisations

The culture of an organisation is determined by people in it and people often come into conflict with each other and this leads to cultural clashes. Strong organisations often have a clearly positive culture and a clash of cultures tends to compromise this.

## Reasons for culture clashes

- **Organisation growth** – When an organisation changes, new employees often join it and they bring with them their own ideas from previous employers that are likely to be different from the organisation they join. For example, a social media company brings in a group of new software engineers from a particular computer software business.

- **Mergers and takeovers** – A merger or takeover of one company by another can cause cultural conflict as two sets of management with different corporate ideas are brought together.

- **Crisis and shock** – The organisation experiences a crisis or shock putting the management under pressure. These difficult situations can often lead to management differences on how to deal with the problem. The social media company, for example, may suffer very bad publicity because of unethical use of its services.

- **New leadership** – When a new CEO is appointed to an organisation, they often cause a change in the corporate culture. This change in culture can lead to a clash in the organisation particularly if the senior managers and employees are resistant to the change.

## Consequences of cultural clashes

- **Decision-making** – This can be slowed down and its effectiveness reduced because the people who have to make the decision work are not moving in the same direction. The CEO of a social media company,

**Table 2.5.1**

| Type | Definition | Nature of culture | Example |
|------|-----------|-------------------|---------|
| Power culture | Decision-making is centralised around the CEO or a few senior managers who have a great deal of control over the organisation. | • Autocratic leadership approach<br>• Strong personality of CEO or senior managers<br>• High-pressure working environment<br>• Reliance on financial incentives to motivate employees. | An investment bank dominated by a very powerful CEO. |
| Role culture | Decision-making is based on a small number of senior management positions where the position rather than the person has control. | • Bureaucratic organisations with strict rules and policies<br>• Formal hierarchical organisation structure<br>• Managers and employees have precise roles they need to fulfil<br>• Decision-making is slow and lacks flexibility. | A government-run organisation that manages healthcare. |
| Task culture | Decision-making is focused on specific jobs or projects where workers are organised in teams. | • Matrix organisation structure<br>• Decentralised decision-making<br>• Team identity is more important than the individual<br>• Importance of highly skilled employees in key positions. | Computer software business continuously looking to develop new products. |
| Person culture | Decision-making is focused on specific individuals and exists to benefit those individuals' rather than wider business objectives. | • Organisation structure that lacks power over the individual<br>• Decentralised decision-making<br>• Individual influence is more important than the team<br>• Rare in organisations. | Research organisation that employs highly skilled scientists. |

for example, is trying to launch a new product and some of the directors slow the process down because they do not like the way the decision was made.

- **Productivity** – Culture clashes can reduce productivity if conflict has a negative effect on employee motivation.

- **Corporate image** – If there is a more public clash of culture, there may be open disagreements that external stakeholders become of aware of and that

damage the firm's corporate image. The investors in the social media business, for example, are concerned that conflict in the organisation is damaging its brand.

- **Labour turnover** – Employees often find it difficult to work in cultural environments where there are clashes and they might leave, which increases labour turnover. Increased labour turnover is often associated with increased costs and more instability.

# 2.5

**Gillette and Procter & Gamble**

When two of the world's leading consumer products businesses, Gillette and Procter & Gamble, merged, this was seen by many as the perfect match. But the management of the newly merged business found huge difficulties in integrating the two organisations. Insiders said there were no 'deep-seated differences in values or mission' but the two businesses had very different methods of communicating and making decisions. Gillette managers used a written-memo-based approach whereas P&G used face-to-face meetings. Gillette was always quick to make decisions, while P&G's decision-making was much slower.

**Progress questions**

1   Describe two reasons for culture clashes that occurred following the merger of Gillette and P&G. [4 marks]

2   Analyse two possible consequences of the culture clash that might arise from the merger of Gillette and P&G. [6 marks]

# How corporate culture influences individuals

The values, philosophy and behaviour of the whole organisation will impact on an individual who works for that organisation in positive and negative ways depending on the culture.

Impact of a culture:

*   **Motivation** – Workers feel more motivated and strive to achieve more in their work if the prevailing culture encourages this. In a social media business, for example, a strong team- or task-based culture might successfully develop new products.

*   **Behaviour** – A positive culture encourages employees to behave in a way that enhances

the 'positive feeling' experienced by different stakeholders when they deal with the organisation.

*   **Loyalty** – Workers will feel more connected to an organisation with a culture they like and can identify with. This means they are more likely to stay with the business and this reduces staff turnover.

*   **Conflict** – Where employees identify with and feel good about the culture in their working environment then they are less likely to be in conflict with other workers and management, which leads to greater stability and a more cohesive and effective business.

Where a business has poor corporate culture that negatively affects employees, they are likely to be less motivated, behave negatively in the workplace, be disloyal to the organisation and be involved in conflict.

# How individuals influence corporate culture

Organisations are a collection of individuals who all make some contribution to its corporate culture. These are the factors that affect the influence an individual has on corporate culture:

*   **Size of the organisation** – The smaller the organisation is, the more impact one individual will have on its culture. In a very large organisation, it is difficult for any one individual, even senior managers, to have as much effect on culture.

*   **Position in the organisation** – The more senior an individual's position is in a business, the more influence they are likely to have on its culture. In, for example, the social networking business, the CEO is seen to have most influence on its culture.

*   **Personality traits** – Individual employees are likely to have more impact on corporate culture if they have a strong personality.

*   **Gender** – If the gender balance of a business moves more towards women or men then it may have an impact on corporate culture.

- **Ethnicity/nationality** – The larger the number of a particular ethnic group or those of a particular nationality, the more effect they are likely to have on corporate culture.

# Exam practice questions

## Paper 1 question (HL)

### The Juice Truck

The Juice Truck is one of the leading mobile beverage businesses in India. It has received a number of business awards and praise in the media for its approach to its employees. The business has four core principles when it comes to the workforce: reward them fairly, train them superbly, empower them and make their work meaningful. HR director, Surender Singh describes the business as a 'role culture'. This has created a culture that attracts people to come and work for the business.

**a** Outline two characteristics of role culture that might apply to The Juice Truck. [4 marks]

**b** Analyse two benefits to the The Juice Truck of having a positive corporate culture. [6 marks]

[Total 10 marks]

### Exam tip

The 'outline' command term in this question means giving a brief account or summary of two characteristics of SEN that suggests it is a power culture.

## Paper 2 question (HL)

### SRE Global

SEN is a hedge fund based in New York founded by its CEO Mark Branner, a former investment banker. The business is a partnership with ten partners and 30 other employees. One employee described the corporate culture as 'ruthless and fiercely competitive'. Mark Branner is a very autocratic leader and a very demanding person to work for. All the staff who are not partners are on three-month contracts and if they do not make their sales targets then they get fired. The office is well-known for conflict and open arguments between employees. Mark Branner always looks to employ intelligent, highly competitive young graduates from Ivy League US universities.

In return for working in what is seen as a 'power culture', employees get paid very well. All the partners are multimillionaires and Branner is said to be worth $800 million. One 26-year-old MIT graduate earned $400 000 in his first year with the business.

**a** Define the term 'power culture'. [2 marks]

**b** Outline two characteristics of SEN that suggest it is a power culture. [4 marks]

**c** Explain two ways individuals at SEN have contributed to its corporate culture. [4 marks]

**d** To what extent might SEN's success be the result of its corporate culture? [10 marks]

[Total 20 marks]

## Key concept question

With reference to one organisation that you have studied, examine what changes corporate culture might have on ethics and innovation. [20 marks]

# Industrial/ employee relations (HL only)

## 2.6

**What you should know by the end of this chapter:**

- The role and responsibility of employee and employer representatives (AO2)

- The following industrial/employee relations methods used by:

    - employees: collective bargaining, slowdowns/ go slows, work-to-rule, overtime bans and strike action

    - employers: collective bargaining, threats of redundancies, changes of contract, closure and lock-outs (AO3)

- Sources of conflict in the workplace (AO2)

- The following approaches to conflict resolution: conciliation and arbitration, employee participation and industrial democracy, no-strike agreement, single-union agreement (AO3)

- Reasons for resistance to change in the workplace (such as self-interest, low tolerance, misinformation and interpretation of circumstances) (AO2)

- Human resource strategies for reducing the impact of change and resistance to change (such as getting agreement/ownership, planning and timing the change and communicating the change) (AO3)

- How innovation, ethical considerations and cultural differences may influence employer– employee relations in an organisation (AO3).

**Chapter illustrative example**
A train operating company

# The role and responsibility of employee and employer representatives

**Key term**
**A trade union** is an organisation set up by employees to represent the views and protect the rights of those employees.

## Employees' representatives – trade unions

**Trade unions** have the following functions:

- **Representing the view of employees to employers** – It communicates with an employer on a regular basis to discuss the views and mood of the employees it represents. The union representing the workers at the train operating company, for example, has explained to the managers that its members are unhappy about changes to its shift patterns.

- **Safety and security at work** – Unions put pressure on employers to make sure the workplace is safe and secure for workers.

- **Protecting pay and conditions** – Trade unions often use collective bargaining where they negotiate on behalf of their members with employers on pay and conditions. For example, the union representing the workers at the train operating company enter collective bargaining with management if it tries to negotiate a 3% pay increase for all its members.

- **Industrial action** – When employees are in dispute with their employers, trade unions negotiate with the employers to try and resolve the dispute. If the dispute cannot be resolved, the union may organise industrial action to try and push the business's management to make a resolution in favour of the employees.

## Employers' representatives

Employers are generally represented by HR managers appointed by the organisation to work with trade unions on issues relating to its workforce and how this affects the organisation. There are also employers' associations representing groups of employers in a particular industry.

---

### CASE STUDY

**IG Metall**
IG Metall is Germany's biggest trade union representing 3.7 million workers. It has 70 000 engineering workers who are members working for companies like BMW, Mercedes and Daimler. In 2015, IG Metall was acting for its 70 000 engineering members in pay negotiations. It was dealing with an employers' association that represented the 300 employers involved.

**Progress questions**

1 Define the term 'trade union'. [2 marks]

2 Outline two roles of trade unions. [4 marks]

3 Explain why an employers' association might act for the engineering employers involved. [4 marks]

---

# Industrial relations methods used by employees

Table 2.6.1 summarises the different industrial relations methods trade unions might use in a conflict situation.

In the train operating company, for example, the union tried to negotiate a 4% wage rise using collective bargaining and then embarked on a period of work to rule and overtime bans when negotiations stalled. A settlement was finally made on a 3% pay increase without a strike.

**Table 2.6.1**

| Industrial relations method | Definition | Impact on employers | Impact on employees |
|---|---|---|---|
| Collective bargaining | Unions negotiate on behalf of their members with employers' representatives on pay and conditions of employees. | Easier to deal with employees collectively rather than as separate individuals and groups. | Gives employees greater bargaining power when they negotiate together. |
| Slowdown/go slow | Where employees work at the minimum pace required by their contract. | Can disrupt production and lead to poor customer service. | Employees may lose money if pay is based on achieving certain production or sales targets. |
| Work to rule | Employees refuse to do any work that is outside their employment contact. | This will affect production where employers rely heavily on uncontracted work. | Workers who rely on additional payments for uncontracted work will lose income. |
| Overtime ban | Unions stop workers completing extra work outside their contracted hours of work. | Could disrupt production where overtime work is needed to meet production targets. | Workers who do a significant amount of overtime work will lose pay. |
| Strike action | Unions instruct their members to stop working for a certain period of time. | This can be very disruptive for a business and may even force it to stop operating during a strike period. | Can lead to a significant drop in income for workers and can mean conflict between workers. |

**Table 2.6.2**

| Industrial relations method | Definition | Impact on employers | Impact on employees |
|---|---|---|---|
| Collective bargaining | Employer's team negotiate on behalf of the business with the trade union on employees' pay and conditions. | Easier to deal with employees collectively rather than as separate individuals and groups. | Gives employees greater bargaining power when they negotiate together. |
| Threat of redundancies | Employer says they will have to make some workers redundant if an agreement is not reached as some employees' jobs will no longer exist without an agreement. | Redundancies may reduce costs, which release funds to make a deal with remaining workers. | Some employees will lose their jobs and incomes. |
| Changes of contract | Employer changes employment contract of an employee, such as making workers go on a one-year contract. | A change in employment contract allows the firm to be more flexible managing employees in the future. | Changes in employment contracts could worsen workers' working conditions and increase vulnerability. |
| Lock-outs | Employer can prevent employees from entering the premises to do their work. | Employers would save money during a dispute period. | Employees would lose income during the dispute period. |
| Closure | Employer threatens to shut the office or plant down unless an agreement is reached. | Employers reduce cost and problems of managing a difficult part of their business. | Employees face redundancy and loss of income from closure of their work. |

# Industrial relations methods used by employers

Table 2.6.2 summarises the methods employers can use in negotiating situations to try and reach a settlement in the best interest of the employer.

In the train operating company example, the business's negotiating team used collective bargaining with the representative trade union to reach an agreement on the pay increase of 2%. Part of the process involved offering a 2% pay offer and then moving to 3% when the union agreed to contract changes that meant workers had to work more flexible hours.

# Sources of conflict in the workplace

Short-term and long-term conflict situations are challenges to businesses and can have significant negative implications for the performance of the operation such as lost profits and reputation for the business and low morale for the workforce.

Common causes of conflict:

- **Changes in the business environment** – In a recession, for example, firms often cut costs and output by reducing wages or making redundancies.

This can cause acute levels of conflict between a trade union that is trying to protect its members and the management that is trying to keep their business profitable or just survive the recession.

- **Change management by the organisation** – If a business embarks on strategic change then this often unsettles workers and causes conflict. The train operating company, for example, put in place a new electronic ticketing system that reduced the need for so many ticketing staff who were redeployed onto the trains to sell and check tickets. This changed the way large numbers of its staff had to work and they were very resistant to the change.

- **Pay and working conditions** – If the pay and working conditions of a business's employees is below their expectations then this is likely to lead to conflict because workers will feel dissatisfied and demotivated.

- **Different personalities** – Conflict in organisations is often about how people and groups of people relate to each other. If personalities clash with each other, it will lead to conflict – particularly if it is at a senior level.

- **Poor communication** – Conflict between individuals in organisations often occurs because of breakdowns in communication. The train operating company, for example, has several cases of changes being made to employees' working hours without them being told first.

# 2.6

**French air traffic control unions SNCTA and UNSA**

There has been a six-month dispute between trade unions representing air traffic controllers and the French government. Two of the main unions involved are the SNCTA and the UNSA, who are unhappy about the pay and conditions of their members. They also say reductions in the number of air traffic control staff and outdated equipment are threats to passenger safety. The dispute, which has involved a number of strikes, is against a background of the French government trying to change labour laws that, in the opinion of the unions, leave their members worse off.

**Progress questions**

1 Define the term 'strike'. [2 marks]

2 Outline two other methods of industrial relations the SNCTA and UNSA unions could use in the dispute situation. [4 marks]

3 Analyse two reasons why the French air traffic controllers might have gone on strike. [6 marks]

**Exam tip**

An 'analyse' command term means breaking down the two reasons why the air traffic controllers have gone on strike to bring out the essential reasons.

## Approaches to conflict resolution

There will always be conflict in businesses and successful organisations develop effective systems to resolve conflict.

- **Conciliation** – This is where a third party is called into conflict situation where there is an industrial dispute to help the employer and the trade union to provide a compromise solution.

- **Arbitration** – This is where a third-party court is called into an industrial dispute to make a judgement on the dispute that has to be followed by both parties.

- **Employee participation and industrial democracy** – One approach to conflict in businesses is to introduce all employees into the decision-making process. This could be having employee representatives on the board of directors or using quality circles where groups of workers are involved in the strategic decision-making process.

- **No-strike agreement** – This is where a trade union agrees not to strike in return for greater involvement in a business's decision-making process.

- **Single-union agreement** – This is when an organisations and its employees agree that one union should represent all the employees of the business. This may reduce conflict in the organisation because there are only two parties involved in the collective bargaining process.

To reduce conflict in the train operating company example, there is a single union agreement and union agreement employee representatives are present at certain board meetings. The union and management have also agreed to use conciliation and arbitration in serious dispute situations.

## Impact of change on human resources

Change constantly occurs in organisations and it is something employees can find difficult and can lead to conflict. The new electronic ticketing system in the example train operating company has caused unhappiness and some conflict among some employees.

Reasons why employees may resist organisational change:

- **Self-interest** – Some employees may feel their own pay and working conditions along with their future prospects are poorly affected by a change.

- **Low tolerance** – Employees just find it difficult to deal with a change in their situation, particularly those who have done the same job for a long time.

- **Misinformation** – When there is a threat of change in an organisation it often comes with lots of rumours and information that is not true and causes unease among workers.

- **Interpretation of circumstances** – If workers do not understand the reasons for a change they are more likely to resist it.

# Human resource strategy for change management

### Key term

**Change management** is planning, implementing and controlling the transition of a business as it moves from its current situation to a new one.

The train operating company is facing considerable change with growing customer demand and the need to invest in new trains and operating methods. Table 2.6.3 sets out a strategy on how this change might be managed.

**Table 2.6.3**

| Step | Importance | Approach | Challenges |
|------|-----------|----------|-----------|
| **1** Agreement and ownership | This makes all employees have a say in and feel part of the decision-making process involving the change. | • Consultation with the workforce through documents and meetings<br>• Ask workers their views and take on board their suggestions<br>• Communicate with workforce on how their input has been used. | • Possible negative reaction from the workforce<br>• Workforce suggestions may not be workable in the strategy<br>• Might slow down the decision change process, which may need to be quick. |
| **2** Planning and timing | Once the change strategy has been decided, employees are likely to feel less resistant if it is clear to all employees when changes are going to take place and there is clear plan on implementation. | • Meeting with employees to say when changes will take place<br>• Documentation given to employees clearly sets out the dates and nature of changes<br>• Regular updates communicated to employees. | • Employees may not react positively to plans<br>• Industrial action can be planned by the union to resist the changes. |
| **3** Communicating changes | A plan of how the communication of changes being made needs to be effectively set out for the whole change process. | • Face-to-face meeting with employees<br>• Written documentation available in hard and electronic copy<br>• Electronic updates of progress. | • If the tone the communication is wrong it may increase resistance<br>• Giving too much information may make change more difficult. |

# 2.6

## Possible impacts on employer–employee relations

### Innovation

Innovation can affect employer–employee relations in the following ways:

- creates more organisation change that can lead to more conflict

- development of email and social media increases the quantity of information but it can make managers feel more distant.

### Ethical considerations

Ethical considerations can affect employer–employee relations in the following ways:

- If management and workers both become more ethical, it is likely to improve relations between the two, reduce conflict and make conflict resolution easier. A difficult management decision, however, may need to be made that is ethical but hard on some employees so conflict may not be avoidable.

- A more ethical approach by businesses may bring managers into conflict with workers in certain situations. The train operating company, for example, makes its train staff enforce a policy of not allowing bicycles and pushchairs in the space for wheelchair passengers, which train staff do not like enforcing when there are no wheelchair users on the train.

### Cultural differences

Cultural differences can affect employer–employee relations in the following ways:

- If businesses that operate in overseas markets use their own countries' managers to manage employees, the cultural differences between managers and workers can lead to conflict.

- Migrant workers that work for a business in a country may challenge the employee/employer relationship. Some unethical managers may discriminate against migrant workers, which can cause conflict.

## Exam practice questions

### Paper 1 question (HL)

#### The Juice Truck

The Juice Truck is one of the leading mobile beverage businesses in India. The workers at the Juice Truck are represented by a single union that is involved with service sector workers in retail organisations. CEO Aarti Sen is happy to deal with a single union and industrial relations are generally good with two mobile unit employees being allowed to attend board meetings. There has, however, been a dispute this year with a new computerised payment system being introduced into the mobile units. Many of the unit operators are resistant to the new technology and are worried about new financial monitoring and targets being introduced.

**a** Outline two ways that The Juice Truck has used industrial democracy to reduce industrial conflict. [4 marks]

**b** Analyse two reasons why The Juice Truck operators might resist the change associated with a computerised payment system. [6 marks]

[Total 10 marks]

### Paper 2 question (HL)

#### Aztec Mattresses

Aztec Mattresses is a medium-sized company based in Peru with 200 workers operating in one major production plant just outside Lima. Aztec's CEO is a paternalistic leader with an autocratic management style. He is very reluctant to allow union representation among his workers. His new HR director thinks differently. She wants some union representation and greater use of industrial democracy. She also wants to move the business to collective bargaining between Aztec's managers and its workforce. She has been brought in because the previous HR director has been increasingly unpopular because of his abrasive management style and poor communication. Under his management, conflict at Aztec had deteriorated badly. Aztec is about to undergo considerable change as it plans to move production to a new state-of-the-art factory. The current facility is outdated. The new factory will, however, mean workers having to travel further to get to work and may also involve some redundancies.

a Define the term 'collective bargaining'. [2 marks]

b Outline two reasons for conflict between management and employees at Aztec. [4 marks]

c Explain how the use of industrial democracy might reduce conflict at Aztec. [4 marks]

d Evaluate an HR strategy Aztec might use to manage the change to the new factory successfully. [10 marks]

[Total 20 marks]

**Exam tip**

The 'evaluate' command term in this question means making an appraisal of the HR strategy used by Aztec to consider its strengths and limitations.

# Unit
## 3

**Finance and Accounts**

# 3.1 | Sources of finance

**What you should know by the end of this chapter:**

- Role of finance for businesses: capital expenditure, revenue expenditure (AO2)

- The following internal sources of finance: personal funds, retained profit, sale of assets (AO2)

- The following external sources of finance: share capital, loan capital, overdrafts, trade credit, grants, subsidies, debt factoring, leasing, venture capital, business angels (AO2)

- Short-, medium- and long-term finance (AO1)

- The appropriateness, advantages and disadvantages of sources of finance for a given situation (AO3).

**Chapter illustrative example**
A shampoo manufacturer

# 3.1

## Role of finance for businesses

There are two types of business expenditure that need to be **financed**: capital expenditure and revenue expenditure.

## Capital expenditure

The funds required to finance **capital expenditure** can be very significant to the business, particularly when it is being set up or expanding. Examples of capital expenditure by the shampoo manufacturer include:

- buildings for the shampoo manufacturer's production plant
- machinery that makes up the production line
- equipment to support the operation of the organisation such as computers
- fixtures and fittings such as the office equipment in the shampoo firm's offices.

## Revenue expenditure

**Revenue expenditure** is the day-to-day finance an organisation needs to operate. Examples of revenue expenditure by the shampoo manufacturer include:

- raw materials costs
- wages of labour
- administration
- marketing
- overheads such as heat and light.

Table 3.1.1

| Type | Definition | Advantages | Disadvantage |
|------|-----------|-----------|-------------|
| Personal funds | When a sole trader uses their own money to put finance into a business. | • Owner/business keeps control<br>• No interest to pay. | • Limited amount<br>• Owner risks losing money<br>• Returns (interest) given up from alternative use. |
| Retained profit | Profit made by a firm after tax and payments have been made to shareholders. | • Owner/shareholders keep control<br>• No interest to pay. | • Less income paid to owners/shareholders<br>• Relies on the business making a profit. |
| Sale of assets | Finance generated by selling things such as equipment, land and buildings. | • Owners/shareholders keep control<br>• No interest to pay<br>• Significant funds generated quickly. | • Asset cannot be used to generate future income<br>• Fall in balance sheet value of the business. |

# Internal sources of finance

**Key term**
**Internal finance** is funds generated by the operation of the business itself.

When, for example, the shampoo manufacturer makes and sells its products, **internal finance** comes into the business. Table 3.1.1 shows the different forms that internal finance can take.

## External sources of funds

**Key term**
**External sources of funds** for an organisation come from sources outside the business in the form of loans (debt) and/or investment (equity).

Note: A secured loan is where the value of the loan is covered by the value of a borrower's asset and if the loan is not repaid the lender takes the asset in place of the outstanding debt.

See Table 3.1.2 for the different forms of **external sources of funds**.

**Table 3.1.2**

| Type | Definition | Advantages | Disadvantage |
|---|---|---|---|
| Overdrafts | A short-term bank loan where a business is allowed to draw more money from its account than there is in the account. | • Flexible for day-to-day funding of activities<br>• Covers short-term cash flow problems, such as a debtor who has not paid. | • High interest charges<br>• Can be called in at any time by the bank, which could cause the business to fail. |
| Trade credit | Where a business receives goods or services on credit and agrees to pay for it at a point in the future (normally 30–90 days). | • Flexible way to fund day-to-day purchasing<br>• Cash is not tied up and can be used for other activities. | • Firm misses out on discounts offered to businesses that pay on time<br>• Non/late payment can cause poor relations with suppliers. |
| Debt factoring | A business can sell the debts that are owed to it by customers to a debt factoring agency. | • Quickly generates funds<br>• Covers short-term cash flow problems, such as a debtor who has not paid. | • Firm receives less than the full value of the debt owed to it. |
| Leasing | This is used by a firm to acquire assets such as vehicles without having to purchase them, but make a series of payments over the lease period to a leasing company. | • No initial payment is needed, which is often a significant cash outflow<br>• Business can have up-to-date capital. | • Leasing costs often work out more expensive than purchasing costs overtime<br>• The business does not own the asset, which reduces its balance sheet asset value. |
| Loan capital | These are long-term loans businesses receive that have a set repayment period (more than one year), have interest costs and are often secured against an asset. | • Effective for long-term projects such as asset purchases<br>• Set repayments and interest payments help planning<br>• Owners/shareholders retain control over the business. | • Interest payments adds to business costs<br>• Repayment are a drain on cash flow<br>• Security against an asset risks losing it. |

**(continued)**

**Table 3.1.2 (continued)**

| Type | Definition | Advantages | Disadvantage |
|---|---|---|---|
| Debentures | Unit loans sold by the business to lenders to raise long-term loan funding. | • Effective for long-term projects such as asset purchases<br>• Set repayments and interest payments help planning<br>• Owners/shareholders retain control over the business. | • Interest payments adds to business costs<br>• Repayments are a drain on cash flow<br>• Can be difficult to set up and sell. |
| Share capital | A business sells shares in itself to raise funds. | • Effective for long-term projects and business expansion<br>• No interest costs<br>• No repayment of funds<br>• Can introduce outside expertise to support the business. | • Dividends/profits have to be paid to the new shareholders<br>• Some control over the business is lost. |
| Venture capital | This is share capital finance that is provided by specialist investment organisations looking to take some ownership in a small or medium-sized company. | • Effective for expansion of the business<br>• No interest costs<br>• No repayment of funds<br>• Can introduce outside expertise to support the business. | • Dividends /profits have to be paid to venture capitalists<br>• Some control over the business is lost. |
| Business angels | These are wealthy individual investors who use their own funds to invest in small and medium-sized companies. | • Effective for expansion of the business<br>• No interest costs<br>• No repayment of funds<br>• Can introduce outside expertise to support the business. | • Dividends /profits have to be paid to venture capitalists<br>• Some control over the business is lost. |
| Grants | This is an amount of money given to a business that does not have to be repaid and that is used to fund a particular project or activity. | • Effective financial assistance for a project<br>• No repayment<br>• No interest costs. | • Can be difficult to access<br>• Limited to projects and not for operational funding<br>• May have some political ties if given by a government. |
| Subsidy | Funds governments paid to businesses to contribute to paying their operating costs over a given time period. | • Effective for financing day-to-day operating costs<br>• No repayment<br>• No interest costs. | • Can be difficult to access<br>• Limited to operating costs and not for project funding<br>• May have some political ties if given by a government. |

## CASE STUDY

**AIROD**

AIROD is a Malaysian aerospace business that specialises in aircraft servicing, repair and overhaul. AIROD currently serves 77 customers across more than 30 countries, including Libya, Pakistan, Bangladesh and South Africa. It is now looking to expand its services further by moving into new overseas markets including Taiwan, Thailand and Japan. The firm's CEO Ibrahim Bahari is looking to expand the business by moving into other countries where it can develop new revenue streams and spread its customer base.

**Progress questions**

1 Outline two internal sources of finance AIROD could use to fund its further expansion into overseas markets. [4 marks]

2 Explain two reasons why AIROD might use share capital to fund its further expansion into overseas markets. [4 marks]

3 Analyse the possible implications of AIROD using a government grant and a subsidy to support its further expansion into overseas markets. [6 marks]

**Exam tip**

The 'explain' command term in this question means give a detailed account of the reasons why AIROD might use share capital to fund its expansion.

# Short-, medium- and long-term finance

The length of time an organisation needs to access finance for is important in determining the source of funding they choose. The business – for example, the shampoo manufacturer – funds its day-to-day operational costs with short-term funding such as an overdrafts and trade credit. For longer-term projects such as buying new machinery it has used secured bank loans.

## Short-term finance

Short-term finance refers to funds a business raises for its normal operational activities that have a repayment period of less than 12 months. It includes the following sources:

- overdrafts
- trade credit
- debt factoring.

## Medium-term finance

Medium-term finance is where a business raises funds for a period of three to five years to fund particular projects. It includes the following sources:

- medium-term loans
- leasing
- grants
- subsidies.

## Long-term finance

Long term finance is where a business raises funds for a period of more than five years to funds major projects and growth of the business. It includes the following sources:

- loan capital
- share capital
- venture capital
- business angels.

# 3.1

## CASE STUDY

### Crowdmix

Social music start-up business Crowdmix is a community-based music app where users can join different groups based around music genres and share music, discussions and view charts of the most popular tracks. The app also connects to a user's streaming service such as YouTube, iTunes and Spotify. Crowdmix has 160 employees and offices in London and Los Angeles. The business was started with $18.5 million in venture capital funding. The firm has, however, been struggling to raise money after difficulties in its early development. It has had problems paying its employees following cash flow shortages.

### Progress questions

1 Define the term 'short-term finance'. [2 marks]

2 Outline two types of short-term finance Crowdmix could use to cover its cash flow difficulties. [4 marks]

3 Explain why the $18.5 million of venture capital Crowdmix has raised is considered to be long-term finance. [4 marks]

# Sources of finance for different situations

There are a number of different internal and external sources of finance a business can use to fund its operations in the short, medium and long term. Here are three scenarios the example shampoo manufacturer has faced and the funding choices it made.

## Business start-up

A small business can access funds in the following ways:

- personal funds from each partner
- business angel investment
- overdraft arranged with the bank
- trade credit arranged with suppliers.

If a business owner chooses to put their own funds into a business, they risk losing their own money but if they use a business angel they might get the funds needed but lose some control over decision-making.

## Opening a new factory

Once a business is established it might want to raise funds, for example, to open a new factory. To do this it can use the following sources of funds:

- retained profit
- bank loan
- leasing vehicles
- government grant.

The long- and medium-term funding used for a new plant, for example, can be a mix of retained profit and secured bank loan. The loan will need to be repaid and there are interest payments but current owners do retain control over decision-making.

## International expansion

After a period of time, a business may want to embark on a major expansion that may, for example, mean opening a factory abroad. The funds for this can be sourced by:

- public sale of shares on the stock market (going public)
- debenture issue
- retained profit.

If this type of strategic business decision is funded through a share issue, it would bring significant amounts of money into the business although the owners would lose a lot of control and would now be answerable to shareholders.

# Exam practice questions

## Paper 1 question (HL and SL)

### Preciso Limited

Preciso is a watch manufacturer based in Argentina. It was established in 1974 by the Kempes family. It is a medium-sized business employing 300 people, with a revenue of $30 million and a net profit of $7 million. Its success is based on a quality product that can match any of the leading brands in the market, even the most prestigious. Preciso is considering the purchase of new machinery that will improve both the efficiency of production and the quality of the watches it produces. The firm's finance director, Eduardo Matinez is looking at three options of funding the machinery, which costs $850 000. The options are:

1 secured bank loan

2 leasing

3 retained profit.

   a   Describe two of the finance options available to Preciso. [4 marks]

   b   Analyse two reasons why Preciso might choose to fund the new machinery by leasing it rather than using retained profit. [6 marks]

[Total 10 marks]

### Exam tip

The 'discuss' command term in this question means offering a considered and balanced review that includes a range of arguments of the factors associated with Seven Trees' long-term funding decision.

## Paper 2 question (HL and SL)

### Seven Trees Advertising

Seven Trees Adverting is a small advertising business based in Australia. The company was launched six months ago by two partners, Mark Turner and Helen Stacey. Like any new business, the early development phase is challenging for the new firm because it did not have a significant amount of owners' capital or a track record for outside investors and lenders to make a funding judgement. Seven Trees has two pressing finance issues to deal with:

1 the need to raise extra cash to pay wages and outstanding trade creditors

2 funding to update computers and IT.

   One principle that Mark Turner and Helen Stacey will have to deal with is their desire to keep control of the business. A business angel has offered them finance but they are resistant to this because they want to keep control.

   a   Define the term 'trade creditors'. [2 marks]

   b   Outline two problems Seven Trees may have using a bank overdraft to pay wages and trade creditors. [4 marks]

   c   Describe how Seven Trees could use leasing to fund updated computers and IT. [4 marks]

   d   Discuss the factors associated with the long-term funding decision Seven Trees is looking to make. [10 marks]

[Total 20 marks]

# Costs and revenues

**What you should know by the end of this chapter:**

- The following types of cost, using examples: fixed, variable, semi-variable, direct, indirect/overhead (AO3)

- Total revenue and revenue streams, using examples (AO3).

**Chapter illustrative example**
A business that manufactures guitars

# Importance of cost and revenue

An important financial aspect of an organisation's operations is an understanding of the cost of its operations and the revenue it generates from selling its product. This is because the revenue–cost relationship gives the profit or loss position of the business.

# Cost

**Key term**

A **business cost** is the monetary value of resources used by a business to produce and sell a good or service.

In order to produce a product, a firm needs to employ workers, use raw materials and use capital and these all need to be paid for.

## Cost centre

**Key term**

A **cost centre** is an area of the business that is responsible for generating expenses.

In the guitar business, for example, the section that manufactures electric guitars and the marketing department are both **cost centres**.

## Cost per unit

Cost per unit produced by an organisation is calculated by:

total cost / units produced

The cost per unit for the guitar manufacturing business, for example, is $85 per unit. This is an important piece of cost information because it can be used by a business to set prices and to measure its production efficiency.

**Singapore Airline**

Singapore Airlines is a leading Singaporean business that is majority-owned by the government. It flies all over the world and is one of the leading airline brands. It had revenues in 2016 of $16 billion and employs 23 000 people. In the first quarter of 2016, its profit almost tripled as lower oil prices significantly reduced its operating costs.

**Progress questions**

1 Define the term 'business cost'. [2 marks]

2 Explain how you would calculate Singapore Airlines's cost per unit. [4 mark]

3 Explain how a fall in oil prices might have led to an increase in profits for Singapore Airlines. [4 marks]

## Types of cost

Table 3.2.1 sets out the different types of costs.

# 3.2

**Table 3.2.1**

| Type | Definition | Examples for a guitar manufacturer |
|------|------------|-----------------------------------|
| Fixed | Costs that do not change as a business changes output. | Rent, machinery, management salaries and insurance. It does not matter how many guitars a guitar-maker produces, these costs do not change. |
| Variable | Costs that do change as output changes. | Raw materials and piece rate wages. The guitar manufacturer uses wood, metal and plastic to make its guitars and these costs change with output. |
| Semi-variable | Costs that can change with output but not in a direct way because there is a fixed and variable element. | Maintenance, energy costs and workers paid using overtime. The workers on the guitar production line are paid overtime above their basic pay if they work more than 35 hours a week. |
| Direct costs | Costs that can be clearly linked to each unit of output produced by a business or a cost centre of the business. | Direct labour refers to workers who work on the production line making guitars, and direct materials refers to the wood used to make the guitars. |
| Indirect cost/ overheads | Costs that cannot be clearly linked to each unit of output produced by a business or a cost centre of the business. | Indirect labour in the guitar business is the administration, HR and marketing employees. Its other indirect costs are energy and interest on loans. |

## CASE STUDY

### Taco Bell

The fast food chain Taco Bell is a subsidiary of the huge restaurant organisation Yum!, which also owns Pizza Hut and KFC. Its menu focuses on Tex-Mex products such as tacos, burritos and nachos. It targets the value end of the restaurant market and the majority of its outlets are franchise-owned. It is a large multinational chain that employs 175 000 people and has revenue of $1.9 billion.

### Progress questions

1  Define the term 'direct cost'. [2 marks]

2  State two examples of fixed costs. [2 marks]

3  Outline two examples of indirect costs at Taco Bell. [4 marks]

4  Explain what happens to Taco Bell's fixed and variable costs as it serves more customers. [4 marks]

### Exam tip

The 'state' command term in this question means giving a specific name to the examples of fixed costs.

# Revenue

**Key term**
**Revenue** is the income a business receives from selling its products.

For the guitar business, for example, it earns **revenue** from selling guitars. It is important not to confuse revenue with profit, which is revenue less cost.

## Total revenue

**Key term**
**Total revenue** is the total amount of income a business receives from selling its products.

**Total revenue** is calculated by:

units sold × selling price = total revenue

The guitar manufacturing firm's total revenue is calculated as:

0.8 million × $200 = $160 million

# Revenue streams

### Key term

A **revenue stream** is the different ways a business generates income from its activities.

The guitar manufacturer, for example, has the following different **revenue streams**:

- guitar sales

- other instruments (banjos and ukuleles)

- accessory sales (strings, cases, tuners and straps)

- guitar amplifiers.

Businesses often see different revenue streams as important because they allow a business to earn income from a number of different segments of a market and it spreads risk. For the guitar firm, for example, guitar revenues have not been increasing but the banjos and ukuleles section has seen a big increase in revenue.

# Exam practice questions

## Paper 1 question (HL and SL)

### Preciso Limited

Preciso is a watch manufacturer based in Argentina. It was established in 1974 by the Kempes family. The average price of a Preciso watch is $400 and they are incredibly popular in the Argentinean market but they export very few watches. The marketing director, Sofía Garcia, wants to create new revenue streams by trying to market Preciso watches in the US. The CEO, Mario Fernandez, is concerned about this because he likes the traditional nature of the business and he is concerned about the additional fixed costs of selling in the US such as export licences, shipping and insurance.

**a** Outline why export licences, shipping and insurance are considered fixed costs of Preciso exporting to the US. [4 marks]

**b** Analyse two benefits to Preciso creating new revenue streams. [6 marks]

[Total 10 marks]

## Paper 2 question (HL and SL)

### Auberge Books

Auberge Books is a small publishing company based in Nigeria. It specialises in academic publications and non-fiction books. The business is struggling with falling sales and profits as online publications have become increasing attractive to its core market, which is university students and professional studying for further qualifications. Auberge's management are looking to reduce unit costs to make their selling price competitive. They have particularly focused on reducing indirect labour costs and the price they pay for paper as a raw material. The new marketing manager, Edward Malwani, wants to develop a new revenue stream by creating an online publishing platform to sell the firm's books digitally.

**a** Define the term 'indirect labour cost'. [2 marks]

**b** Outline two ways Auberge might reduce its indirect labour costs. [4 marks]

**c** Explain two ways Auberge might be able to reduce its paper costs. [4 marks]

**d** Evaluate Edward Malwani's proposal to develop a new revenue stream by selling books online. [10 marks]

[Total 20 marks]

### Exam tip

The 'outline' command term in this question means giving a brief account or summary of the reasons why export licences, shipping and insurance are considered fixed costs.

# Break-even analysis

# 3.3

## What you should know by the end of this chapter:

- Total contribution versus contribution per unit (AO2)

- A break-even chart and the following aspects of break-even analysis: break-even quantity/point, profit or loss, margin of safety, target profit output, target profit and target price (AO2, AO4)

- The effects of changes in price or cost on the break-even quantity, profit and margin of safety, using graphical and quantitative methods (AO2, AO4)

- The benefits and limitations of break-even analysis (AO3).

## Chapter illustrative example
A business that manufactures high-quality garden furniture

# Break-even analysis

**Key term**
**Break-even analysis** is a business planning tool that applies cost and revenue data to support decision-making.

The term '**break-even**' refers to the level of output a firm needs to achieve where total revenue equals total costs and the business starts to make a profit.

# Contribution

## Total contribution

**Key term**
**Contribution** is the surplus of revenue over variable costs a business makes that goes towards paying its fixed costs.

Total **contribution** is calculated as:

sales − variable cost = contribution

The garden furniture business, for example, has revenue from selling its tables of $600 000 and the variable cost is $380 000:

$600 000 − $380 000 = $220 000 contribution

The garden furniture business can then use the $220 000 to pay for fixed costs such as capital, administration, marketing and rent.

## Contribution per unit

**Key term**
**Contribution per unit** is the surplus of the selling price of a product over the unit variable cost of producing it.

**Contribution per unit** is calculated as:

selling price − unit variable cost = contribution per unit

The garden furniture business, for example, has a planned selling price for the tables of $1200 and the variable cost per table is $650:

$1200 − $650 = $550 unit contribution.

The contribution per unit is a useful financial statistic because it tells a business the financial implications of selling more units or fewer units. If, for example, the garden furniture firm decided to sell an extra 20 tables it would make $11 000 (20 × $550) towards paying its fixed costs.

# The break-even chart (diagram)

**Key term**
A **break-even chart** is a graphical representation of the costs and revenues associated with producing a good or service.

A **break-even chart** graphs the following variables against the business' output or units sold:

* total revenue
* total cost
* fixed cost.

**Exam tip**
The 'calculate' command term means obtaining a numerical break-even answer showing the relevant stages in the working.

# 3.3

**Frame-it**

Frame-it is a small business that manufactures picture frames. As a small business, it is very concerned with managing its costs, revenues and profits as effectively as it can, and it uses break-even analysis to support its business planning. Frame-it has a maximum output of 4500 units and has set a target output of 4200 units. It has forecast following cost and revenue figures for 2017:

|  | $ |
|---|---|
| Selling price | 12.50 |
| Direct materials per unit | 2.80 |
| Direct labour cost | 1.70 |
| Fixed cost | 35 000 |

**Progress questions**

1   Calculate the number of units Frame-it has to sell in order to break-even. [4 marks]

2   Construct a fully labelled break-even chart for Frame-it. Indicate the break-even point and the margin of safety and calculate the forecasted profit from the sale of selling 4200 units. [6 marks]

## Constructing a break-even chart

These are the steps for the garden furniture business example constructing a break-even chart for its new tables.

### 1   Calculate and plot the total revenue

- The units sold is the maximum number the business can sell from producing its good or service.

- The maximum number of tables it can produce is 2000 at a selling price of $1200. The total revenue would be: 2000 × $1200 = $2 400 000

- The total revenue is plotted onto the break-even chart shown in Figure 3.3.1.

### 2   Plot the fixed cost

- The fixed costs such as capital, administration do not change with output so the fixed cost line is drawn horizontally at the fixed cost value.

- The garden furniture firm has fixed costs of $700 000.

- The fixed cost is plotted onto the break-even chart shown in Figure 3.3.1.

## 3 Calculate and plot the total variable cost

- The total variable cost such as direct materials is calculated by multiplying variable costs by the maximum number of units the business can produce of its good or service.

- In the garden furniture business, the variable cost is direct labour and direct materials, which is $650 per table.

- The total variable cost is: 2000 × $650 = $1 300 000

## 4 Calculate and plot the total cost

- The total cost is calculated by adding the fixed cost to the total variable cost at the maximum number of units the business aims to produce.

- For the garden furniture producer this is: $700 000 + $1 300 000 = $2 000 000

- Remember the total cost line starts from the y-axis at the fixed cost value because a business will have its fixed costs even if it produces zero output.

- The total cost is plotted onto the break-even chart shown in Figure 3.3.1.

## 5 Find the break-even quantity or output

- If a firm produces more than this level of output it will make a profit and if it produces less than this output it will make a loss.

---

**Key term**

The **break-even quantity** is the level of output a business reaches where total cost equals total revenue.

- The **break-even quantity** can be calculated using the equation:
  fixed cost ÷ (selling price – unit variable cost) = break-even quantity

- In the garden furniture business example, the break-even quantity for the tables it plans to produce is:
  700 000 ÷ ($1 200 - $650) = 1273 units

- The break-even quantity is plotted onto the break-even chart shown in Figure 3.3.1:

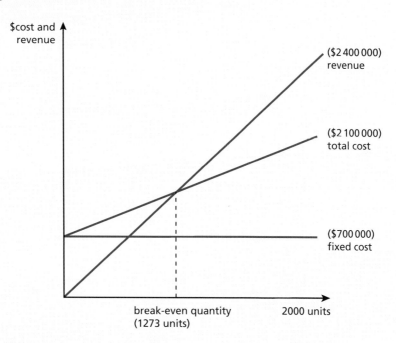

**Figure 3.3.1** Break-even diagram.

## 6 Establish the profit or loss

- The profit or loss on the output produced by an organisation is the difference between total revenue and total cost at a given level of output.

- Businesses will have a maximum amount they can produce, which is set by the production capacity they have and they will have a target output or quantity they will aim to produce.

- For the garden furniture company, for example, the maximum output is 2000 tables per year but it has set a target output of 1800 tables per year based on forecasted consumer demand.

- The target profit the firm would achieve at this level of output is shown in Table 3.3.1:

**Table 3.3.1**

|  |  | $000s |
|---|---|---|
| Revenue | 1800 × $1200 | 2160 |
| Variable cost | 1800 × $650 | 1170 |
| Fixed cost |  | 700 |
| **Profit** |  | **291** |

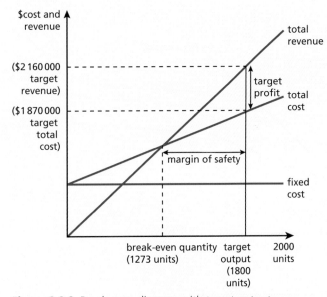

**Figure 3.3.2** Break-even diagram with target output, target profit and margin of safety

## 7 Establish the margin of safety

**Key term**

The **margin of safety** is the difference between the target level of output a business aims to achieve and the break-even quantity or output.

- It is calculated as: target output – break-even output = margin of safety.

- For the garden furniture business, the margin of safety on the new tables would be: 1800 units – 1273 units = 527 units

## 8 Calculate a target profit

- A business can set a target profit and use break-even analysis to calculate the output it needs to produce to achieve the target profit.

- The output that achieves the target profit can be calculated by the equation: (fixed cost + target profit) ÷ (selling price – unit variable cost) = output to achieve a target profit.

- The garden furniture business has set a target profit $400 000. This output is calculated as: (700 000 + 400 000) ÷ ($1200 - $650) = 2000 units

## 9 Calculate a target price

- An organisation may want to know what target price to set to achieve the break-even output.

- This can be calculated by: (fixed cost ÷ break-even output) + unit variable cost = target price.

- For the garden furniture business the target price for its new table to break-even would be: (700 000 ÷ 1273) + $650 = $1200. This is shown in Figure 3.3.2:

## Using break-even analysis to examine the effects of changes in price and cost

If any of the cost and revenue variables change, it will affect the firm's break-even output, margin of safety and the profit and loss.

### Changes in price and cost calculation

The business producing garden furniture, for example, has changed the data on price and variable cost:

- The price it plans to sell the new tables has increased from $1200 to $1300

- The variable cost per unit of producing the tables has increased from $650 to $700.

The break-even output change has fallen from:

$700\,000 \div (\$1200 - \$650) = 1273$ units ⟶
$700\,000 \div (\$1300 - \$700) = 1167$ units

### Changes in price and cost diagram

Each of the changes in price and costs shown in Figure 3.3.3 is made assuming each other factor remains constant. For example, if price changes then fixed and variable costs are assumed to be unchanged.

**Table 3.3.2**

| Change | Diagram | Break-even output | Profit | Margin of safety |
|---|---|---|---|---|
| Rise in price | | Falls to a lower output. | Increases – the profit at the target output rises. | Increases – the difference between the break-even output and the target output rises. |
| Fall in variable cost | | Falls to a lower output. | Increases – the profit at the target output rises. | Increases – the difference between the break-even output and the target output rises. |
| Fall in fixed cost | | Falls to a lower output. | Increases – the profit at the target output rises. | Increases – the difference between the break-even output and the target output rises. |

# 3.3

## Alp Dairy

Alp Dairy is dairy farm based in the Austrian Alps. It is a relatively large firm and specialises in producing milk. Like many milk producers, it has struggled against falling prices in the past two years. It has the following costs and revenue data.

| | $ |
|---|---|
| Selling price | 0.60 |
| Direct materials per unit | 0.05 |
| Direct labour cost | 0.19 |
| Fixed cost | 38 000 |

### Progress questions

1   Alp Dairy has set a target profit of $20 000. Calculate the number of units it needs to sell to achieve this profit. [4 marks]

2   If the milk price at Alp Dairy falls below $0.60, analyse the impact this will have on its break-even output and profit. [6 marks]

# The benefits and limitations of break-even analysis

## Benefits of break-even analysis

- **Supports decision-making** – The cost, revenue, break-even and profit data that arise from a decision help managers see the financial impact of a decision.

- **Simplicity** – The break-even model is relatively straightforward to construct and for different stakeholders to interpret.

- **Pictorial view** – The break-even diagram is an effective way of presenting information to be used in presentation on a project.

- **Flexibility** – Break-even data can be easily changed to show the financial impact of changes in different variables such as price and cost.

## Limitations of break-even analysis

- **Assumption of linear variable costs** – In many cases variable costs do not stay constant as output changes. Buying raw materials and components, for example, in larger quantities can get a bulk buying discount, which means the variable cost per unit falls as output increases.

- **Assumption of linear revenue** – The selling price of a good or service might change as a business changes the amount it sells. The garden furniture business, for example, may need to offer discounts to a large retailer to buy some of its new tables.

- **Semi-variable cost** – The break-even model does not work as effectively with costs that change with output in an unpredictable way, such as maintenance of machinery.

- **Forecasted data** – Break-even data on revenue, cost and output is often forecasted and is very likely to change when a project is actually in operation.

# Exam practice questions

## Paper 1 question (HL and SL)

### Preciso Limited

Preciso is a watch manufacturer based in Argentina. It was established in 1974 by the Kempes family. Preciso's marketing director Sofia Garcia is looking to market a watch in the US. She is very positive about this market and feels they could increase their selling price in this market compared to the Argentinean market from $400 to $500. The finance director, Eduardo Martinez has been asked by the CEO, Mario Fernandez to set out the financial details associated with an additional production run of an extra 2000 watches a year to be exported to the US market. The finance details are:

- selling price $500

- direct material costs per watch $120

- direct labour cost per watch $240

- fixed costs $210 000.

a   Calculate the break-even output of Preciso watches at a selling price of $400 and $500. [4 marks]

b   Analyse two ways the firm could reduce the break-even output of the watches it aims to market in the US. [6 marks]

[Total 10 marks]

## Paper 2 question

### Medical Conference Ltd

Medical Conference Ltd is an organisation that organises conferences for medical professionals including doctors, pharmaceutical company executives and medical research scientists. Medical Conference Ltd organises three-day events in prestigious hotels and then sells tickets to the events. The financial information on the next events is set out as:

- delegate ticket selling price $3500

- hotel charges $1800 per delegate

- direct labour cost per delegate $110

- fixed costs or overheads of the event $255 000.

The capacity for the event is 300 delegates and Medical Conference has sets a target of 270 delegates. The business uses break-even analysis as a planning tool for all its conferences.

a   Explain why the hotel charges per delegate is considered a variable cost. [4 marks]

b   Construct a fully labelled break-even chart for Medical Conference Ltd as part of its planning for the next conference. Calculate and indicate the break-even point and the margin of safety and calculate the forecasted profit from the sale of 270 delegate tickets. [6 marks]

c   Discuss the effectiveness of Medical Conference using break-even analysis as part of its planning for events. [10 marks]

[Total 20 marks]

**Exam tip**

The 'construct' command term in this question means displaying the break-even in diagrammatic form.

# Final accounts

**What you should know by the end of this chapter:**

- The purpose of accounts to different stakeholders (AO3)

- The principles and ethics of accounting practice (AO3)

- Final accounts:

    - profit and loss account

    - balance sheet (AO2, AO4)

- Different types of intangible assets (AO1)

- Depreciation using the following methods: straight line method, reducing/declining balance method (AO2, AO4)

- The strengths and weaknesses of each method of depreciation (AO2).

**Chapter illustrative example**
A business that manufactures surfboards

# The purpose of accounts to different stakeholders

Each year businesses produce a set of accounts, which are a statement of their financial position for that year. The two most important parts of final accounts are the **profit and loss account** and the **balance sheet.**

**Key terms**

- The **profit and loss account** is a statement of a business's performance over a year in terms of revenue gained through sales less the costs of generating those sales.

- The **balance sheet** is a statement of the value of a business at a particular point in time in terms of its assets, liabilities and equity.

Table 3.4.1 illustrates why different stakeholders would be interested in a business's final accounts.

**Table 3.4.1**

| | Profit and loss account | Balance sheet |
|---|---|---|
| Employees and managers | • How their work has contributed to the firm's financial success<br>• Job security based on profit performance<br>• How much income they might receive from profit-related pay<br>• If they are also shareholders, the dividends they might receive. | • How the liquidity/cash position affects their job security<br>• If they are shareholders, how the net asset value of the company has changed. |
| Shareholders | • How successful the CEO and directors they appointed have been in managing the business<br>• Dividends they will receive<br>• Security of their shareholding based on profit. | • How the liquidity/cash position affects the security of their shareholding<br>• How the net asset value of the business they own has changed. |
| Customers | • Profit performance of the business in terms of security of supply. | • Liquidity position of the business in terms of security of supply. |
| Suppliers | • Profit performance of the business in terms of being paid and continued sales. | • Liquidity position of the business in terms of security of being paid and continued sales. |
| Government | • The sales and profit the business makes is used to calculate how much tax it can collect<br>• Sales figures can be used to compile national statistics. | • Net asset value can be used for national statistics. |
| Banks and other creditors | • Profit performance of the business in terms of repayment of loans and interest. | • Liquidity position of the business in terms of repayment of loans and interest<br>• Net asset value for security of loans made. |
| Local community | • Profit performance of the business in terms of employment and related business activity. | • Liquidity position of the business in terms of employment and related business activity. |
| Competitors | • Profit performance of the business in terms of measuring their own performance. | • Net asset and liquidity in terms of measuring their own position. |

# The principles and ethics of accounting practice

- **Integrity** – Stakeholders must be able to trust the financial data in the accounts. To do this, all the financial information contained in an organisation's accounts must be presented in an honest way that gives an accurate reflection of its financial position.

- **Objectivity** – Final accounts are prepared in an objective way by independent accountancy firms in a process known as auditing. Auditing firms are used so that an independent, unbiased profit and loss account and balance sheet can be produced for a business that stakeholders can trust.

- **Professional competence and due care** – Accounts should be prepared according to the law and rules and regulations of the country they are produced in. Every country has standard accountancy practice that needs to be followed and accountants must make sure they prepare an organisation's accounts based on these standards.

- **Confidentiality** – While lots of financial information has to be published, the principle of accounting is for accountants to deal with the preparation of information for the accounts in a confidential way.

# Profit and loss account

The profit and loss account reports profits in the following ways:

## Gross profit

Gross profit is calculated as:

sales revenue – cost of goods sold = gross profit

### Sales revenue

- Sales revenue is recorded as the income from the goods and services sold during the year.

- Sales are recorded even if the goods are not paid for because the profit figure is supposed to relate to the trading period of the year when the goods or services were sold.

- Recording sales in this way shows how the cash figure for a business is going to be different from the profit figure.

- Goods and services sold during the year and not paid for in that year are called debtors.

### Costs of goods sold

- These are the direct costs of producing a good or service sold during the year.

- They include direct labour, finished goods, components and raw materials.

- Direct costs are recorded even if they have not been paid for because they relate to the trading performance of the year when the goods or services were sold.

- Recording the cost of goods sold in this way shows how the profit and cash position of a business will be different.

## WORKED EXAMPLE

The surfboard business has the following trading details for 2016:

- 45000 surfboards sold
- Sales price $120
- Direct labour cost $900000
- Direct material cost $2520000.

The gross profit figure in the business's profit and loss account would be set out as shown in Table 3.4.2.

## Net profit

The net profit figure is calculated as:

Gross profit – expenses = net profit

### Expenses

- These are the indirect costs or overheads associated with a firm selling goods or services during the year.
- Expenses include things such as: indirect labour, management salaries, marketing costs, administration and capital costs.

The surfboard manufacturer had total expenses during the year of $995000.
The net profit figure in the business's profit and loss account would be set out as in Table 3.4.2.

## Interest, tax and dividends

Once the net profit figure has been determined, the way that profit is used to pay following stakeholders is set out:

- interest to be paid to the bank and other creditors
- tax paid to be paid to the government
- dividends to be paid to the shareholders.

The surfboard company has the following figures for 2016:

- Interest $200000
- Tax $150000
- Dividends 235000.

**Table 3.4.2** Surfboard manufacturer profit and loss account

|  | **$000s** |
| --- | --- |
| Sales revenue | 5400 |
| Cost of goods sold | 3420 |
| **Gross profit** | **1980** |
| Expenses | 995 |
| **Net profit** | **985** |
| Interest | 200 |
| **Net profit before tax** | **785** |
| Tax | 150 |
| **Net profit after tax and interest** | **635** |
| Dividends | 235 |
| **Retained profit** | **400** |

### ARP Mowers

ARP is a business based in Russia that specialises in manufacturing lawn mowers for domestic and commercial use. It is a medium-sized company, employing 600 employees based in a production plant near Moscow. The year 2016 has been a good one for the business with:

- direct costs labour costs of $18.5 million

- overhead expenses of $16.1 million

- direct labour costs of $14.4 million

- interest expense of 6.6 million

- profits tax set at 25%

- turnover of $75 million.

### Progress questions

1 Define the term 'gross profit'. [2 marks]

2 From the financial data provided, construct a profit and loss account for ARP. [8 marks]

### Exam tip

The 'construct' command term in this question means display revenue, cost and profit data in a logical form.

# The balance sheet

The balance sheet is a statement of the value of a business at a particular point in time in terms of its **assets**, liabilities and equity. The 'point in time' is often called its balance sheet date, which is at the end of its trading year. For the surfboard firm, for example, its balance sheet date for the trading year 2016 is 31.12.16.

# Assets

### Key term

The **assets** of a business are the value of what it owns at the balance sheet date.

Assets are broken down into two types, fixed assets and current assets. The monetary amount of fixed and current assets entered into the balance sheet are based on their value at the balance sheet date. The surfboard firm, for example, has a balance sheet date of 31.12.16 so the value of its assets will be set on this date.

# Fixed assets

### Key term

**Fixed assets** are the permanent assets of the business used to facilitate its operations.

**Fixed assets** are valued using the historic cost of the asset, which is its purchase price less accumulated depreciation at the balance sheet date.

The surfboard firm, for example, has vehicles with a purchase cost of $500 000 less $200 000 of accumulated depreciation at 31.12.16. This means $200 000 would be entered into its balance sheet.

Organisations have the following types of fixed assets:

- **tangible fixed assets** – including buildings, machinery, equipment and fixtures and fittings

- **intangible fixed assets** – including patents, copyrights and trademarks.

The surfboard business has the following fixed assets:

- Buildings $7 000 000

- Machinery $5 000 000

- Equipment £3 000 000

- Patents £2 000 000.

The figures for the fixed asset section of surfboard firm's balance sheet for year ending 31.12.16 are set out in Figure 3.4.3.

# Current assets

**Key term**
**Current assets** are assets of a business that are constantly changing during its normal course of operations.

**Current assets** are called liquid assets because of the ease with which they can be used by the firm to fund its activities. The most liquid asset is cash. Businesses have the following types of current assets:

- **Stock or inventories** – This is the value of raw materials, components and finished goods.

- **Debtors or accounts receivable** – This is the value of outstanding money owed to the business by its customers at the balance sheet date.

- **Cash** – This is the value of funds held by the business in physical money and in the bank at the balance sheet date.

## WORKED EXAMPLE

The surfboard business has the following current asset:

- stock $750 000
- debtors $240 000
- cash $270 000

The current assets for the surfboard business would be set out in its balance sheet for year ending 31.01.16 are in Table 3.4.3.

# Liabilities

**Key term**
**Liabilities** is the value of funds a business owes to its lenders and creditors at the balance sheet date.

**Liabilities** are broken down into current liabilities and long-term liabilities.

# Current liabilities

**Key term**
**Current liabilities** are the value of funds a business owes to its lenders and creditors with a repayment period of less than 12 months at the balance sheet date.

Organisations have the following types of **current liability**:

- **Overdraft** – This is where the money a business has drawn from its bank account is greater than the amount it has in the account so that account value is negative.

- **Creditors or accounts payable** – This is where a business buys stock or services from a supplier and agrees to pay for the stock or services at some point in the future. This is normally 30 to 90 days.

- **Short-term loan** – Any loans a business has with less than 12 months to pay.

## WORKED EXAMPLE

The surfboard business has the following current liabilities:

- overdraft $210 000
- creditors $290 000
- short term loan $100 000

# Net current assets or working capital

Working capital is the short-term liquidity a business has to fund its everyday operations. It is calculated by:

current assets − current liabilities = net current assets or working capital

The current liabilities and net current assets for the surfboard business would be set out in its balance sheet for year ending 31.01.16 in Table 3.4.3.

## Long-term liabilities

### Key term

**Long-term liabilities** are the funds a business owes to lenders that have a repayment period of more than 12 months at the balance sheet date.

Businesses can have the following types of **long-term liability**:

- **Unsecured loans** – These are loans that are not secured against the value of an organisation's assets.

- **Secured loans** – These are loans that are secured against the value of an organisation's assets and are sometimes called mortgages.

- **Debentures** – These are loans sold by a business to lenders and are sometimes called corporate bonds.

The surfboard business has the following long-term liability:

- Secured loan $5 500 000.

## Equity

### Key term

**Equity** is the value of the funds put into a business by its owners in terms of the share capital invested in the business plus its accumulated retained profit.

- **Share capital**—This is the value of shares issued by the business.

- **Accumulated retained profit**—This is the addition of retained profit the firm makes each year.

The **equity** of the surfboard business is made up of:

- share capital $8 500 000

- retained profit $3 660 000.

**Table 3.4.3**

|  |  | $000s |
|---|---|---|
| **Fixed assets** |  |  |
| Tangible fixed assets |  |  |
| Buildings | 7 000 |  |
| Machinery | 5 000 |  |
| Equipment | 3 000 |  |
|  |  | **15 000** |
| Intangible fixed assets |  |  |
| Patents | 2 000 | **2 000** |
| **Total** |  | **17 000** |
| **Current assets** |  |  |
| Stock | 750 |  |
| Debtors | 240 |  |
| Cash | 270 |  |
| **Total** |  | **1260** |
| **Current liabilities** |  |  |
| Overdraft | 210 |  |
| Creditors | 290 |  |
| Short-term loan | 100 | **600** |
| **Net current asset** |  | **660** |
| **Long-term liabilities** |  | **5 500** |
| **Net asset** |  | **12 160** |
| **Equity** |  |  |
| Share capital | 8 500 |  |
| Retained profit | 3360 |  |
| **Total** |  | **12 160** |

**Seetha Cosmetics**
Seetha Cosmetics is based in Kenya and produces mid-range cosmetics products for the domestic market and for export. Its products include makeup and skin creams. It is a large company that employs 3 600 people and had sales in 2016 of $467 million. The following information is from its balance sheet in 2016:

|  | $000s |
|---|---|
| Cash | 11 000 |
| Machinery | 110 000 |
| Share capital | 145 000 |
| Debtors | 21 000 |
| Creditors less than 12 months | 35 000 |
| Stock | 25 000 |
| Loans more than 12 months | 80 000 |
| Buildings | 140 000 |
| Retained profit | 47 000 |

**Progress questions**

1 Define the term 'balance sheet'. [2 marks]

2 Explain why debtors and stock appear as assets in Seetha's balance sheet. [4 marks]

3 Using the balance sheet data provided, construct a balance sheet for Seetha for 2016. [8 marks]

# Depreciation (HL only)

**Key term**
**Depreciation** is the method businesses use to account for the fall in the value of fixed assets over time when they are producing the balance sheet and profit and loss accounts.

There are two methods for calculating **depreciation:** the straight line and declining balance methods.

Fixed assets depreciate for two reasons:

- wear and tear from their use over time

- they become obsolete as newer machines, for example, are more technologically advanced.

## Use in the final accounts

### Balance sheet

In the balance sheet, depreciation is used to give a realistic value of fixed assets for the overall valuation of an organisation's total asset value. In the surfboard firm, for example, a $100 000 machine bought two years ago has depreciated to a value of $70 000 so this would be the more realistic asset value to enter into the balance sheet. In the balance sheet, the fixed asset value less depreciation is the asset's net book value.

### Profit and loss account

In the profit and loss account, depreciation is a way of spreading the cost of an asset over its life so it can be deducted from the revenue it generates. In the surfboard firm, for example, a $100 000 machine depreciates on average $15 000 per year, so this should be the cost deducted from the firm's profit and loss account.

## Two methods of depreciation

**Key term**
**Straight line depreciation** means an equal amount of fall in an asset's value is allowed for in each year of its life.

1 **Straight line method**

It is calculated by using the following equation:

(historic cost of the asset − residual value) / useful life = annual depreciation cost

- Historic cost is the purchase cost of an asset.

- Residual value is the estimated value of an asset at the end of its life.

## 3.4

### WORKED EXAMPLE

The surfboard manufacturer has the following figures for a new vehicle it has purchased:

- Historic cost $65 000
- Residual value $33 000
- Useful life four years.

The annual depreciation expense would be:

($65 000 − $33 000) / 4 years = $8 000 per year

In the balance sheet, the vehicle's value would be $57 000 ($65 000 − $8 000) at the end of its first year, and in the profit and loss account $8000 per year would be deducted as a cost from gross profit under expenses.

- Useful life is the forecasted life of an asset in years.

### The strengths of straight line depreciation:

- It is a simple method to calculate and understand.
- The predictable fall in value of an asset each year makes an effective method for forecasting.

### The weakness of straight line depreciation:

- It is unrealistic because assets often depreciate more in the early years of their life, which makes assets look more valuable than they are.
- The useful life and residual value are forecasted values and may be different in reality, making depreciation calculations inaccurate.

2 Declining balance depreciation method

### Key term

The **declining balance method** of depreciation is a technique that reduces the value of an asset by a constant percentage each year.

The depreciation rate for an asset will always be given in the IB examination. The depreciation rate for the example surfboard firm's asset would be 16%.

This means the depreciation of the asset's value in its first year would be:

$0.16 \times \$65\,000 = \$10\,400$

This reduces the vehicle's value to ($65 000 − $10 400) $54 600 at the end of its first year and this value is entered into the balance sheet. In the profit and loss account, $10 400 is subtracted as an expense from the firm's gross profit. In its second year, the asset would depreciate by another 16%, giving an annual depreciation expense of:

$0.16 \times \$54\,600 = \$8\,736$

This gives a net book value at the end of its second year of ($54 600 − $8 736) $45 864.

### The strengths of declining balance depreciation:

- It provides a more realistic valuation of an asset's value over its life because assets tend to lose more value in their early years.

### The weakness of declining balance depreciation:

- It is a complicated method to calculate and more difficult to interpret than straight line depreciation.
- The useful life and residual value are forecasted values and may be different in reality.

### CASE STUDY

**Delhi Express Coach Travel**

Delhi Coach Travel is local travel company based in the city of Delhi. The business operates 20 luxury coaches. The business looks to replace four coaches a year, so the entire stock is replaced every five years. The useful life of a coach is five years. The next coach the company is buying costs $180 000 and has a resale value after five years of $70 000.

**Progress questions**

1 Using the straight line method of depreciation, calculate the annual depreciation expense on the new coach. [4 marks]

2 Analyse two reasons why the bus company might choose to use straight line depreciation rather than declining balance depreciation. [6 marks]

# Exam practice questions

## Paper 1 question (HL and SL)

### Preciso Limited

Preciso is a watch manufacturer based in Argentina. It was established in 1974 by the Kempes family. As part of Preciso's plan to establish a presence in the US market, they are looking at the possibility of buying a small watch-making business based in Los Angeles. Preciso's finance director, Eduardo Martinez, has received some financial data for 2015 for the business they are looking to buy:

- revenue $830 000

- indirect costs $200 000

- gross profits $440 000

- interest costs $30 000

- profit tax in the US is 15%.

There are some concerns about the financial information of the business, however, and Eduardo Martinez has decided to investigate further to see how accurate the data is.

a  Using the data on the business Preciso is looking to buy, construct a profit and loss account for the business. [6 marks]

b  Explain how the profit after tax of the business Preciso is looking to buy might be distributed. [4 marks]

c  Discuss the different accounting principles that need to be followed when the accounts of the business Preciso is looking to buy are being prepared. [10 marks]

[Total 20 marks]

## Paper 2 question (HL and SL)

### ALS

ALS is a courier business based in Sweden. The business has grown dramatically in the last four years because of the growth in internet shopping and the delivery work that goes with this. ALS is a medium-sized business that needs to compete with much larger multinational operators such as Federal Express and DHL. ALS has been approached by one of the multinational competitors on the basis of a possible friendly takeover. The buying company needs to value ALS and has asked to see its balance sheet data for 31.12.16. This is set out below:

|  | $000s |
|---|---|
| Debtors | 34 |
| Cash | 25 |
| Retained profit | 45 |
| Share capital | 693 |
| Stock | 9 |
| Creditors less than 12 months | 14 |
| Vehicles | 540 |
| Loans more than 12 months | 76 |
| Buildings | 220 |

a  Define the term 'fixed asset'. [2 marks]

b  Using the data provided by ALS construct a balance for it for 31.12.16. [6 marks]

c  Explain why share capital is part of equity in the balance sheet. [2 marks]

d  Evaluate the usefulness of ALS final accounts to three of its stakeholders. [10 marks]

**Exam tip**

The 'evaluate' command term in this question means making an appraisal of the usefulness ALS final accounts by weighing up their strengths and limitations.

# Profitability and liquidity ratio analysis

# 3.5

**What you should know by the end of this chapter:**

- The following profitability and efficiency ratios: gross profit margin, net profit margin, return on capital employed (AO2, AO4)

- Possible strategies to improve these ratios (AO3)

- The following liquidity ratios: current, acid-test/quick (AO2, AO4)

- Possible strategies to improve these ratios (AO3).

**Chapter illustrative example**
A business that manufactures bottled water

# Use of ratio analysis

Financial ratios are an important part of analysing an organisation's accounts for different stakeholders so they can make judgements about the performance and value of the organisation. Ratios can be broken down into three groups:

- profitability
- efficiency
- liquidity.

# Profitability and efficiency ratios

This group of ratios is used to consider a business's performance in terms of the profits it makes and how efficiently it generates profits from its assets.

## WORKED EXAMPLE

The ratios in this section are based on the final accounts produced by the bottled water business example on 31.12.16. This is shown in Table 3.5.1.

**Table 3.5.1**

| Profit and loss account 31.12.16 | $000s |
|---|---|
| Sales revenue | 7 600 |
| Cost of goods sold | 4 110 |
| **Gross profit** | **3 490** |
| Expenses | 2 200 |
| **Net profit** | **1 290** |
| **Balance sheet 31.12.16** | **$000s** |
| Fixed assets | 24 000 |
| Current assets | 2 500 |
| Current liabilities | 1 800 |
| Net current asset | 700 |
| Long term liabilities | 9 400 |
| Net Assets | 15 300 |
| Equity | 15 300 |

# Gross profit margin

**Key term**
**Gross profit margin** is the percentage of gross profit (sales revenue – cost of goods sold) a firm earns on each dollar of sales it makes.

- **Gross profit margin** is calculated using the equation: gross profit / sales revenue $\times$ 100 = gross profit margin.

- The gross profit margin analyses a business's profit performance in term of direct costs.

- In the bottled water business example this would be: 3490 / 7600 $\times$ 100 = 45.9%. This means for each dollar of sales it makes $0.46 of gross profit.

- The interpretation of this ratio is the higher the percentage of gross profit margin the better the performance of the business in terms of generating gross profits from sales.

# Net profit margin

**Key term**
**Net profit margin** is the percentage of net profit (gross profit – expenses) a firm earns on each dollar of sales it makes.

- **Net profit margin** is calculated using the equation: net profit/sales revenue $\times$ 100 = net profit margin.

- Net profit margin analyses the profit performance of the business taking into account direct and indirect costs.

- In the bottled water business example, this would be: 1290/7600 $\times$ 100 = 17%. This means for each dollar of sales it makes $0.17 of net profit.

- The interpretation of this ratio is the higher the percentage of net profit margin, the better the performance of the business in terms of generating gross profits from sales.

# 3.5

# Return on capital employed (ROCE)

## Key term

**Return on capital employed** measures the percentage of net profit a business earns on each dollar of capital employed in the business.

- Capital employed is the total long-term funding of an organisation made up of: long-term liabilities + equity.

- It is calculated using the equation: net profit / capital employed × 100 = ROCE.

- In the bottled water business example this would be: 1 290 / 24 700 × 100 = 5.2%. This means for each dollar of capital employed in the firm, it makes $0.05 of net profit.

- The interpretation of this ratio is the higher the ROCE, the better the performance of the business in generating net profit from the capital employed in the business.

**Clear Sight PLC**

Clear Sight PLC manufactures glasses. It is a global business selling their low-cost reading glasses in more than 30 countries. It is a big company, employing 4000 people and with production based in five different plants in Asia. Its summary balance is as follows:

| Profit and loss account 31.12.16 | $m |
|---|---|
| Sales revenue | 250 |
| Cost of goods sold | 145 |
| **Gross profit** | **105** |
| Expenses | 62 |
| **Net profit** | **43** |

| Balance sheet 31.12.16 | $000s |
|---|---|
| Fixed assets | 650 |
| Current assets | 230 |
| Current liabilities | 140 |
| Net current asset | 90 |
| Long-term liabilities | 210 |
| Net assets | 530 |
| Equity | 530 |

## Progress questions

1   State the equations for gross profit margin and net profit margin. [2 marks]

2   Explain what gross profit margin and net profit margin show. [4 marks]

3   Calculate the following ratios: gross profit margin, net profit margin, return on capital employment. [6 marks]

**Table 3.5.2**

| Strategy | Impact | Evaluation |
|---|---|---|
| Increase selling price | A higher price directly increases the gross and net profit margin on each unit sold. | This might increase the margin on each unit sold but total revenue might fall as consumers reduce demand because of the higher price. If revenue falls then net and gross margins will fall and so will ROCE. |
| Decrease selling price | This might increase sales revenue and profit as more consumers are attracted to buy the product. | This will reduce gross and net profit margin on each unit sold but if not enough extra units are sold profits will fall. |
| Increase sales revenue through advertising and promotion | An increase in consumer demand might increase sales and profits, which increases gross and net margins as well as ROCE. | For profits to increase, the increase in revenue generated by the advertising and promotion needs to be greater than the extra expenditure on advertising and promotion. |
| Reduce labour costs | Lower labour costs may increase profits, which leads to higher gross and net margins as well as ROCE. | This may increase margins, but might lead to redundancies and reduced wages for workers, which leads to lower motivation that adversely affects efficiency and customer service. This could lead to lower sales and profits. |
| Reduce raw material and component costs | Lower direct material costs may increase profits, which leads to higher gross and net margins as well as ROCE. | This may increase margins and profits successfully if better deals can be made with suppliers. If, however, poorer quality materials are used, the quality of the final product may not be as good. This could lead to lower revenues and profits. |
| Reduce indirect costs | This could be through reduced administration expenses, which increases net profits. | If the firm can reduce administration costs through efficiency savings then this could successfully increase margins and net profits. If, however, the cost savings make the business less efficient then customer service will not be as good and profits may fall. |

# Possible strategies to improve profitability and efficiency ratios

Table 3.5.2 sets out the strategies a business might use to improve the gross and net profit margins, and the return on capital employed.

# 3.5

### Col Cycles

Col Cycles is a chain of bicycle shops based in Belgium, which has 15 shops located in Belgium and Holland. The management have some concerns about the business's financial performance and this is reflected in the ratios shown in the table below.

| % | 2014 | 2015 | 2016 |
|---|---|---|---|
| Gross profit margin | 42 | 35 | 32 |
| Net profit margin | 21 | 18 | 17 |

### Progress questions

1  Explain two reasons why Col cycles gross profit margin might have fallen. [4 marks]

2  Evaluate the methods Col Cycles could use to increase its gross and net profit margins. [10 marks]

# Liquidity ratios

### Key term
**Liquidity** is the ease with which a business can turn its assets into cash.' Has this been removed deliberately or accidentally?

These two ratios are used to measure an organisation's ability to access funds for its everyday operation.

## Current ratio

### Key term
The **current ratio** measures the amount of currents assets a business has to funds its current liabilities.

- **The current ratio** is measured by the equation: current assets / current liabilities = current ratio.

- Current assets are the most liquid of a firm's assets and current liabilities are the debts that need to be paid most quickly.

- The bottled water company example the current ratio is: $2500 / $1800 = 1.39. This means for every $1 of current liabilities, the bottled water company has $1.39 of current assets to pay them.

- The guide for a safe current ratio is normally about 1.5.

- If the ratio is too low, the business may risk going bankrupt because it may not be able to cover its debts.

- If the ratio is too high, the business may be tying up current assets in an unprofitable way.

# Acid-test/quick ratio

### Key term
The **acid test ratio** measures the amount of the most liquid of currents assets a business has in cash and debtors to fund its current liabilities.

- **The acid-test/quick ratio** is measured by the equation: cash + debtors / current liabilities = acid test ratio.

- In the bottled water company example, the current ratio is: $1900 / $1800 = 1.06. This means for every $1 of current liabilities, the bottled water company has $1.06 of cash and debtors to pay them.

- The guide for a safe acid test ratio is normally about 1.0.

- If the ratio is too low, the business may risk going bankrupt because it may not be able to cover its debts.

- If the ratio is too high, the business may be tying up current assets in an unprofitable way.

## CASE STUDY

### Daily Post

*The Daily Post* is a regional newspaper based in New Zealand. It has a solid base of loyal readers but it is struggling to attract new readers as more people get their news from the internet. It is struggling with its cash flow position because it is not generating enough cash from sales and its costs are rising. The following information is from its balance sheet.

| Balance sheet 31.12.16 | $ |
| --- | --- |
| Fixed assets | 163 000 |
| | |
| Current assets | |
| Stock | 16 000 |
| Debtors | 5 700 |
| Cash | 1 800 |
| | 23 500 |
| Current liabilities | 23 400 |
| Net current asset | 100 |
| Long-term liabilities | 57 400 |
| Net assets | 105 700 |
| Equity | 105 700 |

### Progress questions

1 State the equations for the acid test and current ratios. [2 marks]

2 Calculate the acid test and current ratios for the *Daily Post*. [4 marks]

3 Analyse what the *Daily Post's* current ratio and acid test ratios tell us about its liquidity. [6 marks]

### Exam tip

The 'analyse' command term in this question means giving a breakdown of the current and acid test ratios and what they tell us about *Daily Post's* liquidity.

## Possible strategies to improve liquidity ratios

Table 3.5.5 sets out the strategies a business might use to improve its current and acid test ratios.

### Table 3.5.5

| Strategy | Impact | Evaluation |
| --- | --- | --- |
| Keep more cash in the business by leasing fixed assets. | Fixed assets can be sold generating cash and large amounts of cash are not used on fixed asset purchases. More cash available in the business improves both the current and acid test ratios. | Leasing assets can be more expensive than owning them in the long run, which reduces profitability. |
| Increase cash in the business through a loan. | A loan brings immediate cash into the business, which improves the acid test and current ratios. | Loans have to be repaid and there are interest payments. This is a drain on cash flow in the future and interest costs reduce future profits. |
| Increase cash through selling new shares. | A new share issue brings more cash into the business increasing the current and acid text ratios. | Issuing new shares may mean the influence of existing shareholders is reduced and more money has to be paid in dividends, which is a future drain on cash flow. |

# 3.5

## Exam practice questions

### Paper 1 question (HL and SL)

#### Preciso Limited

Preciso is a watch manufacturer based in Argentina. It was established in 1974 by the Kempes family. The CEO of Preciso, Mario Fernandez, is concerned with the liquidity position of the business as it looks to expand into the US. The current ratios and acid test ratios for the business are set out in the table below.

|  | 2014 | 2015 | 2016 |
|---|---|---|---|
| Current ratio | 1.4 | 1.2 | 1.1 |
| Acid test ratio | 0.9 | 0.85 | 0.8 |

a Explain what a fall in the current and acid test ratios for Preciso tells us about its liquidity position. [4 marks]

b Analyse two ways Preciso could increase its current and acid test ratios. [6 marks]

[Total 10 marks]

### Paper 2 question

#### Premium Air Conditioning

Premium Air Conditioning manufactures air conditioning units in Vietnam. The business is relatively new, being launched three years ago. It has always struggled with liquidity and it has come under particular pressure this year. Despite the fact it produces a good product and has plenty of regular orders, its cash flow is constantly under strain. Its balance sheet for 2016 is set out below:

| Balance sheet 31.12.16 | $ |
|---|---|
| Fixed assets | 129 000 |
|  |  |
| Current assets |  |
| Stock | 22 000 |
| Debtors | 4 200 |
| Cash | 900 |
|  | 27 100 |
| Current liabilities | 26 200 |
| Net current asset | 900 |
| Long-term liabilities | 74 000 |
| Net assets | 55 900 |
| Equity | 55 900 |

a Define the term 'liquidity'. [2 marks]

b Calculate the current and acid test ratios for Premium Air Conditioning. [4 marks]

c Explain what the values of Premium Air Conditioning's current and acid test ratios tell you about the firm's liquidity. [4 marks]

d Recommend the strategies Premium Air Conditioning could use to improve its acid test and current ratios. [10 marks]

[Total 20 marks]

#### Exam tip

The 'define' command term in this question requires you to give the precise meaning of the term liquidity.

# 3.6 | Efficiency ratio analysis (HL only)

**What you should know by the end of this chapter:**

- The following further efficiency ratios: inventory/ stock turnover, debtor days, creditor days, gearing ratio (AO2, AO4)

- Strategies to improve these ratios (AO3).

**Chapter illustrative example**
A business that manufactures perfume

# 3.6

## Measuring efficiency

This section focuses on how efficiently a business manages its resources in certain key areas to maximise the overall performance of the business. The following efficiency ratios measure the performance of an organisation in terms of the way it manages its:

- **stock** – stock turnover ratio

- **debtors** – debtor days' ratio

- **creditors** – creditor days' ratio

- **long-term finance** – gearing ratio.

### WORKED EXAMPLE

The ratios in this section are based on the final accounts produced by the perfume business example on 31.12.16. This is shown in Table 3.6.1.

**Table 3.6.1**

| Profit and loss account 31.12.16 | $000s |
|---|---|
| Sales revenue | 2 750 |
| Cost of goods sold | 1 310 |
| **Gross profit** | **1 440** |
| Expenses | 850 |
| **Net profit** | **590** |
| **Balance sheet 31.12.16** | **$000s** |
| **Fixed assets** | **12 050** |
| Current assets | |
| Stock | 220 |
| Debtors | 130 |
| Cash | 90 |
| **Total** | **440** |
| **Current liabilities** | |
| Creditors | 190 |
| Net current asset | 250 |
| **Long-term liabilities** | **1 500** |
| **Net assets** | **10 800** |
| **Equity** | **10 800** |

## Efficiency ratios

### Stock or inventory turnover

**Key term**
**Stock turnover** measures the number of times on average the stock of the business is sold or 'turned over' during the accounting year.

- **Stock or inventory turnover** is calculated by either: cost of goods sold / stock = stock turnover, or stock / cost of goods sold × 365 = stock turnover in days.

- For the perfume business example, the stock turnover is: $1310 / $220 = 5.96. This means the stock of the firms is sold 5.96 times on average during the accounting year.

- For the perfume business example, the stock turnover in days is $220 / $1310 × 365 = 61 days. This means the business sells its stock in 61 days on average this year.

- A high stock turnover figure and smaller number of days it takes to sell stock means the business is managing stock more efficiently. This results in less money being tied up in stock, which can then be used more profitably in other areas of the business.

- This ratio varies from industry to industry depending on factors such as the perishable nature of stock. A food processing business would need to turn stock over more quickly than a furniture manufacturer.

- If the stock turnover figure is too high, the business may suffer from holding too little stock, which may lead to it running out of stock.

### Debtor days

**Key term**
**Debtor days** is the average amount of time it takes customers who have bought goods on credit to pay a business during the accounting year.

- **Debtor days** is calculated by the equation: debtor / sales × 365 = debtor days.

- For the perfume business example, the debtor days would be: $130 / $2750 × 365 = 17 days to pay.

- The lower the debtor days, the more efficiently the business manages its outstanding debts and the more secure its cash flow position will be.

- If the debtor days is too low, the business may be operating a credit policy to its customers that is too strict and it could lose out on potential sales.

## Creditor days

**Key term**
**Creditor days** is the average amount of time it takes a business to pay for the goods it has bought on credit from its suppliers during the accounting year.

- **Creditor days** is calculated by the equation: creditors / cost of goods sold × 365 = creditor days.

- For the perfume business example, the creditor days would be: $190 / $1 310 × 365 = 53 days.

- The higher the creditor days figure, the more efficiently the business is in managing its creditors in terms of holding cash in the business by not paying creditors too quickly.

- It may mean, however, that the business misses out on early payment discounts and develops bad relationships with its suppliers.

## Gearing ratio

**Key term**
**Gearing ratio** is the proportion of an organisation's capital employed that is financed by long-term borrowed finance.

- **The gearing ratio** is measured by the equation: long-term liabilities / capital employed × 100 = gearing ratio (capital employed = equity + long-term liabilities).

- For the perfume business this would be: 1500 / 12 300 × 100 = 12.2%.

- A business that manages a low gearing ratio is often seen to manage its capital more efficiently because higher gearing means a larger proportion of funds are borrowed, which have to be repaid, and it also incurs interest costs.

- Low gearing does, however, mean after-tax profits may be distributed among a smaller number of shareholders.

### CASE STUDY

**Norton and Teller**
Norton and Teller manufactures tools for car repairs and maintenance. It is a medium-sized, established business but it has had some recent cash flow problems. The finance director is investigating some of the causes and has produced the following ratio data:

| | 2014 | 2015 | 2016 |
|---|---|---|---|
| Stock turnover ratio | 5.4 | 4.8 | 4.3 |
| Debtor days' ratio | 27 days | 31 days | 36 days |
| Creditor days' ratio | 28 days | 27 days | 25 days |
| Gearing ratio | 22% | 25% | 28% |

**Progress questions**

1 Calculate the stock turnover days for Norton and Teller in 2014, 2015 and 2016. [3 marks]

2 State how Norton and Teller's debtor days is calculated. [1 mark]

3 Explain why Norton and Teller's creditor days might have fallen. [2 marks]

# 3.6

**Table 3.6.2**

| Strategy | Impact | Evaluation |
|---|---|---|
| Reduce the stock levels a business holds. | This increases stock turnover assuming the same level of sales and reduces the funds a business ties up in stock. | Holding lower stock levels might increase the costs associated with a firm running out of stock where frustrated customers buy from more reliable suppliers. |
| Reduce the credit period an organisation gives its customers to pay. | This will reduce debtor days period and increase the flow of cash into the business and improve its liquidity. | Customers may be reluctant to pay more quickly because they are looking to protect their own liquidity position and they could go to other suppliers, which reduces sales revenue and profit. |
| **Strategy** | **Impact** | **Evaluation** |
| Increase the time a business takes to pay its suppliers. | This will increase the creditor days period and means the business will hold cash for longer and improve its liquidity. | The business may miss out on early payment discounts and their relationship with suppliers might deteriorate making managing supply more difficult. |
| Reduce long-term borrowing by increasing funds from outside investors. | If outside investment funds are used to reduce debt the gearing ratio of the business will fall. This will mean fewer repayments and less interest payments. | Bringing in additional funding from outside investors may mean a reduction in the control existing owners have on the business and profits have to be shared out among more shareholders. |

## Exam tip

The 'state' command term in this question means giving a specific equation to how debtor days is calculated.

## Possible strategies to improve the efficiency ratios

Table 3.6.2 sets out the strategies a business might use to improve stock turnover, debtor days, creditor days and the gearing ratio.

# Exam practice questions

## Paper 1 question (HL)

### Preciso Limited

Preciso is a watch manufacturer based in Argentina. It was established in 1974 by the Kempes family. The CEO of Preciso, Mario Fernandez, is investigating the cash flow position of the business as it looks to expand into the US. He is focusing on debtors and creditors.

**a** Outline what the debtor days' and creditor days' ratios show. [4 marks]

**b** Analyse one reason why the debtor days might have fallen and the creditor days might have increased. [6 marks]

[Total 10 marks]

### Exam tip

The 'outline' command term in this question means giving a brief account or summary of what debtor days' and creditor days' ratios show.

## Paper 2 question (HL)

### Ever Sport

Ever Sport Clothing is a sports clothing manufacturer. It is based in Indonesia where it produces clothing for some of the leading sports clothing brands. The final accounts of the business are set out below:

| Profit and loss account 31.12.16 | $000s |
|---|---|
| Sales revenue | 4 125 |
| Cost of goods sold | 1 560 |
| **Gross profit** | **2 565** |
| Expenses | 1 390 |
| **Net profit** | **1 175** |

| Balance sheet 31.12.16 | $000s |
|---|---|
| **Fixed assets** | **10 193** |
| Current assets | |
| Stock | 320 |
| Debtors | 150 |
| Cash | 100 |
| **Total** | **570** |
| **Current liabilities** | |
| Creditors | 450 |
| Net current asset | 120 |
| **Long term liabilities** | **3 500** |
| **Net Assets** | **6 813** |
| **Equity** | **6 813** |

The business has been approached by an outside investor that is looking to inject cash into the business but wants 10% return on their shareholding.

**a** Define the term 'creditors'. [2 marks]

**b** Calculate the following ratios: stock turnover, debtor days, creditor days and gearing for Ever Sport. [8 marks]

**c** Discuss the view that the best way to reduce Ever Sport's gearing ratio is to accept the funds from the outside investor. [10 marks]

[Total 20 marks]

# Cash flow

**What you should know by the end of this chapter:**

- The difference between profit and cash flow (AO2)

- The working capital cycle (AO2)

- Cash flow forecasts (AO2, AO4)

- The relationship between investment, profit and cash flow (AO2)

- The following strategies for dealing with cash flow problems: reducing cash outflow, improving cash in-flows, looking for additional finance (AO3).

**Chapter illustrative example**
A fast food restaurant that specialises in Mexican food

# Importance of cash flow

**Key terms**

**Cash flow** is the continuous movement of money in and out of a business resulting from its operations.

**Bankruptcy** is a legal position where a business does not have enough cash to pay an outstanding debt and is forced to stop trading.

Managing **cash flow** effectively is one of the most important aspects of the work finance managers do, because if a business runs out of cash it is at risk of **bankruptcy**.

Cash flows take two forms:

1   **Cash inflows** refers to money that comes into an organisation through sources such as:

   • cash sales

   • payments from debtors

   • sale of assets

   • investment from shareholders

   • loans from banks.

2   **Cash outflows** refers to money that flows out as the organisation spends funds on things such as:

   • paying wages

   • buying stock using cash

   • paying creditors

   • repaying a loan to the bank

   • paying tax to the government.

# The difference between profit and cash flow

The profit a business makes on its trading and the cash flow that that moves through a business are different things. The reason for this is credit trading, where sales and costs occur at different times to cash being received and paid.

## Credit sales and costs

A firm counts a good or service as sold as soon as it is delivered to the customer whether the good has been paid for or not. This means there will be a revenue figure in the firm's profit and loss account for goods sold even if they have not been paid for and no cash has been received.

### WORKED EXAMPLE

• In the fast food example, the business sells 20 meals at $7 each to a local business that has an account with the restaurant. This will be a revenue figure of (20 x $7) $140 in the restaurant's profit and loss account even though no cash has been received.

• To calculate the gross profit on the sale of the meals, the direct labour and raw material costs of producing the meals would be deducted.

• In this case the direct labour and material is $3 per meal, which means the total direct cost of the meals is (20 x $3) $60. This is counted as cost in the profit and loss account even though the materials for the meal had not been paid for and the wages to the workers had not been paid.

• The gross profit from selling the 20 meals is shown in Table 3.7.1:

**Table 3.7.1**

|  |  | $ |
|---|---|---|
| Sales revenue | 20 × $7 | 140 |
| Cost of goods sold | 20 × $3 | 60 |
| **Gross profit** |  | **80** |

• The cash flow figure would be completely different to this because the meals have not been paid for and the costs associated with producing the meals have also not been paid.

# 3.7

## CASE STUDY

### Davos Dairy Farm

Davos Dairy Farm's cash balance fell significantly this year. Milk prices have dropped by around 6 cents per litre over the year, leading to significant falls in its revenues. This is led to significant cash flow problems for the farm as production costs have increased as well.

### Progress questions

1 Define the term 'cash flow'. [2 marks]

2 Explain two reasons why Davos's cash flow might have deteriorated. [4 marks]

3 Explain two reasons why a fall in Davos's cash flow might be important to the business. [4 marks]

# Working capital

### Key term

**Working capital** is the short-term liquidity a business has to fund its everyday operations.

**Working capital** is calculated as current assets less current liabilities. This means that working capital is critical in affecting the cash flow position of a business.

The fast food restaurant, for example, has current assets of $200 000 and $120 000 of current liabilities, which gives a working capital of $80 000. This is a current ratio of ($200 000 / $120 000) 1.67, which means the fast food restaurant has $1.67 of cash, debtors and stock to cover each $1 of short-term loans and creditors. This appears to be secure in terms of cash flow because the business has access to enough money to cover its short-term debts.

## The working capital cycle

### Key term

The **working capital cycle** is the constant change in current assets and current liabilities as a business goes through its normal course of trading.

The **working capital cycle** is the flow of funds that occurs when a business buys stock on credit, uses the stock to produce a good, sells the good to a customer on credit and then receives the cash from the customers. The working capital cycle is shown in Figure 3.7.1.

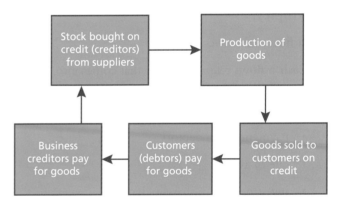

**Figure 3.7.1** The working capital cycle.

## Managing working capital

All organisations need to manage working capital and the working capital cycle to make sure they have the right amount of cash flow needed to fund their operations. There are two aspects to this managing of the cash flow to make sure a firm:

- has enough cash to pay its everyday expenses and debts

- does not have too much cash that is then tied up unprofitably.

## WORKED EXAMPLE

Table 3.7.2 sets out an example of a cash flow forecast for the fast food restaurant example.

These are the list of cash transactions and their timings for January to June 2017:

- revenue $40 000 per month
- cost of buying stock $8 000 per month
- wages paid $12 000 per month
- indirect expenses $11 000 per month
- interest payment $2 000 per month
- loan repayment $20 000 paid in March
- tax payment of $8 000 in April.

The opening cash balance on 1 January 2017 is $15 000.

Over the six-month period, the cash flow position of the fast food restaurant drops to a low point of $15 000 but increases by $7000 over the period to $29 000. The finance department would need to monitor the cash flow position to make sure the figure did not get too low and risk the business's liquidity or get too high and have cash tied up unprofitably.

**Table 3.7.2**

| $000s | Jan | Feb | Mar | Apr | May | Jun |
|---|---|---|---|---|---|---|
| Inflow | | | | | | |
| Revenue | 40 | 40 | 40 | 40 | 40 | 40 |
| Outflow | | | | | | |
| Stock buying | 8 | 8 | 8 | 8 | 8 | 8 |
| Wages | 12 | 12 | 12 | 12 | 12 | 12 |
| Indirect expenses | 11 | 11 | 11 | 11 | 11 | 11 |
| Interest | 2 | 2 | 2 | 2 | 2 | 2 |
| Loan Repayment | | | 20 | | | |
| Tax | | | | 8 | | |
| Total outflow | 33 | 33 | 53 | 41 | 33 | 33 |
| **Net cash flow** | **7** | **7** | **(13)** | **(1)** | **7** | **7** |
| Opening balance | 15 | 22 | 29 | 16 | 15 | 22 |
| **Closing balance** | **22** | **29** | **16** | **15** | **22** | **29** |

# Cash flow forecasts

## Key term

A **cash flow forecast** is a statement produced by a business that sets out the flow of cash into and out of the business over a given time period.

## Steps to producing a cash flow forecast

1 **Time** – Set out the time period for the cash flow forecast, which could be weekly or monthly.

2 **Opening cash balance** – Start with the cash balance value the business has at the start of the forecasting period.

## 3.7

3 **Cash inflows** – List the cash inflows into the business setting out the amount of cash coming into the business and the timing of the cash inflow.

4 **Cash outflows** – List the cash outflows from the business setting out the amount of cash going out of the business and the timing of the cash outflow.

5 **Net cash flow** – Work out the net cash flow of the business for the time period in the forecast, this could be weekly or monthly.

6 **Closing cash flow** – Add the net cash flow to the opening cash balance for the time period in forecast to give the closing cash balance.

### CASE STUDY

**Angelino's Coffee Shop**
Angelino's Coffee is a small coffee shop that serves a local area in central Milan. The owner is very concerned to manage the cash of the business following significant cash flow problems. He has decided to draw up a cash flow forecast for the first six months of 2017 based on the following information:

- revenue $23 000 per month
- cost of buying stock $4 300 per month
- wages paid $6 200 per month
- indirect expenses $5 500 per month
- interest payment $1 000 per month
- new machine purchase $9 000 paid in February
- tax payment of $3 000 in April
- opening cash on 1.01.17 $3 000.

**Progress questions**

1 Define the term 'working capital'. [2 marks]

2 Describe Angelino's working capital cycle. [4 marks]

3 Construct a cash flow forecast for Angelino's for the first six months of 2017. [8 marks]

**Exam tip**
The 'describe' command term in this question means giving a detailed account of the way Angelino's working capital cycle works.

# Investment and cash flow

When organisations invest in new capital such as buildings, machinery and equipment or in projects such as launching new products, this often involves significant outflows of cash from the business. The fast food restaurant, for example, is investing in a new oven that will cost $150 000. This money will flow out of the business when the oven is purchased.

To make sure a business's liquidity position remains secure it will need to organise finance to the cash outflow this may come from:

- reserves of cash a business builds up over time
- investment from new shareholders
- long-term bank loan
- leasing new equipment or buildings.

The fast food restaurant, for example, has decided to fund its new ovens from cash reserves and a bank loan.

# Strategies for dealing with cash flow problems

Table 3.7.3 sets out the possible strategies a business might use to deal with cash flow problems that can arise during its everyday operations.

**Exam tip**
The 'construct' command term means display the cash flow information in a table form. This needs to be clearly set and the process for the cash flow statement needs to be logically shown.

**Table 3.7.3**

| Strategy | Impact | Evaluation |
|---|---|---|
| Cutting labour and raw material costs. | Cutting costs reduces cash payments and cash outflow from the business. | Reducing wages might have a negative impact on employee motivation and reducing material costs might reduce the quality of the final product. Both effects might reduce a firm's sales and ability to generate future cash inflows. |
| Additional advertising spending to increase sales. | Increased advertising might raise consumer demand and lead to higher sales and greater cash inflows. | Expenditure on promotion will lead to an initial cash outflow, which causes a firm's cash flow to deteriorate in the short run although more cash may come in from sales in the long run. |
| Arranging an overdraft. | This gives a firm a constant source of short-term funding to cover cash flow problems. | Overdrafts have relatively high interest expenses that need to be paid, which are a drain on cash flow and banks can call in overdrafts, which can lead to severe cash flow problems when they need to be repaid. |
| Taking a long-term bank loan. | There is an injection of cash into the business from the bank loan. | In the long run, the bank loan incurs interest expenses and loan repayments that are a drain on future cash flow. If the loan is secured against an asset, there is the risk of losing the asset if the loan is not repaid. |

# Exam practice questions

## Paper 1 question (HL and SL)

### Preciso Limited

Preciso is a watch manufacturer based in Argentina. It was established in 1974 by the Kempes family. Finance director Eduardo Martinez is extremely conscious of cash flow and prepares Preciso's cash flow forecasts meticulously.

**a** Outline two things Preciso needs to include when preparing a cash flow forecast. [4 marks]

**b** Analyse two strategies Preciso could use to deal with a cash flow problem. [6 marks]

[Total 10 marks]

## Paper 2 question (HL and SL)

### Aspen Fury Autos

Aspen Fury Autos is a car dealership based in Baltimore. Its main business is selling cars that are less than two years old and have relatively low mileage. The accounting department are producing a monthly cash flow forecast for the coming year. The forecast is based on the following situation:

- revenue $220 000 per month
- cost of buying stock $105 300 per month
- wages paid $35 200 per month
- indirect expenses $46 600 per month
- interest payment $12 000 per month
- new machinery purchased $85 000 paid in June
- tax payment of $30 000 in May
- opening cash on 1.01.17 $20 000.

  **a** Define the term 'working capital cycle'. [2 marks]

  **b** Construct a cash flow forecast for Aspen Autos for the first six months of 2017. [6 marks]

  **c** Explain how a new asset purchase could cause cash flow problems for Aspen Fury Autos. [2 marks]

  **d** Evaluate the strategies Aspen Autos could use to improve its cash flow. [10 marks]

[Total 20 marks]

# Investment appraisal

## What you should know by the end of this chapter:

- Investment opportunities using payback period and average rate of return (ARR) (AO3, AO4)

- Investment opportunities using net present value (NPV) (AO3, AO4).

**Chapter illustrative example**
A passenger ferry company

# Investment and finance

## Business investment

**Investment** decisions often involve large cash outflows for an organisation and so investment decisions need to be carefully planned.

## Types of investment project

Organisations can be involved in a number of different types of investment project:

- **New machine** – Used to make production more efficient, which reduces production costs and improves the quality of a product.
- **New factory** – Increases the production capacity of a business, allowing it to increase revenues and profits.
- **Refurbishing a building** – For service organisations like retailers, this can improve the customer experience and increase sales and profits.
- **Research and development** – This could develop a new product for a business that could lead to sales and profits in the future.

The passenger ferry business, for example, is planning to buy a new ferry to open up a new route.

## Business investment and cash flows

Investment projects can affect a business's cash flows in the following ways:

- **Initial cash outlay** – This involves funds being used, for example, to buy a new piece of machinery.
- **Annual cash outflows** – These are the funds that are used to pay for the running cost of an investment decision such as labour and raw materials.
- **Annual cash inflows** – These are the cash inflows an investment project generates such as the revenues from selling a product produced by a new machine.
- **Annual net cash flow** – Investment annual cash inflows less annual cash outflows.

---

WORKED EXAMPLE

In the passenger ferry business example, the investment in the new ferry is associated with the following cash flows set out in Table 3.8.1.

**Table 3.8.1**

| $000s | Year 0 | Year 1 | Year 2 | Year 3 | Year 4 | Year 5 |
|---|---|---|---|---|---|---|
| Initial outlay | 4000 | | | | | |
| Annual cash inflows | | 1800 | 2100 | 2200 | 2200 | 2200 |
| Annual cash outflows | | 900 | 1000 | 1100 | 1200 | 1300 |
| Net annual cash flows | (4000) | 900 | 1100 | 1100 | 1000 | 900 |

The 'year' figures in the table refer to cash flow at the end of the year. For example, year 1 net annual cash flow is recorded at the end of year 1. Year 0 is the start of the project, when the initial cash outlay occurs.

# 3.8

## WORKED EXAMPLE

The payback for the ferry business example where the business invests in a new ferry is shown in Table 3.8.2.

**Table 3.8.2**

| $000s | Year 0 | Year 1 | Year 2 | Year 3 | Year 4 | Year 5 |
|---|---|---|---|---|---|---|
| **Initial outlay** | 4000 | | | | | |
| **Net annual cash flows** | (4000) | 900 | 1100 | 1100 | 1000 | 900 |
| **Cumulative cash flow** | (4000) | (3100) | (2000) | (900) | 100 | 1000 |

### Calculating and interpreting payback

- In this example, the project pays back the initial investment of £4 million in year 4 when the cumulative cash flow becomes positive.

- The exact payback time in year 4 can be calculated by the equation: (outstanding net cash flow at the start of the payback year / net cash flow in the payback year) × 365 = payback in days

- The precise payback for the ferry project would be: $900 000 / 1 000 000 × 365 = 37 days or 4 years 37 days.

- The shorter the payback period for an investment, the more desirable the investment.

# Methods of investment appraisal

## Payback period

### Key term
**Payback** is the time it takes an investment project's net cash inflows to cover the initial outlay of the investment.

**Payback** is often used by businesses because of the cash flow pressure an investment can put on a business's cash flow when the initial outlay on an investment is made until the project has generated sufficient net cash inflow to cover the investment.

Payback is calculated by deducting the annual net cash flow from the net cash flows year by year until the initial cash outlay is covered.

### Evaluation of the payback method
Strengths of payback:

- simple to calculate and interpret
- paybacks of different projects can be compared and judgements made
- useful for small and medium-sized businesses, where cash flow is more pressurised.

Weaknesses of payback:

- only considers cash flows to the payback time and ignores what might be significant net cash flows after the payback period
- ignores the overall cash return of a project and may make manager focus on the short term
- takes no account of the time value of money.

## Average rate of return (ARR)

### Key term
**Average annual rate of return** is the average annual net cash flow or profit of an investment project expressed as a percentage of the initial investment.

Profit is often used in place of net cash flow when the average rate of return **(ARR)** method is used so the profitability of a project can be appraised.

This method of appraisal is useful to businesses that want to assess the cash returns or profit over the whole life of a project relative to the size of the initial investment.

The ARR is calculated using the equation:

(total net cash inflow or profit − initial outlay / project life) / initial outlay × 100 = ARR

### WORKED EXAMPLE

The ARR for the ferry business example would be:

($000s)

(900 + 1 100 + 1 100 + 1 000 + 900 − 4 000 / 5) / 4 000 × 100 = 5%

The ARR of 5% means the investment in the new ferry yields an annual net cash flow of $0.05 on each $1 invested in the project.

The higher the ARR, the better the return on the investment in terms of the net cash flow it yields relative to the initial outlay.

## Evaluation of the ARR method

**Strengths of the method:**

- ARR considers the returns or profits for the entire life of a project.

- Percentage return or profit the investment yields means projects of different sizes can be compared.

- Returns or profits of investment projects are important pieces of decision-making information.

**Weaknesses of the method:**

- ARR does not account for the timings of net cash flows that are important to firms with cash flow constraints.

- Relies on an accurate forecast for the life of a project, which can be difficult to make.

- No allowance is made for the time value of money.

### CASE STUDY

**The Boot Maker**
The Boot Maker is a business that manufacturers different types of boots. It has, up to now, focused on boots but it wants to move into the shoe market. To do this it will need to expand by investing in new machinery and taking on new employees. Cash flow data for the investment project is set out below:

| $000s | Year 0 | Year 1 | Year 2 | Year 3 | Year 4 |
|---|---|---|---|---|---|
| Initial outlay | 750 | | | | |
| Net annual cash flows | | 200 | 300 | 400 | 400 |

**Progress questions**

1 Define the term 'investment'. [2 marks]

2 For the Boot Maker's project, calculate the payback and ARR. [6 marks]

3 Outline two advantages for the Boot Maker of using the payback method to appraise the project. [4 marks]

**Exam tip**
The 'calculate' command term in this question means giving a numerical answer for payback and ARR clearly showing the relevant stages in the working.

## Net present value method (NPV) (HL only)

**Key term**
The **net present value (NPV)** of an investment is the sum of discounted net cash flows of a project less the initial outlay of the investment.

Discounting is a method used with investment projects that generate net cash flows over a period of years to allow for the time value of money. Money has a time value because it is worth more in the present than it is

# 3.8

in the future because money now could be put into a bank account to earn a rate of interest.

For example, $1000 could be put in a bank for a year and earn 5% interest so it would be worth $1050 after one year – $1000 received after one year is not worth as much.

Because investment projects have net cash flows received years into the future, the net cash flows are not worth as much as if the cash was received now so the future net cash flows are discounted.

The net cash flows associated with an investment are discounted by the equation:

discount factor × net cash inflow = present value of the net cash flow

The new ferry investment has a positive NPV of $4000, which means the project yields a positive return on a discount rate of 8%. If the aim of management was for the new ferry project to yield a positive NPV at an 8% discount rate the project may go ahead. The greater the positive NPV on a project, the more desirable it is in

terms of discounted rate of return. The discount factors associated with a particular interest rate are always given in the examination.

## Evaluation of the NPV method

Strengths of the method:

- NPV considers the time value of money, which is important for projects that last a number of years.

- NPV considers the discounted returns for the entire life of a project.

- NPVs can be used to compare different projects.

Weaknesses of the method:

- NPV does not account for the timings of net cash flows, which are important to firms with cash flow constraints.

- It is a relatively complex method and more difficult to interpret than payback and ARR

- It relies on an accurate forecast for the life of a project, which can be difficult to make.

**WORKED EXAMPLE**

The NPV for the ferry business example where the business invests in a new ferry is shown in Table 3.8.3.

**Table 3.8.3**

| $000s | Year 0 | Year 1 | Year 2 | Year 3 | Year 4 | Year 5 |
|---|---|---|---|---|---|---|
| Initial outlay | 4000 | | | | | |
| Net annual cash flows | (4000) | 900 | 1100 | 1100 | 1000 | 900 |
| Discount factor 8% | 1 | 0.93 | 0.86 | 0.79 | 0.74 | 0.68 |
| Present value of net cash flows | (4000) | 837 | 946 | 869 | 740 | 612 |

$000s

837 + 946 + 869 + 740 + 612 = 4004 (total present value)

4004 – 4000 = 4 NPV

## CASE STUDY

### Metro Stop

Metro stop operates bus services in cities in Asia. It is currently looking at a major investment in one city that involves the buying a new fleet of buses. The cash flows associated with the project are set out in the table below.

| $000s | Year 0 | Year 1 | Year 2 | Year 3 | Year 4 | Year 5 |
|---|---|---|---|---|---|---|
| Initial outlay | 8100 | | | | | |
| Net annual cash flows | | 1800 | 1900 | 2100 | 2100 | 2100 |
| Discount factor 5% | 1 | 0.95 | 0.90 | 0.86 | 0.82 | 0.78 |

### Progress questions

1 Describe the net present value method of investment appraisal. [4 marks]

2 Calculate the NPV and payback of Metro Stop's new investment. [6 marks]

3 Analyse two advantages of using the NPV method to appraise Metro Stops investment project. [4 marks]

# Exam practice questions

## Paper 1 question (HL and SL)

### Preciso Limited

Preciso is a watch manufacturer based in Argentina. It was established in 1974 by the Kempes family. It is a medium-sized business employing 300 people, with a revenue of $30 million and a net profit of $7 million. The finance director, Eduardo Martinez, has a policy of looking at investment projects where he would expect a project to payback within four years and have an ARR that exceeds 15% for it to be feasible.

a Explain what an ARR of 15% shows and a payback within four years shows. [4 marks]

b Analyse the benefits of using ARR and payback to appraise investment projects. [6 marks]

[Total 10 marks]

## Paper 2 question (HL)

### Bespoke Furniture

Bespoke Furniture is a small business that manufactures high-quality furniture specifically for customers who are part of the design process. The furniture is made in the firm's factory, which normally works on a three-month time from order to delivery. The business is looking into buying a new computer system with the latest design software. The investment will lead to cost savings and raise revenue, which will bring cash flows into the business. The cash flow forecasts for the projects are set out in the table below:

| $ | Year 0 | Year 1 | Year 2 | Year 3 | Year 4 |
|---|---|---|---|---|---|
| Initial outlay | 70000 | | | | |
| Net annual cash flows | | 22000 | 27000 | 31000 | 31000 |

a State two things that would be part of the initial outlay for Bespoke Furniture's investment. [2 marks]

b Calculate the payback and ARR of Bespoke Furniture's investment. [6 marks]

c Outline what the ARR figure you have calculated tells you about Bespoke Furniture's investment. [2 marks]

d To what extent are investment appraisal techniques such as ARR and payback effective tools to help make decisions about investment projects. [10 marks]

[Total 20 marks]

## Key concept question

With reference to one organisation that you have studied, examine what changes globalisation and innovation bring about in investment decisions. [20 marks]

### Exam tip

The 'to what extent' command term in this question means consider the advantages and disadvantages of payback and ARR for making investment project decisions.

# Budgets (HL only)

## 3.9

**What you should know by the end of this chapter:**

- The importance of budgets for organisations (AO2)
- The difference between cost and profit centres (AO1)
- The roles of cost and profit centres (AO2)
- Variances (AO2, AO4)
- The role of budgets and variances in strategic planning (AO2).

**Chapter illustrative example**
An ice cream manufacturing business

# The importance of budgets for organisations

## Budgeting

**Key term**
A **budget** is a plan for the future costs, revenues and use of resources by a business.

The important elements for setting up a **budget** by a business are:

- Budgets are set for the coming year during the current year.

- Firms start by forecasting sales, which sets the budgeted revenue and determines how much the firm needs to produce.

- Once the production level is determined, the business can set budgets for the raw materials and labour it will need and it can then budget for direct and indirect costs.

- After costs and revenues have been budgeted, the budgeted profit and loss account can be fixed.

- Alongside the budgeted costs and revenues, the business can budget for changes in assets and liabilities. Setting a cash budget is an important part of this.

- Once the budget is fixed for the whole organisation, it is communicated to the managers who are responsible for carrying it out.

## Importance of budgets

Budgets are an important part of effective financial management and overall management of any successful organisation for the following reasons:

- **Controlling revenue and cost** – Part of an organisation's corporate objectives will include aiming to achieve a target level of profit, which means reaching a budgeted revenue and keeping costs to budgeted levels. The production manager in the ice cream manufacturer, for example, needs to keep spending on raw materials within a certain budgeted level if the firm is going to achieve the target profit set out as a corporate objective.

- **Managing resources effectively** – It is crucial for businesses to have resources in the right amounts and in the right place to be efficient. This is particularly crucial with the cash budget where running out of cash can threaten the firm's future.

- **Setting targets** – Budgets provide managers and employees with targets that can motivate them to work effectively. A sales budget for the ice cream manufacturer, for example, can be effective in motivating sales staff.

- **Measuring performance** – The whole organisation and individual parts of the organisation can be judged on the success or failure to achieve the targets provided by budgets. If the cost of producing the product by the ice cream manufacturer, for example, is higher than budgeted then the production manager may not be performing at a high enough level.

# Cost and profit centres

Different parts of an organisation can be considered cost and profit centres for setting up budgets.

## Cost centres

**Key term**
A **cost centre** is a department within an organisation that does not generate any revenues but is only associated with costs.

A **cost centre** of an organisation could be a production department responsible for maintenance or a service department such as marketing.

In the context of budgeting, the managers of cost centres have a responsibility of keeping the costs of their department within their cost budget. The manager of the transport department in the ice cream business, for example, is responsible for managing the firm's vehicles within a certain budgeted cost.

## Profit centres

### Key term
A **profit centre** is a department within an organisation that is responsible for generating costs and revenues.

A **profit centre** can operate like a separate business within the main organisation. The ice cream manufacturer, for example, has a number of retail outlets that sell the firm's ice cream and have costs and revenues associated with their operation.

In the context of budgeting, profit centres have a responsibility to control costs and revenues to achieve a budgeted profit.

### CASE STUDY

**Carlton Cards**
Carlton Cards is a business that manufactures greeting cards which it supplies to a whole variety of different retailers, including small shops and large supermarket chains. It is a business that works very hard to make its resources work efficiently and the CEO believes very strongly in effective budgeting.

**Progress questions**

1 Define the term 'budget'. [2 marks]

2 Outline the difference between a cost centre and a profit centre. [4 marks]

3 Explain two reasons why budgets are important to Carlton Cards. [4 marks]

**Exam tip**
The 'explain' command term in this question means giving a detailed account of the importance of budgets to Carlton Cards.

## Budgeting and variance

### Variance

**Key term**
A **variance** is where a business has a difference between an actual figure achieved in its operations in an accounting year and a budgeted figure.

**Variances** are used as part of budgetary control by organisations to help evaluate the performance of the organisation and different department within it. The sales manager of the ice cream business, for example, has seen the sales achieved by the business above the budgeted sales – a positive of favourable variance.

On the basis of this variance, it suggests the sales manager and the sales department have been successful in achieving their budgeted target.

# Calculating variances

## Favourable variance

**Key term**
A **favourable variance** is where the actual figure achieved is different to the budgeted figure, which causes the actual profit figure to be higher than the budgeted figure.

### WORKED EXAMPLE

Variances are calculated by subtracting an actual figure a business achieves in an accounting year and the budgeted figure for that year. Table 3.9.1 illustrates how variances are calculated.

**Table 3.9.1**

| $000s | Budget | Actual | Variance | Favourable or adverse |
|---|---|---|---|---|
| Sales revenue | 27 600 | 28 150 | 550 | Favourable |
| Direct materials | 8560 | 9130 | 570 | Adverse |
| Direct labour | 7450 | 7610 | 160 | Adverse |
| **Gross profit** | **11 590** | **11 410** | **180** | **Adverse** |
| Indirect expenses | 3150 | 3100 | 50 | Favourable |
| **Net profit** | **8440** | **8310** | **130** | **Adverse** |

The sales variance, for example, in Table 3.9.1 (\$28 150 000 – \$27 600 000) is \$550 000 favourable because a higher actual sales figure would increase actual profit. A **favourable variance** would be seen as a successful performance for this part of the organisation.

## Adverse variance

**Key term**
An **adverse variance** is where the actual figure achieved is different to the budgeted figure which causes the actual profit figure to be lower than the budgeted figure.

The direct materials variance in Table 3.9.1, for example, (\$8 560 000 – \$9 130 000) is adverse because the actual direct material figure is above the budgeted figure, which leads to a lower actual profit. An **adverse variance** would be seen as an unsuccessful performance for this part of the organisation.

### CASE STUDY

**Ezpectcy Sandwich Shop**
Ezpectcy is a small business based in Cairo that sells a range of fast food in a small local area of the city. The business has just appointed a new accountant to improve the financial performance of the business. Their first task is to look at the firm's performance against its budget.

| | Budget | Actual |
|---|---|---|
| Sales revenue | 65600 | 69430 |
| Direct materials | 15560 | 19540 |
| Direct labour | 14870 | 16.410 |
| Indirect expenses | 13150 | 14200 |

**Progress questions**

1 Define the term 'variance'. [2 marks]

2 Calculate the budgeted and actual gross and net profit figures. [4 marks]

3 Calculate the: revenue, direct material costs, direct labour costs, indirect expenses, gross profit and net profit variances. [6 marks]

4 Analyse what the revenue and direct materials' variance tells Ezpectcy's managers about the performance of the organisation. [6 marks]

# The role of budgets and variances in strategic planning

## Role of budgets

**Key term**
**Strategic planning** is where senior managers in an organisation set out the corporate aims of the organisation and put in place a plan that sets out how the business is going to achieve the corporate aims.

Budgets are an important part of a business's **strategic planning** because they set the precise financial targets needed to achieve the corporate aims of the business. The ice cream business, for example, has an aim of achieving a 9% return on capital employed for 2017. To achieve this aim, it needs to set budgets for costs and revenues that achieve a net profit that would deliver this figure.

## Role of variances

Variances support strategic planning because they give managers the financial information they need to make judgements about the success or failure of different departments in the organisation in achieving the corporate aims and how those departments might be managed in the future.

# Exam practice questions

## Paper 1 question (HL)

### Preciso Limited

Preciso is a watch manufacturer based in Argentina. It was established in 1974 by the Kempes family. Finance director Eduardo Matinez believes in tight control over the organisation's finances and he sees effective budgeting as crucial.

**a** Explain how budgets help Preciso motivate employees in its organisation. [4 marks]

**b** Analyse two reasons why variance analysis might help Preciso measure its performance. [6 marks]

[Total 10 marks]

## Paper 2 question

### Fortuna Heating

Fortuna Heating is medium-sized business based in the Czech Republic. It has produced the following budgeted and actual data for 2016:

| $000s | Budget | Actual |
|---|---|---|
| Sales revenue | 124 600 | 119 450 |
| Direct materials | 38 450 | 37 560 |
| Direct labour | 42 130 | 43 230 |
| Indirect expenses | 26 780 | 27 970 |

**a** Define the term 'variance'. [2 marks]

**b** Calculate the following variances: revenue, direct materials, direct labour, indirect expenses, gross profit and net profit. [6 marks]

**c** Explain two possible reasons for the revenue variance you have calculated. [4 marks]

**d** Analyse two ways budgeting can help Fortuna Heating in its strategic management. [8 marks]

[Total 20 marks]

**Exam tip**
The 'analyse' command term in this question means breaking down how budgeting helps strategic management into its essential elements.

# Marketing

# The role
# of marketing

**What you should know by the end of this chapter:**

- Marketing and its relationship with other business functions (AO1)

- The differences between marketing of goods and marketing of services (AO2)

- Market orientation versus product orientation (AO2)

- The difference between commercial marketing and social marketing (AO2)

- Characteristics of the market in which an organisation operates (AO1)

- Market share (AO4)

- The importance of market share and market leadership (AO3)

- The marketing objectives of for-profit organisations and non-profit organisations (AO3)

- How marketing strategies evolve as a response to changes in customer preferences (AO3)

- How innovation, ethical considerations and cultural differences may influence marketing practices and strategies in an organisation (AO3).

**Chapter illustrative example**
A large soft drinks manufacturer

# Marketing in relation to other business functions

**Key term**
**Marketing** is where a business produces a good or service that satisfies the needs and wants of the customer.

The focus of the **marketing** function in an organisation is to work with all the other functions in the organisation to produce a product that consumers want to buy. The marketing department in the soft drink business, for example, will work with the production department to get the soft drinks produced to the right quality.

# Differences between marketing goods and services

Businesses in the service sector face different challenges to those in the primary and secondary sector. The key differences between marketing goods and services are:

- Goods are tangible and services are not, so consumers can see what they are going to buy.

- With services, the business nearly always comes into direct contact with the consumer so customer service is crucial in marketing services.

- Services are consumed immediately by the buyer, not stored so there is great sales pressure on airlines not to have empty seats on a flight, for example.

- Dissatisfied customers cannot take back a service if the service is poor quality and does not work.

# Market orientation versus product orientation

## Market orientation

**Key term**
**Market orientation** is where an organisation uses an outward-looking approach to marketing by focusing on what the consumer wants and producing a product that satisfies this.

The soft drinks business, for example, does extensive market research to find out about consumer tastes in terms of flavours and packaging.

## Product orientation

**Key term**
**Product orientation** is where a business uses an inward-looking approach that focuses on producing a product that satisfies the business's management.

This often happens with firms in specialist areas who are more concerned with product quality rather than consumer wants.

Businesses often use both market orientated and product orientated approaches but some have greater emphasis on being market orientated and some on being product orientated.

# Commercial marketing and social marketing

## Commercial marketing

**Key term**
**Commercial marketing** focuses on meeting the wants and needs of the consumer so the business can achieve its corporate aims.

The soft drinks business, for example, markets its products to achieve revenue, profit and market share aims.

## Social marketing

**Key term**
**Social marketing** is where businesses markets goods and services to consumers to benefit society as a whole.

The soft drinks business, for example, has marketed sugar-free drinks extensively for the health benefits of their consumers and also the social benefits of a healthier population.

---

### CASE STUDY

**Spotify**
The music streaming service Spotify is a Swedish music, podcast and video streaming service that has achieved phenomenal growth since it was founded ten years ago. It now provides a digital platform where users can listen to more than 30 million tracks for a few dollars a month.

**Progress questions**

1 Define the term 'market orientation'. [2 marks]

2 Outline two ways Spotify can be seen as a market-orientated business. [4 marks]

3 Explain two differences in the way Spotify as a service markets its product compared to a business that sells a physical good. [4 marks]

---

# Characteristics of the market

To successfully market a good or service, an organisation needs to understand the characteristics of the market it operates in. The soft drinks producer, for example, would want to know things like:

* number of consumers in the market

* age of the consumers

* income level of consumers

* consumption habits of the consumers

* main competing firms

* whether the market is growing or not.

If the marketing is shrinking because the consumption of soft drinks is falling and the market has many competitors then this is a challenging marketing environment for the business.

---

# Market share and market leadership

## Market share

**Key term**
**Market share** is the proportion of total market sales revenue one business's sales revenue accounts for.

* Achieving a certain **market share** is often an objective of firms because it gives them a measure of relative performance compared to their competitors.

- Calculating market share:

    business's total annual sales revenue / market total annual sales revenue × 100 = business's market share

- For the soft drinks business example, the business sales in 2016 were $350 million and the total market sales for soft drinks were $1 260 million

    $350 / $1 260 × 100 = 28%

# Market leadership

## Key term
**Market leadership** is where a business achieves the highest market share of all the businesses selling in that market.

The **market leader** in the soft drinks market example is a firm that has a market share of 33%.

The benefits of achieving market leadership:

- strengthens the brand image of the product and further increases its sales

- strengthens the bargaining position of the business, such as the soft drinks firm, when it is negotiating a selling price with retailers

- often implies high levels of output, which leads to economies of scale.

The disadvantages of being market leader:

- attracts negative publicity for achieving things like excess profits

- attracts government intervention if the business looks like it has a monopoly position.

## CASE STUDY

### Nike
Nike is the world's largest manufacturer of athletic shoes, clothing and sports equipment. The business employs 62 000 people worldwide and has a global revenue of $30.6 billion. Its global market share is expected to grow to 27.2 percent by 2020.

**Progress questions**

1 Define the term 'market share'. [2 marks]

2 State how you would calculate Nike's market share. [1 mark]

3 Analyse two benefits Nike might receive from increasing its market share. [6 marks]

**Exam tip**
In this 'define' command term question you need to give the precise meaning of the term 'market share'. A supporting example from the case material would also be useful.

# The marketing objectives of for-profit and non-profit organisations

## For-profit businesses marketing objectives

- increase sales revenue
- increase or maintain market share
- introduce new goods or services
- develop brand awareness and loyalty
- enter new markets.

## Non-profit marketing objectives:

- **Increase income** – For charities, for example, this would be donations.

- **Develop awareness** – For a medical organisation, for example, that wants to prevent an illness.

- **Attract members** – For example, a political party.

- **Develop a positive image.**

- **Create publicity** – For a political organisation, for example, putting pressure on a government.

The key difference between the marketing making profit-making and non-profit-making organisation is that non-profit-making organisations have a wider scope for their objectives than profit-making businesses that have profit as a focus for their objectives. The soft drinks business, for example, has to set marketing objective within the scope of ultimately making a profit.

## How marketing strategies evolve as a response to changes

The soft drinks manufacturer, for example, has set the objective of increasing its market share by two percent next year and it will use a pricing and promotion tactics to try and achieve this.

Table 4.1.1 sets out changes in customer preference for the example soft drinks business and how its marketing strategy might change when dealing with them.

## Influences on marketing

Table 4.1.2 sets out how innovation, ethical considerations and cultural differences might influence marketing strategy in the soft drinks business example.

**Table 4.1.1**

| Change in customer preference | Strategy | Evaluation |
|---|---|---|
| Consumers become more health conscious. | Introduce sugar-free drinks and promote them as healthy alternatives. | This may attract health-conscious consumers but it may make the sugar-based drinks they sell look even more unhealthy and reduce their sales. |
| More consumers going to coffee shops rather than bars. | Change the products, distribution to coffee shops. | Soft drinks may not sell as well in coffee shops where consumers want to drink hot drinks. |
| Growth in consumption of soft drinks among older people. | Change promotion and packaging to target older consumers. | Targeting older consumers may put off younger consumers. |

**Table 4.1.2**

| | Strategy | Evaluation |
|---|---|---|
| **Innovation** – Social media facilitates a new way of advertising products. | The soft drinks business uses Facebook, Instagram and Twitter to promote its products. | Allows promotion and advertising to be more targeted but the promotion message may get lost because of the volume of media information consumers receive. |
| **Ethical considerations** – Need to make consumers aware of the health effects of sugary drinks. | Health guidelines need to be included on packaging and in advertising. | Information may help with image and government regulation but it could lead to a fall in sales if consumers become aware of how unhealthy a product is. |
| **Cultural differences** – Launching soft drink products into overseas markets. | Changing the flavours of products to reflect differing tastes among consumers in different countries. | Developing new flavours may add to production costs and it could affect the image of existing products if the new flavours are not well received by consumers. |

# Exam practice questions

## Paper 1 question (HL and SL)

### Aderson Publishing

Aderson Publishing is an independent, worldwide publishing business that produces fiction and non-fiction books. The business is based in Sweden and has a turnover of $80 million. Along with its published books it also has significant digital content and its online catalogue is increasing in importance. One of its USPs is strong political views. A recent publicity campaign by the business highlighted the problem of violence against women.

**a** Outline two differences Aderson might find between marketing its books and its online content. [4 marks]

**b** Analyse two marketing consequences of Aderson being involved in political campaigns. [6 marks]

[Total 10 marks]

### Exam tip

In this 'outline' command term question you need to give a brief account of two differences between marketing goods and services using Aderson as an example.

## Paper 2 question (HL and SL)

### Médecins Sans Frontières

Médecins Sans Frontières (MSF) is a global humanitarian-aid NGO and Nobel Peace Prize winner. It is known for its medical support in conflict regions and medical challenges in developing countries where it sends in medical professionals and resources to deal with crisis situations.

**a** Define the term 'marketing'. [2 marks]

**b** Outline two possible marketing aims of MSF. [4 marks]

**c** Explain two differences between not-for-profit marketing and for-profit marketing. [4 marks]

**d** Evaluate how ethical and cultural issues might influence the way MSF markets itself. [10 marks]

[Total 20 marks]

## Key Concept question

With reference to one organisation that you have studied, examine how innovation and ethics influence marketing strategy. [20 marks]

# Marketing planning

# 4.2

## What you should know by the end of this chapter:

- The elements of a marketing plan (AO1)

- The role of marketing planning (AO2)

- The four Ps of the marketing mix (AO2)

- An appropriate marketing mix for a particular product or business (AO2, AO4)

- The effectiveness of a marketing mix in achieving marketing objectives (AO3)

- The difference between target markets and market segments (AO2)

- Possible target markets and market segments in a given situation (AO4)

- The difference between niche market and mass market (AO2)

- How organisations target and segment their market and create consumer profiles (AO2)

- A product position map/perception map (AO2, AO4)

- The importance of having a unique selling point/ proposition (USP) (AO2)

- How organisations can differentiate themselves and their products from competitors (AO3).

### Chapter illustrative example
A business that runs a chain of cinemas

# Elements of a marketing plan

**Key term**

A **marketing plan** is where a business sets out the marketing strategies and tactics it is going to use to achieve its marketing objectives.

These are the steps of producing a **marketing plan**:

- Assess the current market situation using PESTLE and SWOT analysis.

- Use market research to establish the target market of consumers and the wants and needs of these consumers.

- Set the marketing objectives.

- Develop the marketing strategies to be used such as pricing and promotion.

- Finalise the marketing tactics to be used as part of strategies such as the nature of promotional methods.

- Set a budget for the plan.

# The role of marketing planning

Marketing plans are important for organisations because they allow:

- a business to clearly focus on the way a business it is going to market its products

- the marketing function of the organisation to achieve its corporate objectives.

# The four Ps of the marketing mix (seven Ps is part of HL)

**Key term**

The **marketing mix** is the way organisations use product, price, promotion and place as part of their marketing plan.

The **marketing mix** consists of:

- **Product** – Nature of the good or service to be sold.

- **Price** – What price the business sets for its product.

- **Promotion** – The communication methods used to sell the product to the consumer.

- **Place** – Where the product is being sold or service located.

# Using an appropriate marketing mix

Using the right marketing mix for a good or service is important for a firm when it is trying to achieve its marketing objectives.

An appropriate marketing mix for the cinema chain example should be based on the research the business has done in terms of what its consumers want:

- **Product** – The quality of the buildings and their fittings where the films are shown along with showing the films the customers want to see.

- **Price** – Setting ticket prices at the appropriate level to attract consumers and cover costs.

- **Promotion** – Advertising the films shown and the facilities they offer to the target audience.

- **Place** – Locating the cinemas in places which are accessible to the target market.

# The effectiveness of a marketing mix

A key factor that will determine the success of a business's marketing mix will be how effectively it interprets its market research and sets the four Ps to meet the needs and wants of the consumer. It will also be affected by how effectively it adapts its marketing mix to changes in the business environment. These could be:

- changes in the marketing strategy of existing competition

- new competition entering the market

- changes in economic growth

- decline or growth in the market

- changes in rules and regulations.

The cinema chain, for example, has had to adapt its marketing mix by reducing prices because an economic recession has reduced demand for tickets.

**Exam tip**
The 'identify' command term in this question means providing an answer from a number of different possible aspects of a marketing plan.

# The difference between target markets and market segments

Part of a business's marketing plan is to work out who its potential consumers are and what they want and need from the product the business is marketing.

## Target markets

**Key term**
A **target market** is the group of consumers a business is looking to sell its good or service to.

The cinema chain, for example, might target customers living within a certain distance from its cinemas who want to watch films in a cinema environment. **Target markets** can be very broad, as in the cinema chain's case, or narrower such as a cinema only showing Art House films.

## Market segment

**Key term**
A **market segment** is the consumers who are part of a market that share certain common characteristics.

**Market segment** can be based on:

- **Demographic factors** – age and gender of people in the market.

- **Psychographic segmentation** – education, income, lifestyle, and beliefs of consumers.

- **Geographic** – where people live (local, regional or national).

- **Behavioural** – way people buy goods and services (online or in a shop).

Two segment factors affecting the cinema chain, for example, is geographic (local to the cinema) and behavioural (how often they attend cinemas to watch films).

## The difference between niche and mass market

The way a firm sets its marketing plan will often be determined by whether it sells to a mass market or a niche market.

## Niche market

**Key term**
A **niche market** is a market segment with a relatively small number of consumers who share certain specific characteristics.

In the cinema market, for example, Art House cinemas that specialise in showing specialist foreign-language films would be selling to a **niche market** of consumers. Consumers with a certain education level and lifestyle would probably form the narrow niche market in this case.

## Mass market

**Key term**
A **mass market** is a very broad market segment where a large number of consumers make up the target market for a business.

Everyday products sold in supermarkets such as washing powder and toothpaste are typical products sold to **mass markets**.

The cinema chain is, for example, selling to a relatively mass market so the marketing mix it uses should reflect this, such as showing blockbuster Hollywood films with a wide appeal.

## Targetting and segmenting markets and consumer profiles

Once a business has fixed the target market it is going to market its product to, it needs to build up profiles of the consumers it is targeting. Not all groups of consumers

**4.2**

in the target market will share the same characteristic, so it is important for a business to set a marketing mix that allows for different consumer profiles.

## CASE STUDY

### R.L. Bhatia & Co

R.L. Bhatia & Co is an India-based manufacturer and supplier of sports goods with cricket equipment as one of its leading products. It produces items such as cricket bats, pads, balls and gloves. Based near New Delhi, it supplies the domestic market and it also exports.

### Progress questions

1  Define the term 'target market'. [2 marks]

2  Describe two possible characteristics of R.L. Bhatia's target market. [4 marks]

3  Outline two possible consumer profiles R.L. Bhatia might face when it markets products. [4 marks]

# A product position map/ perception map

**Key term**
A **product position map** or perception map is a graphical technique used to analyse a consumer's perception of the products in a market based on two characteristics.

The **product position map** is a useful tool to help develop marketing plans because it gives a business an understanding of what the consumer thinks of its product's position in the market relative to competing products. If the firm believes it needs to change the perception, it can adapt its marketing plan to do this.

**WORKED EXAMPLE**

The cinema chain might consider the following types of consumers and how to set the marketing mix to attract them. This is shown in Table 4.2.1.

**Table 4.2.1**

| Consumer type | Profile | Marketing tactic |
|---|---|---|
| Young independent | • Age 16–25<br>• Low income<br>• Flexible attendance time<br>• Likes mainstream films. | Show mainstream films that attract the young independent at discounted prices at off-peak times. |
| Young family | • Parents with children under ten<br>• Time constrained to late afternoon, weekends and school holidays<br>• Likes children's films. | Show children's films scheduled between 4 p.m. and 6 p.m. with special showings at weekends and school holidays. Offer family discounted tickets. |
| Older educated | • Age 50+<br>• High income<br>• Evening attendance<br>• Likes serious/classic films. | Show serious/classic films in the evening and offer premium price tickets for more comfortable seats. |

Table 4.2.2 illustrates a product position map for the cinema chain example based on quality of experience against ticket price. The other competitors in the market are shown by points A, B and C. The example cinema chain might be concerned that its price against competitor B is perceived to be the same but the perceived quality is significantly lower and this may be something it would improve on in its marketing plan.

**Table 4.2.2**

| | | Ticket price | |
|---|---|---|---|
| | | **Low** | **High** |
| **Quality of experience** | High | | X A<br>X B |
| | | | X (example chain) |
| | | X C | |
| | Low | | |

# The importance of having a unique selling point/ proposition (USP)

**Key term**

A **unique selling point (USP)** is the key factor that differentiates a good or service from the competing products in the market.

The soft drinks manufacturer, for example, sees the global perception of its brand as its **USP**.

A USP is important for a business because it:

- is a reason for the consumer to choose the firm's product over its competitors

- provides a focus for a marketing plan

- can be developed by other parts of the business to create a strong brand image

- protects the business against new competition.

### Mast Chocolate

The Mast brothers founded Mast Chocolate in New York in 2007. The business sells the highest quality chocolate using small-batch chocolate-making methods, which allows them to charge $10 a for a bar.

### Progress questions

1 Define the term 'unique selling point'. [2 marks]

2 Explain two ways Mast might have developed its USP for its chocolate. [4 marks]

3 Analyse two changes in consumer taste and preferences Mast might have responded to in marketing their product. [6 marks]

# How organisations can differentiate themselves and their products

A business can use the marketing mix to differentiate itself from its competitors. Table 4.2.3 illustrates how the example cinema chain business could use the marketing mix to differentiate its products.

# Exam practice questions

## Paper 1 question (HL and SL)

### Aderson Publishing

Aderson Publishing is an independent, worldwide publishing business that produces fiction and non-fiction books. The business is based in Sweden and has a turnover of $80 million. Along with its published books it also has significant digital content and its online catalogue is increasing in importance. One area of marketing that has worried its market director Olaf Andersson is the firm's books appear relatively expensive compared to the competition, although the quality of its products is higher.

1 Outline two possible market segments Aderson could target its books at. [4 marks]

2 Analyse two possible ways a product positioning map might help Aderson develop a marketing strategy. [6 marks]

[Total 10 marks]

## Paper 2 question (HL and SL)

### Square Peg

Square Peg is due to launch its range of children's toys in two months' time. It is targeting the parents of children up to the age of five with toys with an education or

### Table 4.2.3

| Method | Strategy | Evaluation |
|--------|----------|------------|
| Product | Improve the quality of the product by investment in new higher specification cinemas that offer a better viewing experience. | The new investment will add to the business's costs, which may lead to higher prices. |
| Price | Set higher prices to reflect the higher quality cinema experience. | Higher prices may make the cinema unaffordable to some consumers and reduce revenue. |
| Promotion | Use advertising to reflect the higher quality of the cinema experience on offer. | The image of higher quality might make the cinema chain exclusive and put off some consumers. |
| Place | Locate a new cinema in a prestigious city-centre location as a 'flagship'. | Central city locations have high development costs, which could make the location unprofitable. |

young learning focus. Its USP is that all its toys are made from recycled materials.

1  Define the term 'USP'. [2 marks]

2  Outline two reasons Square Peg might have targeted the parents of children under five rather than children of all ages. [4 marks]

3  Explain how Square Peg could use promotion and place to react its target market segment. [4 marks]

4  Compare and contrast the methods Square Peg has used to differentiate its products from its competitors in the toy market. [10 marks]

[Total 20 marks]

**Exam tip**

The 'compare and contrast' command term in this question means giving an account of similarities and differences between the methods Square Peg has used to differentiate its products.

# Sales forecasting (HL only)

**What you should know by the end of this chapter:**

- Up to four-part moving average, sales trends and forecast using given data (AO4)

- Seasonal, cyclical and random variation (AO4)

- The benefits and limitations of sales forecasting (AO3).

**Chapter illustrative example**
A business that manufactures suntan lotion

# Importance of sales forecasting

**Key term**
**Sales forecasting** is where a business uses data and other information to predict future sales.

The suntan lotion business example uses its **sales forecast** to plan production levels during the year.

# Moving averages

## Three-part moving averages

**Key term**
A **moving average** is where the mean average in a set of data is continuously recalculated over time to establish a trend in the data.

**Chill-out**
Chill-out produces frozen yogurt that it markets locally in a central district of Mexico City. The business has seen its sales increase over the past six years but there are concerns that the growth in sales has slowed down. Its sales for the past six years are shown in the table below.

| Year | Sales revenue $000s |
|------|---------------------|
| 2011 | 45 |
| 2012 | 56 |
| 2013 | 64 |
| 2014 | 58 |
| 2015 | 65 |
| 2016 | 64 |

**Progress questions**

1 Define the term 'sales forecasting'. [2 marks]

2 Calculate the thee-part moving average for Chill-out for the period 2011–16. [4 marks]

3 Plot the actual sales figures and moving average sales figure for Chill-out for the period 2011–16. [4 marks]

4 Describe the trend in the sales data for Chill-out from 2014 to 2016. [2 marks]

## WORKED EXAMPLE

Table 4.3.1 shows the sales revenue data for the suntan lotion firm example. The three-part moving average is calculated by:

1 **Calculate the three-part moving total** – This is done by adding up the sales revenue for the first three years of data (2010, 2011, 2012) which is 980 + 990 + 1005 = 2975, then repeating the calculation by moving on a

year (2011, 2012, 2013) which is 990 + 1005 + 1010 = 3005. This is repeated through the entire set of data.

2 **Calculate the three-part moving average** – This is done by calculating the mean average for each three-year period in the data, which is calculated by: 3 year total / 3 = 3 year moving average. The moving average for 2011 would be 2975 / 3 = 992.

**Table 4.3.1**

| Year | Sales revenue $000s | 3 year total | 3-year moving average |
|------|---------------------|--------------|----------------------|
| 2010 | 980 | | |
| 2011 | 990 | | 2975 / 3 = 992 |
| 2012 | 1005 | 980 + 990 + 1005 = 2975 | 3005 / 3 = 1002 |
| 2013 | 1010 | 990 + 1005 + 1010 = 3005 | 3040 / 3 = 1013 |
| 2014 | 1025 | 1005 + 1010 + 1025 = 3040 | 3055 / 3 = 1018 |
| 2015 | 1020 | 1010 + 1025 + 1020 = 3055 | 3115 / 3 = 1038 |
| 2016 | 1070 | 1025 + 1020 + 1070 = 3115 | |

3 **Establish the trend** – By graphing the three-year moving average it is possible to forecast sales revenue data in future years by extrapolating the data. The

graph in Figure 4.3.1 shows how the moving average can be used to establish a trend and then this can be used to forecast future sales.

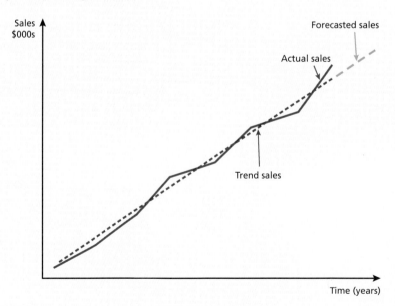

**Figure 4.3.1** Establishing a trend.

# Four-part moving averages

### Key term
A **four-part moving average** means calculating a mean average over a four-period time in a series of data.

## CASE STUDY

### Genius Gift Cards
Genius Gift Cards is a medium-sized gift cards business based in Canada. It is a very seasonal business and this is reflected in its quarterly sales figures.

| Year | Quarter | Sales revenue $000 000s |
|------|---------|-------------------------|
| 2014 | 4 | 27 |
| 2015 | 1 | 16 |
|  | 2 | 19 |
|  | 3 | 22 |
|  | 4 | 28 |
| 2016 | 1 | 15 |
|  | 2 | 18 |
|  | 3 | 20 |
|  | 4 | 29 |

### Progress questions

1 Calculate the four-period moving average for Genius Gift Cards for the period 2014–16. [6 marks]

2 Plot the actual sales figures and moving average sales figure for Genius Gift Cards for the period 2011–16. [4 marks]

3 Calculate the seasonal variation for the period 2014–16. [2 marks]

4 Describe the trend in the sales data for Genius Gift Cards from 2014–16. [2 marks]

### Exam tip
The 'plot' command term in this question means marking the position of actual and moving average sales points on a diagram.

## WORKED EXAMPLE
In Table 4.3.2 the Suntan lotion business example has sales data for 2015 and 2016. The **four-part moving average** is calculated by:

1 **Calculate the four-quarter moving total** (for third quarter 2015 this is: 230 + 270 + 310 + 210 = 2010) for each quarter in the table.

2 **Calculate the eight-quarter moving total** (for third quarter 2015 this is: 1020 + 1030 = 2050) for each possible quarter in the table.

3 **Calculate the four-quarter moving average** (for the third quarter 2015 this is: 2050 / 8 = 256.25) for each possible quarter in the table. This is calculated by:

   8 quarter moving total / 8 = 4 quarter moving average

5 **Calculate the seasonal variation** using the equation: Actual sales revenue – quarterly moving average = seasonal variation. For the third quarter of 2015 this would be $310 000 – $256 250 = $53 750. The seasonal variation is the way data changes in a repeatable and predicable way during the year.

6 **Calculate the average seasonal variation**. This is a way of smoothing out the actual seasonal variations in the data to give a seasonal variation that makes it easier to forecast sales. It is calculated by adding together seasonal variations in a quarter and dividing by the number of times there is data for this quarter. For the third quarter this would be: $53 750 + $65 000 / 2 = $59 375.

## 4.3

| Year | Quarter | Sales revenue $000s | 4 Quarter moving total | 8 Quarter moving total | Quarterly moving average | Seasonal variation |
|---|---|---|---|---|---|---|
| 2015 | 1 | 230 | | | | |
| | 2 | 270 | | | | |
| | 3 | 310 | | | 256.25 | 53.75 |
| | 4 | 210 | 1020 | | 258.75 | −48.75 |
| 2016 | 1 | 240 | 1030 | 2050 | 262.5 | −22.5 |
| | 2 | 280 | 1040 | 2070 | 266.25 | 13.75 |
| | 3 | 330 | 1060 | 2100 | 265 | 65 |
| | 4 | 220 | 1070 | 2130 | | |
| 2017 | 1 | 220 | 1050 | 2120 | | |

**Figure 4.3.2**

7 **Random variation** is used to show how the seasonal variation data differs from the average seasonal variation to show the extent to which actual data differs from the moving average by a factor that cannot be just explained as seasonal. It is calculated by: seasonal variation – average seasonal variation = random variation. For the third quarter this would be: $53750 – $59375 = –$5625. This could be explained by a random factor that affects demand such as poor weather, which means people do not buy as much suntan lotion.

# The benefits and limitations of sales forecasting

## Benefits of sales forecasting

Sales forecasting is important because firms can use it to:

- **Establish future resource needs** – By knowing how much a business can sell, it knows how much to produce and the resources it will need to do this. For example, the suntan lotion business will know how many workers and raw materials it will need.

- **Forecast costs** – Forecasting sales is particularly good at forecasting direct costs such as raw materials because direct costs are related to sales.

- **Forecast profits** – Once sales revenue and costs have been forecast, profit can be forecast. This figure is useful to potential investors and shareholders.

- **Set up budgets** – Sales forecasts are very important in starting the budgeting process because it determines the activity level of the organisation.

- **Support cash flow management** – Sales revenue is a very important source of cash inflow into an organisation and producing a cash flow forecast.

## Limitations of sales forecasting

The problems of trying to forecast sales are:

- **Uncertain future demand for a business's good and services**—The business environment is constantly changing and this will affect a business's sales. For the suntan lotion business example, the recent concerns over sun exposure and skin cancer have increased the demand for its product.

- **Change in costs affecting price** – If the cost of producing a product changes, firms are often forced to change prices and this will affect the sales forecast.

- **Complex moving average calculation** – Producing forecasted sales on the basis of moving averages is quite difficult and time-consuming.

- **No account is taken of non-monetary factors** – In the future, a business may improve the quality of its product or customer service, which will impact on future sales. They are not accounted for when using moving averages.

# Exam practice questions

## Paper 1 question (HL and SL)

### Aderson Publishing

Aderson Publishing is an independent, worldwide publishing business that produces fiction and non-fiction books. The business is based in Sweden and has a turnover of $80 million. Along with its published books it also has significant digital content and its online catalogue is increasing in importance. The general trend in digital book sales over the last four years has been upwards and they are forecast to grow even more strongly in the next three years.

**a** Explain two reasons why sales forecasting is useful to Aderson Publishing. [4 marks]

**b** Analyse two limitations of sales forecasting for Aderson Publishing. [6 marks]

[Total 10 marks]

## Paper 2 question (HL and SL)

### Alpine Ski Lodges

Alpine Ski Lodges own 40 Ski lodges in Austria in the country's major ski resorts. The business is concerned about falling sales and wants to invest in a major refurbishment programme to increase revenues. Its sales figures for the past two years are set out in the table below.

| Year | Quarter | Sales revenue 000s |
|---|---|---|
| 2015 | 1 | 36 |
| | 2 | 18 |
| | 3 | 16 |
| | 4 | 22 |
| 2016 | 1 | 32 |
| | 2 | 17 |
| | 3 | 15 |
| | 4 | 21 |

**a** Define the term 'four-part moving average'. [2 marks]

**b** Calculate the four-period moving average for Alpine Ski Lodges for the period 2015-16. [6 marks]

**c** Calculate the seasonal variation for the period 2014–16. [2 marks]

**d** Evaluate the usefulness of sales forecasting using moving averages for Alpine Ski Lodges. [10 marks]

[Total 20 marks]

### Exam tip
The 'calculate 'command term in this question means obtaining a numerical answer to the four-period moving average showing the relevant stages in the working.

# Market research

## What you should know by the end of this chapter:

- Why and how organisations carry out market research (AO2)

- The following methods/techniques of primary market research: surveys, interviews, focus groups, and observations (AO2)

- The following methods/techniques of secondary market research: market analyses, academic journals, government publications, media articles (AO2)

- Ethical considerations of market research (AO3)

- The difference between qualitative and quantitative research (AO2)

- The following methods of sampling: quota, random, stratified, cluster, snowballing and convenience (AO2)

- Results from data collection (AO2).

### Chapter illustrative example
A manufacturer of high quality shampoo

# Why and how organisations carry out market research

**Key term**
**Market research** is the process where organisations collect information about the consumers and the market they are selling their product to.

**Market research** is important in marketing because it is important for businesses to understand what customers' wants and needs are if the business is going to produce a product to fulfil them.

Businesses can either do their own market research or they can outsource it to a company that specialises in market research. The depth and scope of research depends on the resources the business has.

Market research provides businesses with information that can help them understand the following:

- **Part of marketing strategy** – Helps a business understand the needs and wants of customers when developing marketing strategy.

- **New products** – Identifies marketing opportunities for new products.

- **Problem-solving** – If a firm is experiencing a problem like a fall in sales, market research allows the firm to understand the problem.

- **Growth** – If a business wants to move into new markets or expand in existing ones, then market research provides information to support this.

- **Objective setting** – Knowing about the number of consumers and how much they might spend allows firms to set sales targets.

- **Knowledge of competition** – Tells the firm about other firms they have to compete with in the market.

The shampoo manufacturing company, for example, is currently using market research to develop a marketing plan to launch a new product.

# Methods of primary market research

**Key term**
**Primary market research** is where a business generates its own research data to find out information about the market and the consumer.

## Surveys

A survey is where an organisation gathers market research data by communicating with existing or potential consumers. Surveys normally take the form of a questionnaire that will be completed by the customers that the business has targeted. They are a relatively low-cost way of getting information from a wide audience.

Surveys provide the following types of information:

- **Quantitative data** – Information that can be analysed statistically such as the average amount of money per week, people within the age of 25–35 spend on, for example, shampoo. This kind of information is useful for forecasting potential sales revenue.

- **Qualitative data** – This is information that gives businesses an understanding of consumers' thoughts, beliefs and actions. This has helped the shampoo business, for example, understand why their product has become increasingly popular among men. Qualitative information is good for developing new products or problem-solving.

## Interviews

Direct contact with people through telephone or face-to-face interviews provides similar types of information to a survey but the direct contact allows the market researcher to get more information and to be able to interpret the information of the respondent more accurately.

## Focus groups

### Key term
A **focus group** is where a business selects a group of people to obtain qualitative market research information.

A market researcher leads a discussion based around a specific market research theme and they develop information through open-ended questions. The shampoo business, for example, used **focus groups** to develop ideas for a new advertising campaign.

## Observations

Observations refers to information gained by observing customers and potential customers. This can be done informally by, for example, sales people who can tell a market researcher what products consumers find popular or it can be more formal by researchers actively watching consumers.

# Methods of secondary market research

### Key term
**Secondary market research** is where a business uses data and material prepared by an outside source to generate market research information.

The shampoo business, for example, has been using a report prepared by a market research business to show changes in buyer behaviour in the shampoo market.

## Market analyses

Market analyses refers to information provided by organisations that specialise in generating information about specific markets. They use sophisticated databases, analysis and forecasts to give users a comprehensive picture of what is happening in the market they are operating in.

## Academic journals

Academic journals provide market information and are produced by universities and business schools. They look at market data in a scientific way and can provide information that is useful to businesses. The shampoo business, for example, might use a university report about changing demographics in its target markets.

## Government publications

The government is constantly publishing information that businesses might find useful in their market research. Information, for example, on changes in average earnings will tell businesses about the disposable income consumers have to spend.

## Media articles

Newspapers, magazines and websites have significant business news sections that can provide information that can support a firm's market research.

## Evaluation of methods

The most valuable market research information is specific to the business and the issue the business is facing. Primary research does this most effectively but it comes at a cost. Secondary research is valuable because it gives research information with a wider scope and at a lower cost but it may not be specific enough to the business issue. Many businesses will focus their market research using primary methods and support this with secondary data.

### Twitter

Twitter was started in July 2006 by a partnership between Jack Dorsey, Evan Williams, Biz Stone, and Noah Glass. By May 2015, Twitter had more than 500 million users and a revenue of $2.21 billion. It is said that the Twitter concept came from a brainstorming session led by Jack Dorsey and what followed was a considerable amount of primary and secondary research into the potential for this social media concept.

### Progress questions

1 Define the following terms:

   a Market research. [2 marks]

   b Secondary market research. [2 marks]

2 Outline two types of secondary research the founders of Twitter might have used. [4 marks]

3 Analyse two benefits Twitter might get from using primary research. [6 marks]

### Exam tip

The 'analyse' command term in this question means breaking down the two benefits Twitter might get from primary research into their essential reasons.

# Ethical considerations of market research

These are possible ethical issues involved in market research:

- **Confidentiality** – People involved in primary research interviews give information that may be personal to them, which could be passed on or even sold to other organisations.

- **Disruption** – Primary research may mean using invasive research techniques through telephone surveys and street questionnaires.

- **Plagiarism** – Market research may involve using another business's information without permission.

- **Bias** – Data can be interpreted in different ways and the conclusions drawn can be subject to bias of the people doing the report.

# Sampling

### Key term

**Sampling** is where a business selects a group of people to be part of primary research that represents the market the business is targeting.

Organisations need to sample when they are doing primary research because it is too time-consuming and expensive to cover all consumers in a market. Figure 4.4.1 looks at the different sampling methods.

The shampoo business, for example, uses quota sampling because it is relatively quick and low-cost and has a manageable level of bias.

### Fujitsu

The IT specialist Fujitsu uses focus groups extensively as part of its market research, running focus group sessions with key customers over breakfast, dinner or lunch. They float an idea and have a conversation around what the group thinks of it. Sampling the business people to be part of these groups is a key part of the strategy.

### Progress questions

1 Define the term 'focus group'. [2 marks]

2 Explain two reasons why Fujitsu might use focus groups as part of its market research. [4 marks]

3 Explain how Fujitsu could use quota and snowball sampling to choose the participants of their focus groups. [4 marks]

4 Analyse two difficulties for Fujitsu of using random sampling to choose the participants of their focus groups. [6 marks]

**Table 4.4.1**

| Sampling method | Approach | Strength | Weakness |
|---|---|---|---|
| Quota | Gathering information from a chosen group based on certain criteria. For example: 50 people aged 18–25, 30 women and 20 men. | Effective at precisely covering the target market, which reduces the sample size needed. | Choosing people can distort results because the chosen sample is not representative. |
| Random | Everyone in the target market has an equal chance of being chosen. | Because everyone has an equal chance of being sampled, the results are statistically more accurate than quota sampling. | More people have to be sampled, which is more time-consuming and expensive. |
| Stratified | Target market is divided into subgroups based on criteria such as gender, age and education level. The subgroups are then randomly sampled. | Gives the statistical accuracy of random sampling but cuts down on the numbers needed to be sampled. | More time-consuming and expensive than quota sampling. |
| Cluster | A geographical area such as a town or region and then random sampling within the cluster. | Gives the statistical accuracy of random sampling but cuts down on the numbers needed to be sampled. | More time-consuming and expensive than quota sampling. |
| Snowball sampling | People chosen to be part of a sample are used to recruit other people to form a larger sampled group. | A low-cost method that is simple to use. | Can lead to bias in the sample. |
| Convenience sample | Choosing people to be part of a sample because they are easy for a business to access. | A low-cost method that is simple for businesses to use. | Can lead to bias in the sample. |

# Results from data collection

Once market research has been carried out, it needs to be put into a format that can be analysed by the marketing department to support a marketing plan.

## Qualitative research

Marketing teams work through this and pick out common themes from the respondents who have completed surveys and been part of focus groups. The common theme, for example, from the shampoo business's qualitative research is that target consumers like to 'use the shampoo used by professional hairdressers'.

## Quantitative research

This can be analysed statistically using methods such as:

- bar charts
- pie charts
- line graphs
- histograms
- averages
- percentages.

The shampoo business example produced a market research report for its directors that included pictorial representations to show changes in the buying behaviour in the target market.

# Exam practice questions

## Paper 1 question (HL and SL)

### Aderson Publishing

Aderson Publishing is an independent, worldwide publishing business that produces fiction and non-fiction books. To try and develop its digital content, Aderson did extensive primary research and secondary research and the CEO Victoria Akerman did a major presentation to the shareholders on the results.

**a** Explain two reasons why quantitative market research would have been useful to Aderson Publishing. [4 marks]

**b** Analyse two limitations of market research for Aderson Publishing. [6 marks]

[Total 10 marks]

## Paper 2 question (HL and SL)

### Global defibrillators

The market research specialist, Allied Market Research has produced a report on the defibrillators (used to revive patients after a heart attack) market. It projects that the global defibrillators market would grow to reach $15 billion by 2022. The study said that the US would continue to lead, accounting for more than 40% share of the world defibrillator market in 2015.

**a** Define the term 'secondary market research'. [2 marks]

**b** Outline two reasons Allied Market Research's report might be useful to a firm producing defibrillators. [4 marks]

**c** Explain two other methods of secondary market research a firm producing defibrillators might use. [4 marks]

**d** Should a business rely on a market research specialist like Allied for all its secondary market research? Justify your answer. [10 marks]

**Exam tip**
The 'justify' command term in this question means giving valid reasons or evidence to whether businesses should rely on a market research specialist and come to a conclusion.

# The four Ps of marketing

# 4.5

**What you should know by the end of this chapter:**

- The product life cycle (AO4)
- The relationship between the product life cycle and the marketing mix (AO2)
- Extension strategies (AO3)
- The relationship between the product life cycle, investment, profit and cash flow (AO2)
- Boston Consulting Group (BCG) matrix on an organisation's products (AO3, AO4)
- Aspects of branding: awareness, development, loyalty, value (AO2)
- The importance of branding (AO3)
- The importance of packaging (AO3)
- The appropriateness of the following pricing strategies: cost-plus (mark-up), penetration, skimming, psychological, loss leader, price discrimination, price leadership, predatory (AO3)
- The following aspects of promotion: above the line promotion, below the line promotion, promotional mix (AO2)
- The impact of changing technology on promotional strategies such as viral marketing, social media marketing and social networking (AO3)
- Guerrilla marketing and its effectiveness as a promotional method (AO3)
- The importance of place in the marketing mix (AO2)
- The effectiveness of different types of distribution channels (AO3).

**Chapter illustrative example**
A manufacturer of sports footwear

# The product

## Key term

A **product** is a physical good or a service produced by an organisation to meet the needs and wants of the consumer.

## The product life cycle

## Key term

The **product life cycle** is the change in the sales revenue of a product as it moves through different phases in its life.

Figure 4.5.1 illustrates a typical **product life cycle**.

# Product life cycle and the marketing mix

The product life cycle is a useful model to support marketing strategy because it guides the way the elements of the marketing mix can be adapted at different phases in the product life cycle.

Table 4.5.1 illustrates how the different element of the mix can be used at different phases in the product life cycle.

## Extension strategies

## Key term

An **extension strategy** is the marketing methods a business uses to maintain sales revenue in the maturity phase of the product life cycle.

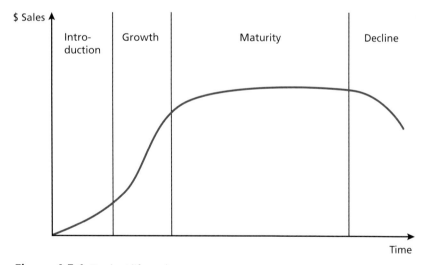

**Figure 4.5.1** Product life cycle.

**Table 4.5.1**

| Phase | Nature of the phase | Product | Price | Promotion | Place |
|-------|---------------------|---------|-------|-----------|-------|
| Introduction | Product is first introduced with low sales and market share. | Adapting design and packaging. | Discounting used to attract consumers. | Initial advertising to attract consumers. | Launch the product through a narrow distribution network. |
| Growth | Rise in sales and market share. | Any changes to the product finalised. | Increase in price as the product becomes established. | Broaden promotion methods as the product becomes established. | Broaden distribution to attract more consumers. |
| Maturity | Sales and market share growth peaks and stays constant. | New versions of the product released to maintain sales. | Periodic discounting to maintain sales. | Regular promotion campaigns to maintain sales. | Explore distribution to new markets to maintain sales. |
| Decline | Sales and market share start to fall. | New versions to reduce the fall in sales. | Discounting to reduce the fall in sales. | Reduce promotion as income from sales decline. | Narrow distribution to markets where sales are still strong. |

Extension strategies are based on the marketing mix:

- **Product** – Redesign and repackage.

- **Price** – Discount the price.

- **Promotion** – New advertising campaign.

- **Place** – Launch the product in a new market.

The sports shoe business, for example, regularly redesigns it sports shoes to extend their product life cycles.

# The product life cycle and investment, profit and cash flow

## Investment

Business investment may change in the following ways as a product moves through its life cycle:

- **Introduction** – Research and development, and capital set-up costs.

- **Growth** – Costs of advertising and promotion.

- **Maturity and decline** – Cost of extension strategies.

## Cash flow

Cash flow may change in the following ways as a product moves through its life cycle:

- **Introduction** – Negative initial cash flow because of the cost developing and launching a product.

- **Growth** – Cash flow becomes positive as cash inflows from sales increases.

- **Maturity** – Positive cash flow as sales peak and costs fall.

- **Decline** – Cash flow can become negative as sales fall.

Figure 4.5.2 shows the relationship between the different phases of the product life cycle and cash flow.

## Profit

This follows a similar pattern to cash flow with initial losses in the introduction and growth phases leading to profits in the maturity phase and losses again in the decline phase.

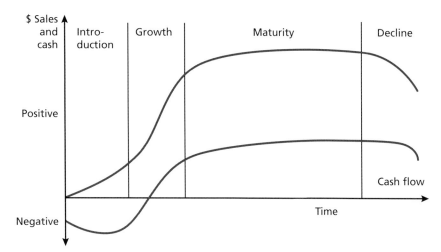

**Figure 4.5.2** Relationship between the different phases of the product life cycle and cash flow.

# Boston matrix

## Key terms
The **Boston Matrix** is a model used by a business to analyse the portfolio of products it sells by using market share and market growth.

**Market share** is the proportion of total market sales that the sales of a business's product accounts for.

**Market growth** is the rate at which sales of the target market are increasing.

- For the sports shoe company, for example, the market shares of five different brands would be put into the matrix.

- The target markets of the five different sports shoe brands of the example sports shoe business can be positioned on their **market growth** and **market share**.

Table 4.5.2 illustrates the Boston Matrix for the example sports shoe business.

## Use of the Boston Matrix
The Boston Matrix supports marketing planning and strategy by:

**Table 4.5.2**

| | | Market share % | |
|---|---|---|---|
| | | **Low** | **High** |
| Market growth % | High | X (2)<br>X (1)<br>**Question marks** | X (3)<br>**Star** |
| | Low | X (5)<br>**Dogs** | X (4)<br>**Cash cow** |

- Allowing the organisation to develop a collective strategy for all the products a business sells. By having products in different segments in the Matrix, the long-term future of the business can be planned. Question mark brands become the new cash cows.

- Effective support for cash flow management. Cash cows can provide the cash to support the development of stars.

## Evaluation of the Boston Matrix and product life cycle
Both methods are useful tools to support marketing strategy but they are often based on average product life cycles and actual life cycles can be very different. Some can last a few months and some many years.

# 4.5

## CASE STUDY

### Colgate-Palmolive Company

Colgate-Palmolive Company is an American worldwide consumer products company that had a sales revenue of $16 billion in 2015 and employed 37 000 people worldwide. One of its leading products is toothpaste and some of its leading toothpaste brands are Colgate, Cibaca, Dentagard, Kolynos and Profiden.

### Progress questions

1 Define the term 'product life cycle'. [2 marks]

2 Describe two elements of the product life cycle for Colgate's products. [4 marks]

3 Analyse how the product life cycle model might help manage its product portfolio. [6 marks]

# Branding

## Importance of branding

**Key term**
**Branding** is where a business creates an identity for its good or service through its marketing characteristics.

**Branding** can be done through things such as design, packaging, name, trademark and advertising. Branding is important in marketing because it distinguishes a product from its competition and creates a USP.

## Brand awareness

**Key term**
**Brand awareness** is how recognisable a business's good or service is in the minds of consumers in the target market.

**Brand awareness** is important for the following reasons:

- attracts consumers when they are making buying decisions
- can be used to sell associated new goods and services
- develops long-term sales through brand loyalty.

## Brand development

**Key term**
**Brand development** is the rise in the sales of a good or service as a proportion of total sales in the target market.

Successful businesses will see their **brand development** rise over time and the example sports shoe business has seen its new basketball shoe achieve a significant brand development through its rise in market share.

## Brand loyalty

**Key term**
**Brand loyalty** is the extent to which the consumer will continue to buy an organisation's good or service over time.

**Brand loyalty** is the key to maintaining sales in the long run and protecting a firm's product from competition.

## Brand value

**Key term**
**Brand value** is the extra amount consumers will pay above the average market price for a business's product because of its brand.

The sports shoe firm, for example, may be able to add 20% to the pair of running shoes because of the strength of its brand name. **Brand value** is useful in generating extra revenue and profit.

## Packaging

A product's packaging is an important part of the product element of the marketing mix because it:

- identifies the product sold in a retail outlet or on the internet
- is used to attract the consumer to the product
- becomes part of the product's appeal in the mind of the consumer
- can be used to advertise the brand.

### CASE STUDY

**Walt Disney Company**

The Walt Disney Company is one of the most recognisable brands in world. The giant US-based multinational mass media and entertainment business is valued at nearly $90 billion and employs 180 000 people.

**Progress questions**

1 Define the term 'brand'. [2 marks]

2 Analyse how Disney might benefit from brand loyalty and brand value. [6 marks]

3 To what extent might the strength of Walt Disney's brand be the most important factor in the business's success. [10 marks]

**Exam tip**

This question uses the 'to what extent' command term, which means considering the relative merits of Walt Disney's brand compared to other reasons for its success.

## Pricing

The pricing element of the marketing mix needs to fit with the other elements of the marketing mix. The sports shoe business, for example, sells a high-quality product so its price needs to reflect this. Table 4.5.3 sets out the different pricing strategies a business can use.

### CASE STUDY

**Sony PlayStation**

The PlayStation 4 is a home video game console developed by Sony Interactive Entertainment. Launched in 2014 it has sold nearly 40 million units worldwide. Sony is known for its price skimming approach when launching successive PlayStation products.

**Progress questions**

1 Define the term 'price skimming'. [2 marks]

2 Explain two reasons why Sony might use skimming as a pricing strategy. [4 marks]

3 Analyse two other pricing strategies Sony could use when marketing the PlayStation. [6 marks]

## Promotion

**Key term**

**Promotion** is the methods used by a business to create awareness, attract consumers and persuade them to buy its products.

## Methods of promotion

The methods of **promotion** can be broken down into two types:

**Key term**

**Above-the-line promotion** is where businesses use mass media to promote brands to their target market.

# 4.5

**Table 4.5.3**

| Method | Definition | Example | Strength | Weakness |
|---|---|---|---|---|
| Cost-plus (mark-up) | Price is set by adding a percentage profit to the unit cost of a product. | Unit cost of training shoe is $20 and a 40% mark-up is added. $20 × 1.4 = $28 price | Ensures the business covers its costs and makes a profit on sales. | It ignores the prices charged by competitors. |
| Penetration | Reducing price to make a firm's goods cheaper relative to the competition and increase its sales. | Sport shoe manufacturer reduces the price of its golf shoes to establish itself in a new market. | Effective at increasing sales volume and achieving growth in market share. | Reduces profit margins and can make goods look poor quality. |
| Skimming | Initially high price to attract consumers who like to buy products when they are first launched. | The very latest football boot launched by the sports shoe business can be set as a skimming price. | High initial profits that can be used to repay development costs. | Only works with products with high demand when launched, such as technology products. |
| Psychological pricing | Setting a price that creates an attractive value for the product in the mind of the consumer. | The sports shoes business sees $80 as a ceiling for its running shoe price so often prices at $79.99. | Price that fits with the marketing principle of meeting the wants of consumers. | Not always easy to establish the psychological price. |
| Loss leader | Setting a low price for a product in order to sell more of its complementary products. | Sports goods retailer might discount its tennis rackets to sell more: balls, clothing, shoes and racket bags. | Effective when the main product sold has large numbers of dependent complements. | Not useful for goods that do not have strong dependent complements. |
| Price discrimination | Selling the same product at different price in different markets. | A sports centre gym may charge different prices at different times of day. High prices at peak times in the evening and lower prices at other times. | Takes advantage of the different prices different groups of consumers are willing to pay for a product. | Only really useful for businesses that can separate their market, which is normally service organisations. |
| Price leadership | Largest firm in market set a price that other firms in the market often follow. | The sport shoe firm, for example, has a leadership position with its brand of running shoe. | Forces other businesses to follow, which prevents price wars that can reduce profits. | The leader can attract government regulation if it exploits its position. |
| Predatory pricing | Firm cuts prices to levels below its competitors to force them out of the market. | The sports shoe firm has been accused of doing this when new competitors have tried to enter the market. | By reducing competition, it maintains market share and enables the firm to increase prices in the long run. | Predatory pricing can attract government regulation. |

**Above-the-line promotion** can use the following types of media:

- television
- internet
- newspapers
- magazines
- trade journals
- billboards.

**Key term**

**Below-the-line promotion** is where an organisation uses techniques that allow it to reach its target market more directly than using mass media.

The **below-the-line promotion** methods include:

- price promotions
- personal selling
- sponsorship
- point of sale material
- public relations
- trade shows.

**Key term**

The **promotional mix** is the different promotion methods a business uses as part of its marketing strategy.

The sports shoe business, for example uses a **promotional mix** that includes:

- **Above-the-line** – TV advert during sports events, sports magazines, banner adverts on sports websites.
- **Below-the-line** – Sponsorship of major sports stars and teams and promotional point of sale material in retailers.

# New developments in promotion

Organisations are continuously developing new methods of promotion to reach the consumer in their target markets. These have been inspired by developments in technology. Table 4.5.4 shows four different methods:

**Table 4.5.4**

| Method | Definition | Example | Strength | Weakness |
|---|---|---|---|---|
| Viral marketing | Promotion methods using social networking website. | The sports shoe business produced a video clip for YouTube that showed street footballers' ball skills. | Achieves a very wide audience at relatively low cost. | Difficult to control the outcome of the promotion method. |
| Social media marketing | Promotion by using social media sites such as Facebook and Twitter. | The sports shoe business has used Instagram effectively to target its younger consumers. | Use of computer cookies allows this to be precisely target at consumers. | Consumers do not always react positively to the volume of advertising on social media. |
| Guerrilla marketing | Promotion that uses unconventional methods to raise consumer awareness. | The sports shoe business set a tennis match between two top tennis players in the square of a city centre. | Achieves a very wide audience at relatively low cost as it goes viral on social media. | Scope for the event to go wrong and for consumers to misunderstand the message. |

# 4.5

**VTM**

To raise publicity for its reality TV show 'The Search For Maria', the Belgian television station VTM used guerrilla marketing when it organised a giant 'flashmob' in Antwerp strain station. It filmed the giant dance routine and the YouTube clip went viral on the internet.

**Progress questions**

1 Define the term 'guerrilla marketing'. [2 marks]

2 Analyse two advantages to VTM of using guerrilla marketing. [6 marks]

3 Explain two other methods of promotion VTM could have used. [4 marks]

# Place

## Importance of place in the marketing mix

**Key term**

**Distribution** is the methods a business uses to get a good or service to the final customer.

Place is the **distribution** element of the marketing mix.

The sports shoe business uses a wide distribution network through sports goods retailers and a significant online presence.

## Effectiveness of different types of distribution channel

**Key term**

A **distribution channel** is the different intermediaries a product passes through to reach the final consumer.

Table 4.5.5 sets out the **distribution channels** a business can use:

**Table 4.5.5**

| Method | Definition | Example | Strength | Weakness |
|---|---|---|---|---|
| Direct supply | Good or service is supplied by the producer to the consumer. | The sports shoe firm sells shoes online. | Without any intermediaries the business can reduce prices and increase sales profits. | Small orders have a relatively high cost to a large producer. |
| Retailers | Organisations that specialise in buying goods from producers and marketing them to final consumers in a shop environment. | The sports shoe firm sells its shoes to sports retailers who then sell them to final consumers. | Manufacturers sell in bulk to retailers which leads to economies of scale and retailers are specialists in marketing goods to consumers. | Retailers may not market the good in the way the producer wants and they add their own cost and profits to the selling price. |
| Wholesalers | Organisations that buy goods from producers and sell them to small retailers. | The sports shoe business sells its shoes to wholesalers who supply small retailers. | Manufacturers can sell in bulk to wholesalers leading to economies. | Wholesalers add their own cost and profits to increase the final selling price. |

# Exam practice questions

## Paper 1 question (HL and SL)

### Aderson Publishing

Aderson Publishing is an independent, worldwide publishing business that produces fiction and non-fiction books. The business is based in Sweden and has a turnover of $80 million. Along with its published books it also has significant digital content and its online catalogue is increasing in importance. Market director Olaf Andersson is concerned about pressure online book sales are putting on the market for conventional books and he has suggested a penetration pricing strategy.

**a** Explain two pricing strategies Aderson Publishing could use other than penetration pricing. [4 marks]

**b** Analyse two problems a penetration pricing strategy might pose for Aderson when selling conventional books. [6 marks]

[Total 10 marks]

## Paper 2 question (HL and SL)

### Shinny Tiles

Shinny Tiles is a leading supplier of ceramics tiles used in kitchens and bathrooms along with tiles for businesses like hotels and retail outlets. It is looking to export to Eastern Europe and is developing a marketing plan to do this successfully.

**a** Define the term 'marketing mix'. [2 marks]

**b** Distinguish between above- and below-the-line methods of promotion Shinny Tiles might use. [4 marks]

**c** Explain two reasons Shinny Tiles might have decided to distribute its products through wholesalers initially. [4 marks]

**d** Discuss how the Boston Matrix model might be useful to Shinny Tiles as it develops its market in Eastern Europe. [10 marks]

[Total 20 marks]

**Exam tip**

This question uses the 'distinguish' command term, which means making clear the differences between above- and below-the-line promotion.

# The extended marketing mix of seven Ps (HL only)

# 4.6

**What you should know by the end of this chapter:**

- People: The importance of employee–customer relationships in marketing a service and cultural variation in these relationships (AO3)

- Processes: The importance of delivery processes in marketing a service and changes in these processes (AO3)

- Physical evidence: The importance of tangible physical evidence in marketing a service (AO3)

- The seven Ps model in a service-based market (AO2).

**Chapter illustrative example**
A chain of high quality restaurants

# People

**Key term**

The **people element** of the marketing mix is the way employees and managers of an organisation interact with its customers.

The **people element** is particularly important in service organisations where satisfying consumer wants is greatly affected by the relationship consumers have with the people representing the organisation. In the restaurant example, the quality of service is often critical in determining the consumer's experience.

## Reason employees and managers come into contact with customers

- **Direct service** – Staff in a retail environment, for example, continuously deal with customers.

- **Sales employees** – Some organisations use direct sales people to sell the product to consumers, particularly in business-to-business sales.

- **Delivery** – Workers in, for example, courier firms deal with customers when they deliver goods.

- **Complaints** – When customers have complaints they often ask to deal with the relevant employees.

- **After-sales service** – If, for example, a product needs support through servicing and maintenance then workers will continuously deal with customers.

## Methods of interaction

There are three methods of interaction between an organisation's employees and its customers:

**1 Face-to-face contact**

This occurs when staff are serving customers and its effectiveness will depend on an employee's:

- use of language
- body language
- personal manner
- dress.

Staff in the example restaurant have extensive training in effective face-to-face contact with the customers they are serving.

**2 Telephone contact**

This happens when employees are taking orders from customers and its effectiveness will depend on:

- voice
- use of language
- personal manner.

**3 Online contact**

This happens when customers email contact with employees about orders and its effectiveness will depend on:

- quality of written language
- speed of reply
- tone of written communication.

## Impact of culture

Globalisation has mean that the interaction between employees' and customers' needs takes into account cultural differences in terms of different:

- languages
- manners
- customs
- expectations of service.

Workers in the example restaurant business are trained in how to deal with the multicultural customers they get in their city centre location.

# 4.6

**Costco**
Costco is an American based, membership-only warehouse club. It has a fantastic reputation for customer service. 'The customer experience at Costco is outstanding' say leading retail analysts. Its sales staff are unbelievably helpful, show great product knowledge and will stop whatever they are doing to help you. If you have a problem with a product, they will just replace it even without a receipt.

**Progress questions**

1  Define the term 'people element of the marketing mix'. [2 marks]

2  Describe two reasons why staff come into contact with customers at Costco. [4 marks]

3  Analyse two benefits to Costco have having such a strong 'people' element in its marking mix. [6 marks]

**Exam tip**
The 'describe' command term in this question means giving a detailed account of two reasons why staff come into contact with customers with Costco.

# Processes

## Importance of processes

**Key term**
**Processes** are the procedures, methods and policies a business puts into place when a good or service is being provided to the consumer.

**Process** needs to be managed efficiently to meet the wants of the consumer effectively.

In the restaurant business example, the process for providing its service to effectively meet the wants of the consumers might be:

- taking online and telephone reservations

- meeting customers when they enter the restaurant

- seating customers

- taking orders

- getting food to the table

- attending customers during their meal

- billing

- taking payment.

## Changes in process

Changes in process can take place because of:

- technology advances

- management changes

- innovation in methods

- employees change

- increased competition.

The restaurant, for example, is changing its ordering system because some customers were using booking apps and payment procedures were altered because so few customers are now paying using cash.

## CASE STUDY

### McDonald's

The fast food retailer McDonald's is known for its incredibly prescriptive food preparation systems. Here is part of their food hygiene procedure: 'All our cooked meat, egg and vegetable products are handled using dedicated colour-coded utensils… at no point must cooked meats be handled with bare hands… restaurant staff who prepare food wash their hands every 30 minutes.'

### Progress questions

1 Define the term 'processes element of the marketing mix'. [2 marks]

2 Outline two elements of the process element of the marketing mix used by McDonald's. [4 marks]

3 Analyse two benefits to McDonald's of having such a strict set of rules on food preparation procedures. [6 marks]

# Physical evidence

### Key term

**Physical evidence** is the physical environment of service-based organisations where the service is delivered to the customer.

For service organisations, this could be a retail outlet, coffee shop, gym or restaurant.

# Importance of physical evidence

For service organisations where the point of delivery is a physical place, the quality of the physical evidence is important in meeting the wants of the consumer and needs to fit with the other elements of the marketing mix. The restaurant example is a high-quality restaurant and part of its appeal is the standard of the fixtures and fittings of the restaurant as well as the architecture of the building.

# Exam practice questions

## Paper 1 question (HL and SL)

### Aderson Publishing

Aderson Publishing is an independent, worldwide publishing business that produces fiction and non-fiction books. CEO Victoria Akerman is very keen to get as many members of the company as she can to go out and meet the people that read the company's books. This is done through book fairs and school visits.

a Explain two reasons the people aspect of the marketing mix is important to Aderson. [4 marks]

b Analyse two ways Aderson might improve the people aspect of its marketing mix. [6 marks]

[Total 10 marks]

## Paper 2 question (HL and SL)

### Spirit Gym

Spirit Gym are a regional chain of high specification fitness centres. They are open 24 hours a day and feature the very latest exercise machines. They also employ top trainers and use advanced software training systems for users. The changing rooms and showering facilities are the best in the market.

a Define the term 'physical evidence element of the marketing mix'. [2 marks]

b Outline two ways Spirit Gym achieves the highest standards with its physical evidence. [4 marks]

c Explain two possible elements of the process part of Spirit Gym's marketing mix. [4 marks]

d Examine the importance of the extended marketing mix to Spirit Gym. [10 marks]

[Total 20 marks]

### Exam tip

The 'examine' command term in this question means giving a detailed consideration of the importance of the extended marketing mix in a way that uncovers its assumptions.

# International marketing (HL only)

## 4.7

**What you should know by the end of this chapter:**

■ Methods of entry into international markets (AO2)

■ The opportunities and threats posed by entry into international markets (AO3)

■ The strategic and operational implications of international marketing (AO3)

■ The role of cultural differences in international marketing (AO3)

■ The implications of globalisation on international marketing (AO3).

### Chapter illustrative example

A luxury fashion brand producing clothing, handbags and perfume

# Methods of entry into international markets

**Key term**
**International marketing** is where a business develops a marketing plan to sell its goods and services in different countries.

Business can enter international markets in the following ways:

- **Exporting** – Where a business produces a good or service in its domestic market and then sells the good or service in an overseas market. The luxury fashion brand, for example, produces its coats in its home country, Italy, and then exports them to the US.

- **Producing abroad** – A business can set up production in another country and then sell its good or service in that country or export it to other countries. The luxury fashion brand, for example, has a factory in China and it exports handbags to other parts of Asia.

- **Joint ventures** – Where a business joins together with a business in another country to produce a good or service in that country. This approach uses the experience of an overseas producer to help develop an effective international marketing plan.

- **Licensing** – When a business gives another business (licensee) in an overseas market permission to produce its product allowing it to use its brand name, trademarks and logo. The organisation benefits from licensing because of the funds paid to it by the licensee.

- **Franchising** – A business can use a franchise agreement to enter an international market by selling the right to produce a product to another business (franchisee). This is often used by fast food businesses as a way of expanding overseas. The business benefits from the payment for the franchise and the franchisee's experience of the overseas market.

## CASE STUDY

**Coca-Cola and Endomondo**
Coca-Cola has a joint venture with Endomondo, a social fitness app with more than 12 million users worldwide. The joint venture combines the global reach of Coca-Cola with that of Endomondo and provides a social network to bring people around the world together with the tools they need to reach their fitness goals.

**Progress questions**

1   Define the term 'joint venture'. [2 marks]

2   Analyse two benefits Endomondo receives from the joint venture as it looks to expand its app into more global markets. [4 marks]

3   Analyse two benefits Coca-Cola receives from the joint venture with Endomondo. [4 marks]

**Exam tip**
The 'analyse' command term in this question means breaking down the two benefits to Endomondo from a joint venture into its essential elements or structure.

# Entry into international markets

## Opportunities

Entry into overseas market has the following opportunities:

- **Sales growth** – Overseas markets provide opportunities for businesses to increase their sales revenue and profits. This is particularly true when selling to growing large countries like India and China when the domestic market may be saturated.

- **Brand awareness and image** – Organisations that sell in international markets can develop a global reputation which makes their brand more attractive. The luxury fashion brand, for example, has 'New York, London, Paris and Milan' on all its packaging.

- **Spreading risk** – Operating in markets in different countries and regions in the world means growth in sales in one country can be used to cover declining sales in another market. For the luxury fashion business example, when Europe and the US were experiencing poor sales in 2009, sales in Asia were able to compensate for this.

- **Lower costs** – Producing in developing countries where labour, land and raw materials may be lower-cost can reduce the costs of the business producing abroad. These lower costs allow the business to produce lower-priced goods. The luxury fashion brand, for example, makes some clothing in Indonesia at a cost that allows them to control prices and increase profit margins.

- **Economies of scale** – International marketing allows a business to expand production as it increases sales to overseas markets. As the firm's output increases, it benefits from economies of scale and its cost per unit of production falls.

## Threats

- **Different consumer tastes and preference** – Marketing to people of different cultures in overseas markets means what works in the domestic market may not work as well with overseas consumers. The luxury fashion business, for example, has had to modify its clothing designs when selling into Middle Eastern countries.

- **Regulations** – Countries operate with different rules, laws and regulations that affect the goods and service a business markets abroad. The luxury fashion business, for example, has to follow rules on the specification of its perfumes when selling into certain markets.

- **Exchanges rates** – This particularly applies when goods and services are being exported. If the domestic currency is relatively strong, then the price of good the firm is exporting will increase, which may reduce the demand for it. Changes in the exchange rate also make sales forecasting difficult. The high value of the euro in Asia increased the price of the example luxury fashion business's handbags.

- **Competition** – International markets can introduce a business to a whole new set of competitors. When an organisation from a developed economy sells to a developing economy this often means facing low-cost competition.

# Strategic and operational implications of international marketing

When marketing goods and services in international markets, a firm can adapt its marketing plan in the following ways:

- **Marketing audit** – Use STEEP and SWOT analysis in the context of the international market the business is expanding into. The luxury fashion brand might look at rising incomes in China as an opportunity to exploit one of its key strengths, which is the prestigious nature of the products they sell.

- **Market research** – Primary and secondary research needs to be carried out in the overseas country. Primary research can be challenging with language and cultural differences between overseas consumers and domestic consumers.

- **Product** – Designing a product that meets local tastes and preferences. The luxury fashion brand, for example, produced a whole new range of designs to meet consumer tastes in China.

- **Price** – Setting a price that is competitive in the local market is important to attract local consumers who may have different disposable incomes and spending patterns to domestic consumers.

- **Promotion** – Using methods that adapt effectively to local culture. The luxury fashion brand, for example, exporting to China has used billboard adverting using Chinese models.

- **Place** – Using appropriate retailers that attract local consumers. The fashion brand business, for example, is using a selection of prestigious retailers in major Chinese cities to sell its products in China.

## CASE STUDY

### Cath Kidston

The UK-based Cath Kidston fashion, accessories and homeware brand has been growing in popularity around the world. They have more than 130 stores outside the UK from Spain to China. It is now opening a store in India and Latin America is next.

### Progress questions

1 Explain two opportunities to Cath Kidston of expanding into international markets. [4 marks]

2 Explain two threats to Cath Kidston of expanding into international markets. [4 marks]

3 Analyse two elements of Cath Kidston's marketing mix that will need to be adapted for entry into global markets. [6 marks]

# Cultural differences in international marketing

Table 4.7.1 illustrates the way different aspects of culture can impact on the marketing mix.

# The implications of globalisation on international marketing

Globalisation is the increasing international influence in the business environment of international trade, movement of labour and multinational organisations. This creates opportunities and threats for organisations when marketing their products internationally.

# Exam practice questions

## Paper 1 question (HL and SL)

### Aderson Publishing

Aderson Publishing is an independent, worldwide publishing business that produces fiction and non-fiction books. Along with its published books it also has significant digital content and its online catalogue is increasing in importance. Aderson has benefited from the international demand for Scandinavian crime thrillers and it has seen a big jump in sales in the US and Asia.

**Table 4.7.1**

| Cultural facto | Nature | Product | Price | Promotion | Place |
|---|---|---|---|---|---|
| Language | Language spoken in the country where the good is marketed. | Packaging should be labelled in the target country's language. | Use of the target country's currency in pricing. | Advertising should use the target country's language. | Retail signs should be in the target country's language. |
| Manner and custom | The way individuals interact with each other such as politeness. | When the employees deal with customers in, for example, retail outlets. | The extent that customers are willing to discuss price and negotiate. | How people interact with people in, for example, television adverts reflects local culture. | The layout in a restaurant, for example, reflects the way people interact. |
| Beliefs and values | The religious or political views customers in the target market have. | Some products may not be acceptable to consumers, such as beef used in a fast food restaurant in India. | In some countries very highly priced prestige products may be less acceptable to consumers. | Some advertising, such as showing women in a particular way, may not be acceptable. | Selling products near, for example, particular religious sites may not be acceptable. |

**Table 4.7.2**

| Factor | Opportunity | Threat |
|---|---|---|
| International trade | Ability to enter overseas markets to increase sales and profits. The fashion brand, for example, has seen a big jump in profits from its entry into the Chinese market. | New competition from businesses entering the domestic market. New competition from competing fashion brands has, for example, entered the domestic market. |
| Movement of labour | Immigration into a country creates a marketing opportunity for producers in that market. The fashion brand, for example, has seen domestic sales rise as the number of overseas workers in its financial sector has increased. | Migrant workers might bring their own taste and preferences that a business might find more difficult to sell to in the domestic market. |
| Growth of MNCs | MNCs can represent potential marketing opportunities for business-to-business marketing. The fashion brand, for example, has been involved in joint ventures with a MNC drinks manufacturer. | When MNCs enter a market they provide competition to domestic businesses who might struggle against such big competitors. |

**a** Explain two reasons why Aderson might export its books into international markets. [4 marks]

**b** Analyse two cultural factors that would affect the way Aderson markets its books overseas. [6 marks]

[Total 10 marks]

# Paper 2 question (HL and SL)

## Shape Headphones

Shape manufactures high-quality headphones and has focused much of its production in its domestic Canadian market up to now but it is looking to expand into the US market and into Asia. It is a young, inexperienced company so it sees certain problems with its first experience of international marketing.

**a** Define the term 'international marketing'. [2 marks]

**b** Outline two methods Shape could use to market its products internationally other than exporting. [4 marks]

**Exam tip**

The `explain' command term in this question means giving a detailed account of how selling in international markets affects promotion and pricing.

**c** Explain how selling in international markets might affect Shape's promotion and pricing elements of its marketing mix. [4 marks]

**d** Evaluate the view that expanding into international markets is the best way for Shape to grow its business. [10 marks]

# Key Concept question

With reference to one or two organisation(s) that you have studied, discuss how international marketing strategy might differ in two cultures that you are familiar with. [20 marks]

# E-commerce

# 4.8

## What you should know by the end of this chapter:

- Features of e-commerce (AO1)

- The effects of changing technology and e-commerce on the marketing mix (AO2)

- The difference between the following types of e-commerce: business to business (B2B), business to consumer (B2C), consumer to consumer (C2C) (A02)

- The costs and benefits of e-commerce to firms and consumers (AO3).

**Chapter illustrative example**
A national league football club

# Features of e-commerce

**Key term**
**E-commerce** is where a business uses the internet and electronic media as part of its marketing of its goods and services.

**E-commerce** affects organisations in the following ways:

- **International exposure** – The global nature of the internet means businesses can instantly access customers all over the world. Many of the overseas fans of the example football club can watch live streamed games.

- **Interaction with the customer** – The use of website and apps allows businesses to continuously interact with their consumers. This adds to the customer experience and is a source of market research. The football club, for example, allows its fans to rate players, club performance and match-day experiences.

- **Personalisation** – The use of software allows the business to target specific consumers with information that is relevant to them. When a football club customer, for example, logs on it might tell them about upcoming club events specific to their age and interests.

- **Process** – Online ordering and booking can improve customer satisfaction with the service the business provides. The football club, for example, has an online ticketing system that allows customers to choose their own seat.

- **Marketing a product range** – The use of websites and apps allows the business to sell related product services through advertising on the webpages. When a supporter, for example, of the website logs on to buy tickets they will see adverts for merchandise.

- **Information-gathering** – Interacting with consumers through websites allows the business to capture huge quantities of information about consumers that can be used by the business to

improve the quality of its marketing. The football club, for example, knows some of the following about their customers: where they live, how often they attend games, their age and the average amount they pay for a ticket.

# The effects of changing technology and e-commerce

Table 4.8.1 shows how changes in e-commerce can affect the different aspects of a business's marketing mix.

## CASE STUDY

The UK-based HSBC is a multinational banking and financial services organisation. It, like so many banks, has been hugely affected by the rise in e-commerce. It is a huge organisation with more than 250 000 employees. A large number of HSBC's customers do not visit their branches anymore and instead interact with HSBC online.

**Progress questions**

1 Define the term 'e-commerce'. [2 marks]

2 Identify two ways e-commerce might have affected HSBC. [2 marks]

3 Analyse how e-commerce might have affected the promotion and product element of HSBC's marketing mix. [6 marks]

**Exam tip**
The 'identify' command term in this question means providing giving two ways HSBC is affected by e-commerce from a number of possibilities.

**Table 4.8.1**

| Change in e-commerce | Nature | Product | Price | Promotion | Place |
|---|---|---|---|---|---|
| Growth | Internet retailing is growing all the time. | Developing products that can be easily sold over the internet such as the downloading of computer software. | Consumers can easily compare prices so a business needs to be price competitive. | Increased used of internet advertising in side bars and embedded video clips. | A business needs to have a presence on the internet when selling its products. |
| Consumer fragmentation | Markets are broken up into smaller segments because the technology helps businesses target them precisely. | Products need to be designed to satisfy more precise target segments. For example, television channels that target particular types of people. | Prices need to be set for certain market segments. Increased use of price discrimination. | Fewer big production adverts and smaller more targeted adverts. | The use of delivery through couriers and downloads means target consumers can be reached accurately. |
| Growth in international e-commerce | Internet means goods and services can be provided from anywhere in the world | Products need to be designed to meet international tastes and preferences and meet global standards. | There is pressure on prices to fall as businesses can access production in low-cost locations. | Needs to reflect cultural differences in the way it is presented. | The use of delivery through couriers and downloads allows for wider distribution. |
| Growth of mobile technology | Increased use of smartphones and tablets. | New products are being developed such as taxis that can be accessed by smart apps. | Consumers can instantly access prices when they are shopping so firms need to be more price competitive. | Adverts can be sent to consumers through their smartphones. | Smartphone apps help consumers locate producers so businesses need to be accessible in this way. |

# The difference between types of e-commerce

## Business-to-business (B2B)

**Key term**

**Business-to-business (B2B)** is where businesses directly market goods and services to other businesses using the internet.

Large supermarkets, for example, operate automatic ordering systems through the internet that buy stock from producers. The football club, for example, uses online ticket agencies to buy some of their tickets that can be sold on to consumers. This has made the buying and selling of goods and services in the supply chain more efficient, which reduces costs.

# Business-to-consumer (B2C)

**Key term**

**Business-to-consumer (B2C)** is where goods and services are directly marketed by businesses to final consumers.

This is where the football club, for example, sells online tickets to its supporters.

# Consumer-to-consumer (C2C)

**Key term**

**Consumer-to-consumer (C2C)** is e-commerce that allows consumers to trade good and services with each other.

The website eBay is one of the most famous examples of how e-commerce has facilitated this type of marketing.

## CASE STUDY

### eBay

eBay is a US-based e-commerce multinational organisation. It specialises in consumer-to-consumer and business-to-consumer sales through the internet. It makes more than $2 billion in profits and employs 35 000 employees.

### Progress questions

1 Define the term 'business to-consumer e-commerce'. [2 marks]

2 Explain two characteristics of eBay's consumer-to-consumer e-commerce. [4 marks]

3 Analyse how a business might benefit from business-to-consumer e-commerce offered by eBay. [6 marks]

# The costs and benefits of e-commerce

## Firms

Firms might benefit from e-commerce in the following ways:

- increased marketing access to consumers through websites

- increased knowledge of consumers means firms can target them more precisely through the marketing mix

- new promotional opportunities through internet advertising

- development of new products such as streaming of films and online books

- selling through the internet reduces costs because, for example, retailers do not need expensive outlets.

Firms might experience the following costs from using e-commerce:

- price comparisons drive down prices and reduce profit margins

- high initial cost of IT platforms needed to facilitate the service

- internet sales may reduce the sales of traditional methods such as retailers who lose conventional sales

- online buying has a higher rate of return for dissatisfied consumers who are unhappy with the products they have purchased.

- internet security is a challenge for any business that markets online.

# Consumers

Consumers might benefit from e-commerce in the following ways:

- the ease and convenience of buying online as opposed to going to a retailer to buy a good or service

- online buying increases consumer choice because so many products are available

- achieving the best price is easier because price comparisons can easily be made

- some goods such as films and books can be immediately accessed

- product information and review is available to help the buyer.

Consumers might experience the following costs from using e-commerce:

- the buying decision may be compromised because consumers cannot physically see or touch

- customer service may not be as effective because the consumer does not directly interact with the business

- buyers can make mistakes when ordering things and do not get the product they want

- relying on goods being delivered may mean goods do not arrive when consumers want them

- consumers may be more open to fraudulent activity when buying online.

# Exam practice questions

## Paper 1 question (HL and SL)

### Aderson Publishing

Aderson Publishing is an independent, worldwide publishing business that produces fiction and non-fiction books. Along with its published books it also has significant digital content and its online catalogue is increasing in importance. Market director Olaf Andersson has worked very hard to achieve one of Aderson's key corporate aims, which is to make Aderson's online presence the best of any publishing company in Europe.

**a** Outline two possible aspects of Aderson's e-commerce. [4 marks]

**b** Analyse two costs to Aderson of the rise in e-commerce. [6 marks]

[Total 10 marks]

## Paper 2 question (HL and SL)

### Citadel Theatre

The Citadel Theatre is a leading national theatre based in a large city. It has many leading plays that draw big audiences and attract large numbers of customers including tourists. It has benefitted from e-commerce through booking and marketing. It is even involved in some business-to-business e-commerce where it sells shows to cinema chains so they can be streamed live to customers.

**a** Define the term 'business-to-business' e-commerce. [2 marks]

**b** Outline how e-commerce has affected the product and place aspects of the Citadel Theatre's marketing mix. [4 marks]

**c** Explain how e-commerce might have affected the Citadel Theatre's promotion mix. [4 marks]

**d** Discuss the view that the rise in e-commerce has only been good for the Citadel Theatre. [10 marks]

[Total 20 marks]

**Exam tip**

The 'discuss' command term in this question means giving a considered and balanced review that the rise of e-commerce has been good for Citadel.

# Operations Management

# The role of operations management

# 5.1

## What you should know by the end of this chapter:

- Operations management and its relationship with other business functions (AO1)

- Operations management in organisations producing goods and services (AO2)

- Operations management strategies and practices for ecological, social (human resource) and economic sustainability (AO3).

**Chapter illustrative example**
A manufacturer of flat screen televisions

# Operations management and its relationship with other business functions

**Key term**

**Operations management** is the way a business plans, organises and coordinates its use of resources to produce its good or service.

The key aim of **operations management** is to produce the highest quality product possible in the most efficient way.

Operations management relates to the other business functions in the following ways:

- **Human resources** – The workforce is an important part of the production or provision of a good or services so it plays a key role in the business's operations. In the TV manufacturer example, production line workers have an important influence on the quality of the TVs produced.

- **Finance** – Financial management is important because it makes sure the business has the financial resources to allow the business to produce efficiently. This might be the funds for a piece of machinery or the cash needed to pay for stock.

- **Marketing** – Effective operations management means the business produces a good product at the lowest possible cost per unit, which gives the product a competitive edge in the market.

# Operations management in organisations

## Production of goods

Operations management affects different stages of the production process in a manufacturing organisation in the following ways:

- **Ordering and taking delivery of stock** – It is important to order and hold stock that allows production to be efficient. The TV manufacturer has an internet-based, automated stock management system for all its components.

- **Manufacturing system** – This sets out how labour and capital are employed to produce products as efficiently as possible. The TV manufacturing business example is a very capital-intensive process with relatively few workers on the production line.

- **Packaging and dispatch** – Once production is completed, the good needs to be packaged and then released to be shipped to its customers. The TV manufacturer example has an automated packaging system that automatically sets up units being put onto vehicles to be dispatched to the domestic and international markets.

## Production of services

Operations management in services differs to goods because both the production and delivery of a service to the consumer take place at the same moment. Operations management affects a business in the following ways:

- **Ordering and taking delivery of stock** – Stock is important to the efficient provision of a service because retailers need stock to sell goods to consumers.

- **Service provision system** – Labour and capital need to be employed and managed in effective ways to produce a high-quality, cost-effective service. A coffee shop, for example, has to have the right number of people serving and the appropriate coffee-producing equipment to satisfy its customers.

- **Service quality** – Operations management needs to make sure the quality of the customer experience is as good as it can be by making sure, for example, the fixtures and fittings, atmosphere and customer service are of the highest standard possible.

## WORKED EXAMPLE

The strategic response of the example flat screen TV producer is shown in Table 5.1.1. The information on a business's ecological, social and economic sustainability is contained in its CSR report.

**Table 5.1.1**

|  | Definition | Strategic response | Benefit | Cost |
|---|---|---|---|---|
| Ecological sustainability | Business activity that does not disrupt the physical environment's ability to meet the needs of people in the future. | The TV manufacturer has set targets to reduce greenhouse gas emissions by a set percentage in each of the next ten years. | • Positive publicity and promotion<br>• Attracts employees<br>• Meets government regulations. | • Increased production costs<br>• Restricts the products a firm can offer<br>• Loss of competitive advantage. |
| Social sustainability | Business activity that satisfies the needs of individuals in society in the short and long term. | The TV manufacturer looks to develop relationships with its suppliers, which the suppliers can base their business models on in the long term. | • Strong relationships with suppliers<br>• Loyal customers<br>• Good relations with the local community. | • Problems with inefficient suppliers<br>• May conflict with the need to increase sales<br>• Can add to business costs. |
| Economic sustainability | Business activity that enables a business to maintain production in the future and contribute to the economic activity of a country in the long term. | The TV manufacturer manages its profitability over time so that it is a sustainable business. | • Long-term profitability in line with business objectives<br>• Good relationships with stakeholders such as employees. | • May reduce risk-taking decisions that lead to innovation<br>• Can conflict with cost-reducing decisions such as outsourcing. |

## CASE STUDY

### Costa Coffee

Costa Coffee is a British multinational coffeehouse company with revenue of $1.1 billion in 2015. It uses a made-to-order production system with a process designed to deliver hot beverages and food as they are required by the customer.

### Progress questions

1   Define the term 'operations management'. [2 marks]

2   Outline the effect the production system for coffee in a Costa Coffee outlet has on its human resources and marketing. [4 marks]

3   Analyse two ways the production of a service like Costa Coffee is different to producing a manufactured good. [6 marks]

### Exam tip

The 'outline' command term in this question means giving a brief account of the effect the production system for coffee in a Costa Coffee outlet has on its human resources and marketing.

# Strategies and practices for ecological, social and economic sustainability

Operations management has been affected by growing awareness of the impact that business activities have on the environment the business operates in. Organisations have adapted their operation management strategies and practices in response to this.

## CASE STUDY

### Samsung

The South Korean multinational Samsung produces a huge range of products from chemicals to consumer electronics products and medical equipment. It produces a sustainability report each year that includes the details of its economic, environmental, and social performance. This information is available to all its different stakeholder groups through its website.

### Progress questions

1   Define the term 'ecological sustainability'. [2 marks]

2   Distinguish between social sustainability and economic sustainability to a business like Samsung. [4 marks]

3   To what extent is Samsung's decision to make sustainability an important aim of its operations management? [10 marks]

### Exam tip

The 'distinguish' command term in this question means making clear the differences between social sustainability and economic sustainability.

# Exam practice questions

## Paper 1 question (HL and SL)

### Complete Cover Security

Complete Cover Security is a medium-sized security business based in Eastern Europe. It manufactures intruder alarm systems that use the most advanced electronic security solutions. The new operations director, Izabel Nemec sees one of her aims as working closely with the business's HR, marketing and finance directors to improve production efficiency and product quality.

**a** Outline two functions of operations management at Complete Cover Security. [4 marks]

**b** Analyse two ways the finance function at Complete Cover Security might be affected by Izabel Nemec's decision to improving production efficiency and product quality. [6 marks]

[Total 10 marks]

## Paper 2 question (HL and SL)

### Asicor Steel

Asicor Steel is a multinational steel plant based in India. It has a turnover of $10 billion and employs 60 000 people worldwide. The price of steel is falling and so are Asicor's profits. To try and address these challenges it has decided to close four unprofitable plants, which will make 7000 workers redundant.

**a** Define the term 'economic sustainability'. [2 marks]

**b** Outline two reasons why effective operations management is important to Asicor. [4 marks]

**c** Explain two ways that Asicor's operations might affect ecological sustainability. [4 marks]

**d** Discuss Asicor's decision to close its unprofitable plants in terms of its ecological, social and economic sustainability. [10 marks]

[Total 20 marks]

# 5.2 | Production methods

**What you should know by the end of this chapter:**

- The following production methods: job/customised production, batch production, mass/flow/process production, cellular manufacturing (AO2)

- The most appropriate method of production for a given situation (AO3).

**Chapter illustrative example**
A bread manufacturer

# 5.2

## Production methods

**Key term**
A **production method** is the processes an organisation uses to turn resource inputs into a final good or service.

For the bread manufacturer example, the production method is using raw materials, labour and capital to produce a loaf of bread. The focus of **production methods** is often on manufacturing organisations but service businesses, such as fast food firms, also rely on production methods.

## Job production

**Key term**
**Job production** is where a business produces a specific unit to meet the wants and needs of a particular customer.

The bread manufacturer example does have a division that makes bread and cakes for particular occasions for corporate customers. **Job production** has the following characteristics:

- **Individual customer needs** – Where the product has to meet specific consumer needs such as architects, surveyors and house builders.

- **Importance of labour** – When a good is produced by skilled labour and cannot be produced using a capital-intensive mechanised process.

- **Higher prices** – Goods such as individually produced artwork are more expensive than mass-produced goods and consumers are willing to pay higher prices.

- **Small businesses** – Job production is often done by small businesses or specialist divisions within large firms because job production does not have significant economies of scale.

## Batch production

**Key term**
**Batch production** is where a business produces a set number of units of a good where the units move through each stage of the production process at the same time.

The bread manufacturer uses **batch production** when a certain number of loaves of bread move from mixing to baking to cooling and then bagging. Batch production has the following characteristics:

- **Manufacturing businesses** – Batch production is used by many small, medium and large manufacturing organisations, such as food production, textiles and chemicals.

- **Short production runs** – Production is often complicated by the need to change and set up production for new batches that need different requirements. For example, the cooking heat and tin size for a different batch of bread needs to be changed.

- **Flexible labour** – Workers need to be able to adapt their skills for the production requirement of different batches. For the bread manufacturer, for example, batches of different types of cakes and breads may need a variety of skills.

## Flow production

**Key term**
**Flow production** is used in mass production when very large numbers of the same product pass continuously through each stage of production.

**Flow production** has the following characteristics:

- **Large-scale manufacturing** – Mass production is used by large organisations manufacturing a standardised product. It can be seen in industries such as car manufacturing and consumer electronics.

- **Continuous production** – Flow production often means producing 24 hours a day and for seven days a week.

- **Low unit costs** – The level of continuous production means low unit costs are achieved because of economies of scale.

- **Capital-intensive** – Large scale capital is used in flow production and the process is highly automated with very limited use of labour on the production line.

# Cellular production

### Key term
**Cellular production** is a manufacturing system where goods are produced using a team of employees that work with a product from the start of the process until the end.

**Cellular production** has the following characteristics:

- **Cell production units** – Capital is organised in a modular way so that teams of workers can complete each production task effectively in a factory.

- **Team working** – Some manufacturing use cellular production because it facilitates team working, which increases employee motivation.

- **Job enrichment** – Employees can work on a particular product completing a variety of tasks, which reduces the monotony of just completing one task on a production line.

- **Set-up costs** – Setting up a cellular production line may be more expensive that the traditional production line.

## CASE STUDY

### Church Shoes
Church Shoes is owned by the Italian luxury brand Prada. It is a UK manufacturer of high quality shoes. The Church Shoe factory is labour-intensive using highly skilled production line workers. The production cycle for a pair of shoes is up to seven weeks. The business uses batch production where output goes through a series of stages where, for example, tanned calf hides are cut and then go through stitching and shaping, until the final product is ready for dispatch.

### Progress questions

1 Define the term 'production method'. [2 marks]

2 Define the term 'batch production'. [2 marks]

3 Outline two possible characteristics of the batch production used by Church Shoes. [4 marks]

### Exam tip
The 'define' command term in this question means give the precise meaning of the term production method.

# The most appropriate method of production for a given situation

The production method an organisation chooses to use will depend on the following factors:

### Nature of the consumer
Where consumers want a more individual product, job production is most appropriate, but if consumers are more concerned about price then batch or flow production is better. People who buy bespoke furniture are often willing to pay a higher price.

## Size of the market

Large mass markets will be supplied by businesses producing goods using flow or cellular production whereas job or batch production is associated with smaller markets.

## Financial resources

Setting up a flow production line requires huge initial set-up costs that are only really available to large firms. Small businesses often choose batch production because of limited investment capital.

## Nature of the product

Standardised products like washing powder and shampoo can only effectively be produced using batch or flow production.

## Approach of management

Some businesses will use a particular type of production because this is what managers feel is more effective for the organisation. Cell production, for example, may well be better for employee welfare and motivation than flow production.

## Evaluation

For all organisations, the choice of production method will depend on a variety of factors and the advantages of the method chosen will be traded off against the disadvantages. The bread manufacturer, for example, has chosen batch production because this gives the highest quality product, the greatest productive efficiency and it meets with the financial constraints of the organisation.

---

### CASE STUDY

**Woods Bagot**

Woods Bagot is an international architecture consulting business with a team of more than 1000 people working across studios in Australia, Asia, the Middle East, Europe and North America. It specialises in areas such as education, science and sport. It is the seventh largest architecture firm in the world.

**Progress questions**

1 Define the term 'job production'. [2 marks]

2 Outline two characteristic of job production. [4 marks]

3 Analyse two reasons why Woods Bagot is likely to use job production. [6 marks]

---

# Exam practice questions

## Paper 1 question (HL and SL)

### Complete Cover Security

Complete Cover Security is a medium-sized security business based in Eastern Europe. It manufactures intruder alarm systems that use the most advanced electronic security solutions. The business's new operations director, Izabel Nemec, is keen to develop innovative production methods. Their products are manufactured using cell production, which has proved to be very successful since it was introduced three years ago.

a Outline two characteristic of cell production. [4 marks]

b Analyse two reasons why Complete Cover Security has chosen to use cell production. [6 marks]

[Total 10 marks]

# Paper 2 question (HL and SL)

## ICT PLC

ICT is a large multinational manufacturer of consumer electronics products. Its biggest market is flat screen TVs and it produces huge numbers of the product which it sells all over the world. It uses flow production in factories that produce 24 hours a day. The management do have some concerns about low morale among its production line workers and is considering a move to cell production.

**a** Define the term 'flow production'. [2 marks]

**b** Outline two characteristics of flow production. [4 marks]

**c** Explain two reasons why ICT uses flow production. [4 marks]

**d** Recommend ICT's decision to move from flow production to cell production. [10 marks]

[Total 20 marks]

### Exam tip

The 'recommend' command term in this question means presenting an advisable course of action with appropriate supporting evidence of ICT's decision to move to cell production.

# Lean production and quality management (HL only)

**What you should know by the end of this chapter:**

- Features of lean production: less waste, greater efficiency (AO1)

- Methods of lean production: continuous improvement (kaizen), just-in-time (JIT), Kanban, Andon (AO2)

- Features of cradle-to-cradle design and manufacturing (AO2)

- Features of quality control and quality assurance (AO1)

- The following methods of managing quality: quality circle, benchmarking, total quality management (TQM) (AO2)

- The impact of lean production and TQM on an organisation (AO3)

- The importance of national and international quality standards (AO2).

**Chapter illustrative example**
A shirt manufacturer

# Features of lean production

**Key term**
**Lean production** is an approach to production that focuses on eliminating waste from all aspects of the production process.

The features of **lean production** are:

- **Waste reduction** – This approach means taking things away from the production process that do not add value to the final product the consumer buys. For the shirt manufacturer example, this might be time wasted by workers who have to constantly change machinery settings when there is a change in a shirt batch.

- **Greater efficiency** – By reducing waste, the output per worker of a firm increases, which leads to lower unit costs and this can be passed on to the consumer in the form of lower prices and it can also increase profit margins.

# Methods of lean production

## Continuous improvement (kaizen)

**Key term**
**Continuous improvement** is where a business adopts an approach where all employees are constantly looking to make small improvements in the way the business produces things.

To achieve **continuous improvement**, the business uses the following approach:

- **Individual workers** – There is a culture that encourages all employees to be involved in the process.

- **Quality circles** – Groups of workers regularly meet to suggest improvements.

- **Incremental improvements** – If many small improvements are made to production methods then significant long-term improvements can be made to efficiency.

A quality circle group at the example shirt manufacturer identified that by changing the order of production, fewer changes in machinery settings need to take place.

## Just-in-time (JIT)

**Key term**
**Just-in-time (JIT)** is a stock management system that aims to increase efficiency and reduce waste through minimising stock levels by only receiving stock when it is needed in production.

Holding minimum levels of stock reduces the cost of managing stock and creates a more efficient production process.

## Kanban

**Key term**
**Kanban** is a stock control system based on coloured cards that signal to production line workers when more stock is needed to maintain production.

In lean production, **Kanban** is an important part of maintaining efficiency on the production line by maintaining a smooth flow of production and preventing interruptions.

## Andon

**Key term**
**Andon** is a manufacturing system used to identify and signal when there is quality or process problems on the production line.

**Andon** means workers and managers can respond quickly to production problems and prevent interruptions to production, which reduce efficiency.

---

### CASE STUDY

#### Toyota

Toyota is one of the biggest car manufacturers in the world producing nearly 17 million vehicles in 2016. Toyota has a production system based on the philosophy of 'the complete elimination of all waste'. Toyota's vehicle production system is based on lean manufacturing and just-in-time (JIT). This production system is based on continuous improvements. The objective of the system is making and distributing vehicles ordered by customers in the quickest and most efficient way.

#### Progress questions

1  Define the term 'lean production'. [2 marks]

2  Describe two possible aspects of Toyota's lean production system. [4 marks]

3  Outline the role Kanban and Andon might have in Toyota's lean production system. [4 marks]

---

#### Exam tip

The 'describe' command term in this question means giving a detailed account of two possible aspects of Toyota's lean production.

# Features of cradle-to-cradle design and manufacturing

#### Key term
**Cradle-to-cradle** is an approach to production that builds sustainability as a central aim of production.

**Cradle-to-cradle** has the following characteristics:

- Products should be designed so they can easily be recycled into something new.

- Materials used in the production process can be reused.

- Production processes should have minimal negative effects on the environment.

- Business activity should have a positive social impact on communities.

The shirt manufacturer example has adopted some cradle-to-cradle practices by using recyclable materials to produce some of its products and by aiming to be carbon neutral by planting trees to balance out its carbon emissions.

# Features of quality control and quality assurance

## Quality control

#### Key term
**Quality control** is continuously monitoring the goods and services produced by a business to ensure they meet a set standard.

The **quality control** approach involves a business:

- setting a required minimum standard for a product

- appointing specific responsibility for carrying out quality control

- developing a testing procedure for the product

- checking each product produced or sampling a certain number

- having a process to deal with products that do not meet the required standard.

## Quality assurance

**Key term**
**Quality assurance** focuses on achieving quality in production by focusing on the consumer and making sure the product meets the quality they want.

**Quality assurance** is a more holistic approach to achieving quality by:

- setting a quality standard to be achieved

- developing a set of policies to make sure all employees continuously work to meet these standards

- ensuring all employees have the task of continuously checking the quality of products they produce against the required standard.

The example shirt manufacturer uses quality assurance rather than quality control because it wants to stop defects occurring in its products earlier and it believes production line workers see more shirts than a quality controller ever could.

# Methods of managing quality

## Quality circles

**Key term**
**Quality circles** are groups or teams of workers organised by a business to identify and offer solutions to quality issues.

**Quality circles** have the following characteristics:

- small groups of employees work together on a particular aspect of production

- led by a supervisor or senior employee

- the group meets regularly to consider issues relating to quality and how improvements can be made

- employees receive training in problem-solving and quality assurance techniques

- findings of quality circles are presented to management.

## Benchmarking

**Key term**
**Benchmarking** is an approach to quality assurance where a business uses the performance standards achieved by other firms to set the quality standards it wants to attain.

**Benchmarking** is achieved by looking at other businesses and firms to get an idea of relative performance along with an understanding of how others achieve quality production. It involves setting performance standards by looking outwards (outside a particular business, organisation, industry, region or country) to examine how others achieve their performance levels, and to understand the processes they use. The benchmarking process involves:

- an appraisal of the organisation's current quality standards

- research into the standards and quality achieved by competitors

- a comparison exercise between the performance standards of the business and its competitors

- developing a strategy to raise standards to the competitor level.

## Total quality management (TQM)

**Key term**

**Total quality management (TQM)** is an approach businesses use to improve the quality of goods and services produced by continuously refining and improving production techniques.

There are four steps to approaching **total quality management (TQM)**:

- **Planning** – By setting out where the problem is and the cause of the problem.

- **Problem-solving** – Managers and employees develop and implement a solution.

- **Checking** – Data analysis is used to see whether the solution has worked.

- **Implementation** – The solution is fully put into practice and relevant employees informed of changes.

- **Review** – Problems are continuously reviewed to see if further improvement can be made.

The shirt manufacturer experienced high product returns on its cheapest shirt range. It used quality circles to investigate the issue and it was found that production line workers lacked care with the lower-priced shirts compared to more expensive ones. The firm then used TQM to develop a quality-checking system with this type of shirt and the number of returns fell.

**Boeing**

Boeing is a multinational company that designs and manufactures aircraft, rockets and satellites. In 2016, its sales revenue was $96 billion and it employed nearly 160 000 people. Boeing has a large manufacturing process based on lean production that is at the heart of the business's success as a leading aircraft producer. Boeing's production is, however, more than lean, it also has to achieve a level of quality that guarantees the safety of its aircraft.

**Progress questions**

1 Define the term 'quality control'. [2 marks]

2 Outline two aspects of quality assurance that might exist at Boeing. [4 marks]

3 Explain two ways quality circles might be used by Boeing to improve the quality of its aircraft. [4 marks]

4 Analyse two reasons why achieving quality is so important to Boeing. [6 marks]

# The impact of lean production and TQM on an organisation

Table 5.3.1 sets out the impact that production and TQM have on different functions in an organisation.

The shirt manufacturer example has benefited from higher sales as the perceived quality of shirts has increased but it has to pay higher wages now to recruit and retain staff who can implement TQM and lean production.

**Table 5.3.1**

| Lean production and TQM | Marketing | HR | Finance |
|---|---|---|---|
| Advantages | • Greater efficiency improves customer satisfaction<br>• Less waste leads to lower costs and prices<br>• High quality becomes a USP and can be promoted. | • Workers feel empowered by techniques like quality circles<br>• Improving quality motivates workers who feel better about their work. | • Higher quality means prices can be increased which increases profit margins<br>• Greater efficiency reduces unit costs and profit margins increase<br>• Higher quality and efficiency leads to a rise in sales which increases revenue and profits. |
| Disadvantages | • Production may become more of a focus than satisfying the consumer<br>• Striving for efficiency may impact on the consumer. For example, JIT means the risk of running out of stock. | • Continuously striving for efficiency puts too much pressure on employees<br>• Processes like benchmarking increases pressure of workers. | • Capital cost of setting up new production systems increased staff training costs<br>• Higher quality workers can be needed which means higher wage costs. |

# The importance of national and international quality standards

Governments put into law regulations that set standards that businesses have to achieve when they are producing goods and services. They do this to ensure:

• Health and safety of consumers

• Health and safety of employees

• Protection of the environment

• Fair competition between firms.

The International Standards Organization (ISO) is an body that promotes standardisation in an international context. One of its key aims is to regulate standards so that international trade in goods and services is fair as all firms are competing using the same standards.

# 5.3

# Exam practice questions

## Paper 1 question (HL)

### Complete Cover Security

Complete Cover Security is a medium-sized security business based in Eastern Europe. It manufactures intruder alarm systems that use the most advanced electronic security solutions. The business's new operations director Izabel Nemec is keen to develop innovative production methods. She is in the process of trying to introduce lean production and adopt the principles of total quality management to Complete Cover Security.

**a** Outline two characteristics of total quality management. [4 marks]

**b** Analyse two ways Complete Cover Security could use benchmarking to improve the quality of its products. [6 marks]

[Total 10 marks]

## Paper 2 question (HL)

### Cilantanyi

Cilantanyi is a leading coffee processing and marketing company based in Uganda. In 2016, the company produced 1.5 million kilograms of coffee per month. The business is currently trying to introduce lean production and trying to empower the workforce in driving quality assurance.

a Define the term 'quality circle'. [2 marks]

b Outline two possible characteristics of quality assurance at Cilantanyi. [4 marks]

c Explain how the use of quality circles at Cilantanyi might increase worker motivation. [4 marks]

d Discuss the advantages and disadvantages of Cilantanyi's decision to introduce lean production. [10 marks]

[Total 20 marks]

**Exam tip**
The 'analyse' command term in this question means breaking down the ways benchmarking can be used to improve quality.

# 5.4 Location

## What you should know by the end of this chapter:

- The reasons for a specific location of production (AO2)

- The following ways of reorganising production, both nationally and internationally: outsourcing/ subcontracting, offshoring, insourcing (AO3).

**Chapter illustrative example**
A pharmaceutical company that produces medicines

# The reasons for a specific location of production

**Key term**
**Location of production** is where a business chooses to produce its good or service.

The reasons for choosing a particular location based on the aim of maximising its profits would be to:

- **Minimise costs** – A location that allows a firm to produce at the lowest possible costs per unit.

- **Maximise revenue** – A location that gives the business access to the greatest number of customers so that it can achieve the highest possible revenue.

## Location factors

The following factors affect a business's location decision:

- **Close to the consumer** – Service businesses need to locate where the market is and they can attract a large number of consumers. A fast food business, for example, will locate in a shopping centre or high street.

- **Access to raw materials** – Some manufacturers that rely on a particular raw material that is difficult to transport will locate near the material. Petroleum producers, for example, will often locate near oil refineries.

- **Availability of employees** – Centres with sizeable populations offer large numbers of workers of different types that can travel easily to the business with an effective travel system.

- **Effective infrastructure** – Infrastructure is large-scale capital that can support business. It includes: roads, rail, ports, airports, power and water supply, as well as the internet. Businesses will often try to locate near important infrastructure to support different business functions.

- **Cost of land** – Businesses want to locate production in a place that allows them access to the resources and market they want at the lowest possible price or rent.

- **Linked industries** – Organisations rely on each other as suppliers and customers. The suppliers of components for car manufacturers often locate near car production plants.

- **Preferences of the owners and manager** – Business will sometimes locate in the place that suits the personal reasons of the owners. It may, for example, be a place where a family business has always been located.

- **Government influence** – Governments can offer tax incentives and grants to firms that choose to locate in a particular location.

The pharmaceutical company, for example, looks to locate its plants where there is good infrastructure, close to other firms in the same industry and where the cost of land is relatively low.

## CASE STUDY

**BASF**
The German chemicals producer BASF has opened its first manufacturing plant in Sri Lanka. The plant is located just outside Colombo and will produce construction chemicals such as those used in concrete. The new plant will allow BASF to better meet the increasing demand for construction chemicals to customers in Sri Lanka.

### Progress questions

**a** Outline two factors that might explain why BASF has chosen to locate near Colombo in Sri Lanka. [4 marks]

**b** Analyse two reasons why BASF's decision to locate in Sri Lanka might lead to a rise in its profits. [15 marks]

# Reorganising production

## Outsourcing

**Key term**
**Outsourcing** is a where a business subcontracts areas of production to an outside producer.

The pharmaceutical company subcontract the cleaning and maintenance of its machinery and equipment.

**Advantages of outsourcing:**

- An organisation can focus on core activities. The pharmaceutical business, for example, can focus on developing new drugs.

- Improved efficiency by using an outsourcing business that specialises in a particular activity.

- Reduced indirect costs when an activity is outsourced such as the labour used to clean and maintain the equipment of the pharmaceutical business.

- Fixed costs can be reduced because the business does not have to invest in machinery. The subcontractor that does the maintenance for the example pharmaceutical business would invest in all the maintenance and cleaning equipment needed.

**Disadvantages of outsourcing:**

- Loss of control over an activity makes it more difficult to manage. The example pharmaceutical business may have problems with the workers who service their equipment but they do not have direct control over them.

- The cost of employing the outsourced business.

- Security because employees who do not work directly for the business may have access to sensitive information.

- The quality of the outsourced business may not be high enough for the business.

## Offshoring

**Key term**
**Offshoring** is when a business moves a business activity to another country.

This could be manufacturing or it could be a service function like accounting. The example pharmaceutical business has moved the manufacturing of a new drug to South America.

**Advantages of offshoring:**

- Lower production costs because of low labour and land costs.

- Reduced tax in an offshore country reduces a business's tax liability.

- Fewer rules and regulation that reduce efficiency. The pharmaceutical business has found some of the rules on drug testing easier to follow when locating in South America.

- It gives a firm access to the market where they offshored production.

**Disadvantages of offshoring:**

- There are extra costs associated with offshoring such as exchange rate changes and transport costs.

- The political environment in the offshore country may be difficult. The example pharmaceutical business has had some difficulties with crime and corruption in the South American country it is dealing in.

- Cultural and language barriers bring some challenges that can make working with an offshore business or workforce difficult.

# 5.4

**Thomas Cook**

One of the world's largest travel companies, Thomas Cook is to outsource part of its booking service for hotels to an Australian online travel agent, Webjet. Webjet will run and manage the booking service using its own computer system and booking agents. The deal will help Thomas Cook to cut costs and boost its profits.

## Progress questions

1 Define the term 'outsource'. [2 marks]

2 Explain two ways Thomas Cook might be able to reduce costs by outsourcing some of its hotel bookings. [4 marks]

3 Analyse two ways Thomas Cook's decision to outsource hotel booking might increase its revenue. [6 marks]

## Exam tip

The 'explain' command term in this question means giving a detailed account of how outsourcing might reduce Thomas Cook's costs.

# Insourcing

## Key term

**Insourcing** is where a business brings a previously outsourced activity back into the organisation by employing a person or department to do the activity.

The pharmaceutical business, for example, has stopped using an outsourced quality control organisation to do its own quality assurance.

## Advantages of **insourcing**:

- Businesses regain management control over an activity.

- Reduced cost of no longer paying for an outsource business.

- Regain control over security.

- An opportunity to do a task more effectively. This is why the pharmaceutical business chose to insource quality assurance.

## Disadvantages of insourcing:

- Increased fixed cost of the insourced activity. The training cost to the pharmaceutical business was, for example, the major disadvantage of their decision to insource.

- Indirect cost of the insourced activity.

- Employees have less time to spend on core activities.

- Employees within the business may not be as effective as the outsource business.

# Exam practice questions

## Paper 1 question (HL and SL)

### Complete Cover Security

Complete Cover Security is a medium-sized security business based in Eastern Europe. It manufactures intruder alarm systems that use the most advanced electronic security solutions. The new operations director, Izabel Nemec, has decided to outsource the transport department of its business. This means it can sell all its vehicles as well as its servicing facility and its equipment. It will then pay an outside business to do all the transport work.

a Outline two ways outsourcing transport will reduce Complete Cover Security's costs. [4 marks]

b Analyse two disadvantages of Complete Cover Security outsourcing its transport. [6 marks]

[Total 10 marks]

## Paper 2 question (HL and SL)

### ERT Insurance

ERT Insurance is considering whether to insource its call centre work. ERT has been using an Asian business to handle customer service enquiries for the past two years but it has run into problems. The outsourcing company has resulted in large numbers of customer complaints and the ERT management feel they are losing customers because of this.

**a** Define the term 'offshoring'. [2 marks]

**b** Explain two reasons why ERT might have used offshoring for its call centre. [4 marks]

**c** Explain human resource problems ERT might have faced when offshoring. [4 marks]

**d** Recommend to ERT whether it should insource its call centre work. [10 marks]

[Total 10 marks]

**Exam tip**

The 'recommend' command term in this question means presenting an advisable course of action on the insourcing decision based on appropriate supporting reasoning.

# Production planning (HL only)

**What you should know by the end of this chapter:**

- The supply chain process (AO2)

- The difference between just-in-time (JIT) and just-in-case (JIC) (AO2)

- Stock control charts based on the following: lead time, buffer stock, reorder level, reorder quantity (AO2, AO4)

- Capacity utilisation rate (AO2), (AO4)

- Productivity rate (AO2), (AO4)

- Cost to buy (CTB) (AO2), (AO4)

- Cost to make (CTM) (AO2), (AO4).

**Chapter illustrative example**
A business that manufactures yachts

# The supply chain process

**Key term**
The **supply chain** is the series of links between a business and its suppliers that allows the production of a product and its distribution to consumers.

In the **supply chain**, a firm takes raw materials and components from suppliers and manufactures them into a product that they sell to a final consumer. For the yacht manufacturer, for example, the supply chain process would be:

- yacht components and raw materials like engines, sails and upholstery
- manufacture yachts
- sell yachts to dealers and end-consumers.

# The difference between JIT and just-in-case (JIC)

**Key term**
**Just-in-time (JIT)** is a stock management system that aims to increase efficiency and reduce waste through minimising stock levels by only receiving stock when it is needed in production.

Holding minimum levels of stock reduces the cost of managing stock and creates a more efficient production process.

To achieve **just-in-time** a firm will:

- **Forecast demand accurately** – This means goods are only manufactured when the consumer orders them.
- **Order stock based on need** – Stock is ordered on the basis of the amount needed to produce what the consumer has ordered.
- **Develop strong supplier relationships** – Reliable suppliers are needed by a business so that stock is delivered when the business needs it in production.

- **Holding minimum stocks** – By minimising stock level, this reduces the cost of holding stock such as insurance and storage facilities.

**Key term**
**Just-in-case (JIC)** is a stock management system where a business keeps enough stock to minimise the probability of running out of stock.

**Just-in-case** reduces stock-out costs where running out of stock might mean:

- interruptions to the production process
- dissatisfied customers who do not receive their order
- customers who do not receive their order might develop a relationship with an alternative supplier
- business develops a reputation for not having stock, which puts off potential customers.

The yacht manufacturer, for example, uses JIT because it has relatively small premises for storage and a tight cash flow situation so it does not want to tie up too much cash in stock.

## CASE STUDY

### Dell
Dell is a technology company that uses a build-to-order process JIT approach to its supply chain and manufacturing process. A Dell computer can be customised and manufactured according to specific customer requests. At Dell they call it 'pull to order'. JIT allows Dell to meet its consumer needs more precisely as well as delivering greater efficiency and lowering production costs.

### Progress questions

1 Define the term 'supply chain'. [2 marks]

2 Describe two aspects of Dell's supply chain. [4 marks]

3 Analyse two benefits to Dell of using JIT. [6 marks]

# Stock control charts

**Key term**
A **stock control chart** is a model that shows a business how the stock level of an organisation changes overtime.

The **stock control chart** allows a business to manage its stock level to balance stock holding costs and stock-out costs and allow the supply chain to function efficiently. Figure 5.5.1 illustrates a stock control chart.

# Capacity utilisation rate

**Key term**
**Capacity utilisation rate** is the proportion of the total production capacity of a business accounted for by the actual level of production.

The **capacity utilisation rate** is measured by the following equation:

actual output per year / maximum capacity output per year $\times$ 100 = Capacity utilisation rate

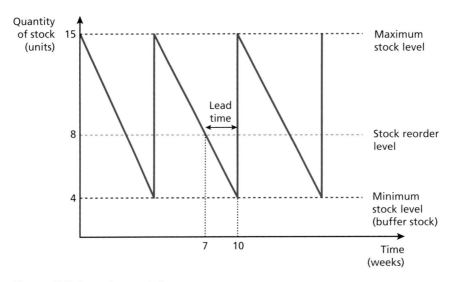

**Figure 5.5.1** Stock control chart.

**WORKED EXAMPLE**

The stock control chart for the example yacht manufacturer shows:

- **Quantity of stock held in units** – Quantity of yacht engines.

- **Time stock is held for** – How long a yacht engine is held for on average in weeks.

- **Maximum stock level (15)** – Highest number of engines the business would stock.

- **Stock reorder level (8)** – Stock of engines when the firm would place a new order.

- **Minimum stock level (buffer stock) (4)** – Lowest level of engine stock the firm plans for to prevent running out of stock.

- **Lead time (3 weeks)** – Time it takes for stock to be delivered.

For the yacht manufacturer that has a maximum capacity of 140 yachts and the actual output of 120 yachts, the capacity utilisation is:

$120 / 140 \times 100 = 86\%$

As a business gets closer to capacity it has the following advantages:

- it is using its assets more efficiently
- unit costs are lower.

As a business gets closer to capacity, it has the following disadvantages:

- risk of machinery breaking down
- risk of not being able to complete or accept orders
- fixed assets depreciate more quickly.

# Productivity rate

**Key term**
**Productivity rate** is a measure of business efficiency that is expressed as output per unit of resource input.

**Productivity rate** can be measured by output per resources such as output per worker or by output per time period such as output per week. The equation used to measure productivity for the yacht business example was output per worker in a year. This was measured by the equation:

**annual output / number of workers = annual output per worker**

**120 / 42 = 2.86 units per worker per year**

The higher the business productivity, the more efficient a business is and the lower the cost per unit will be. Higher productivity can lead to higher profit margins and allow a firm to reduce prices.

**Nissan**
The Japanese car giant Nissan produces nearly 5 million cars a year worldwide and employs 140 000 workers. Its plant in Sunderland in the UK is the most productive car plant in Europe. Output per worker is 118 cars a year from a plant that has a 500 000 car annual capacity.

**Progress questions**

1 Define the term 'productivity'. [2 marks]
2 Explain how Nissan has measured the productivity of its Sunderland plant. [4 marks]
3 Outline how you would measure Nissan's capacity utilisation rate. [4 marks]

**Exam tip**
The 'outline' command term in this question means giving a brief account of how Nissan's capacity utilisation rate can be measured.

# The make or buy decision

Manufacturing organisations often face the decision of whether to make a component themselves or to buy a component in from an outside supplier. The yacht manufacturer, for example, has to decide whether to build yacht hulls itself or buy them in from an outside company.

## Cost to buy (CTB)

**Key term**
**Cost to buy (CTB)** relates to all the costs associated with buying a component from an outside supplier, such as the price of the component and any transport costs that may incur.

# 5.5

The yacht business example pays $20000 for a standard hull and the number it expects to produce this year is 120.

Total cost: $120 \times \$20000 = \$2400000$

The reasons a business would choose to buy a component might be:

- cheaper to buy in a component than make it
- supplier's expertise in manufacturing the component
- avoids the cost of investment in machinery
- business does not have the capacity to produce it.

## Cost to make (CTM)

### Key term
**Cost to make (CTM)** is the total cost to a business of manufacturing a component itself to be used to make a final product.

To make the product itself, a business will incur direct labour and direct material costs along with fixed costs such as machinery. The cost to make is calculated by using the equation:

cost to make (CTM) = fixed costs + (direct cost per unit × expected output)

For the yacht manufacturer this is:

$\$600000 + (\$12000 \times 120) = \$2040000$

On a cost basis, it is cheaper for the yacht manufacturer to produce the hull itself.

The reasons a business would choose to make a component would be:

- cheaper to make the component than buy it in
- business has more control over the quality of component produced
- risk that an outside supplier may not be able to supply the component.

# Exam practice questions

## Paper 1 question (HL)

### Complete Cover Security

Complete Cover Security is a medium-sized security business based in Eastern Europe. It manufactures intruder alarm systems that use the most advanced electronic security solutions. The business's new operations director, Izabel Nemec, is looking to an outside supplier to manufacture infrared sensors for its alarms. The outside supplier will charge Complete Cover Security $5.5 per unit. Complete Cover has the following costs for the sensors:

- Direct labour $1.2 per unit
- Direct labour $2.3 per unit
- Fixed costs $450000
- Total units produced 200000.

a Define the term 'direct labour cost'. [2 marks]

b Calculate
  i The total cost to make
  ii The total cost to buy the sensors. [4 marks]

c Discuss the financial and non-financial factors that might affect Complete Cover Security's decision to make or buy the sensors. [10 marks]

[Total 20 marks]

## Paper 2 question (HL)

### Alzeed Frames

Alzeed Frames buys and sells picture frames for the commercial property market. It deals in the smallest frames right the way up to the largest units needed for commercial display. Figure 5.5.2 sets out its stock control chart.

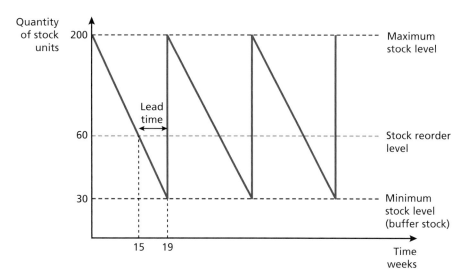

**Figure 5.5.2** Stock control chart for Alzeed Frames.

**a** Define the term 'stock control chart'. [2 marks]

**b** Using the stock control chart for Alzeed state the following:

    **i** How many frames are sold on average per week.

    **ii** The lead time in weeks.

    **iii** The number of weeks when the stock needs to be reordered. [6 marks]

**c** Define the term 'buffer stock'. [2 marks]

**d** Evaluate the view that JIT is the best way for Alzeed to manage its stock. [10 marks]

[Total 20 marks]

**Exam tip**

The 'state' command term in this question means giving a specific value for the: average number of frames sold, the lead time and reorder time.

# Research and Development (HL only)

# 5.6

**What you should know by the end of this chapter:**

- The importance of research and development for a business (AO3)

- The importance of developing goods and services that address customers' unmet needs (AO2)

- Types of innovation: product, process, positioning, paradigm (AO2)

- The difference between adaptive and innovative creativity (AO2)

- How pace of change in an industry, organisational culture and ethical considerations may influence research and development practices and strategies in an organisation (AO3).

**Chapter illustrative example**
A business that produces computer games

# The importance of research and development

## Key term

**Research and development (R&D)** is where an organisation uses resources to explore ways to innovate new products and methods of production.

**Research and development** is important for businesses because it means that businesses can:

- meet changing tastes and preferences among consumers

- develop new products to replace declining products in its portfolio

- respond to R&D by competing businesses

- react to advances in technology in the market

- develop production systems to reduce unit costs

- develop production systems to improve the quality of the product.

The computer games business, for example, is constantly developing new games as technology in the computer games market advances, competitors develop new games and consumer preferences change.

# Developing goods and services that address customers' needs

As markets become saturated as consumer demand stops rising and the number of competing firms in the market increases, there is a need for businesses to develop new products. This often means researching and developing products that meet needs that have not been met up to now. Few business people would have anticipated the consumer need, for example, for the 'selfie-stick'.

## Importance of market research

Market research is a crucial part of product development because it exposes opportunities to develop goods and services to meet new needs. Qualitative research using focus groups can be particularly useful here.

## CASE STUDY

### Ford

The US car manufacturer Ford has announced it will produce a fleet of driverless cars for ride-sharing services such as Uber by 2021. Mark Fields, Ford's CEO, said the next decade will be 'defined by automation of the automobile' and 'the switch to driverless travel will affect society as much as the introduction of the assembly line'. The introduction of driverless cars by Ford follows the company's huge investment in research and development.

### Progress questions

1 Define the term 'research and development'. [2 marks]

2 Explain two reasons why R&D into driverless cars is important to Ford. [4 marks]

# Types of innovation

## Key term

**Innovation** is where a business develops an idea or invention into commercially viable products or production systems.

In the computer game business, for example, **innovation** would refer to the development of virtual reality headsets into a product consumers want to buy. These are the types of innovation:

- **Production innovation** is where a firm develops new goods and services to meet existing and unmet consumer needs. For the computer game business example, this could be new games or products to enhance the consumer's experience when playing the games, such as headsets.

- **Process innovation** is where an organisation develops new production systems to improve the way a good or service is produced. For example, the use of drones in the delivery of goods, which reduces unit cost.

- **Positioning innovation** is where a business takes an existing product and markets it in a new way. This changes the consumer's perception of the product and creates a new target market. The computer game business, for example, could develop a new set of games that were originally designed as leisure games and develop them for educational applications.

- **Paradigm innovation** is where the change in the product sold is so significant that it completely changes the market. The development of game downloading and online playing for example, has, had a huge impact on all businesses in the computer game market.

# Impact of creativity

## Adaptive creativity

### Key term
**Adaptive creativity** is innovation is where an organisation develops existing products in response to changes in market conditions.

The computer game business, for example, is continuously developing the games it sells to meet changing technology in the market such as the introduction of high-definition

screens. **Adaptive creativity** involves small or incremental changes over time.

## Innovative creativity

### Key term
**Innovative creativity** is innovation where a business develops a new product to meet consumer needs or unmet needs.

In the computer game business, for example, this is developing a new way of experiencing computer games such as hand motion sensors. **Innovative creativity** generally involves greater investment in R&D than adaptive creativity.

### CASE STUDY

**Fitbit**
Fitbit is a US company that has developed activity trackers, wireless-enabled wearable technology devices that can be used to help consumers improve their personal fitness and health. The Fitbit wristband enables consumers to measure things such as the number of steps they walk, their heart rate and their quality of sleep. The business grows dramatically as a result of their commitment to innovative creativity.

### Progress questions

1 Define the term 'innovative creativity'. [2 marks]

2 Explain two types of innovation a business like Fitbit might use. [4 marks]

3 Analyse the challenges to Fitbit of using innovative creativity. [6 marks]

### Exam tip
The 'analyse' command term in this question means breaking down the challenges to Fitbit of innovative creativity into its essential elements.

# Influences on research and development

**Table 5.6.1**

| | Nature | Impact | Computer game business example |
|---|---|---|---|
| Market change | The speed at which innovation and consumer taste and preferences change. | The more dynamic a market is, the more time and resources a business will invest in R&D. | The computer game market constantly changes because technological advance and consumer tastes change very quickly. |
| Organisation culture | The willingness of managers and employees to initiate and accept change. | The more people in organisations want to be innovative and change the way a business works, the more time and resources will be put into R&D. | The whole culture in the computer game business is an innovative one. There are brainstorming meetings every week where employees discuss new ideas, no matter how outlandish. |
| Ethics | How moral values and principles among managers and employees affect the new products and systems a business develops. | Ethics can change the products and systems a business might be prepared to develop. | The computer game manufacturer has a strict policy on not developing games with an overly violent nature. |

# Exam practice questions

## Paper 1 question (HL)

### Complete Cover Security

Complete Cover Security is a medium-sized security business based in Eastern Europe. It manufactures intruder alarm systems that use the most advanced electronic security solutions. The business is researching a new product that will allow consumers to monitor their home security online and through an app.

**a** Outline two types of innovation that Complete Cover Security can use. [4 marks]

**b** Analyse two ways market changes might affect R&D at Complete Cover Security. [6 marks]

[Total 10 marks]

## Paper 2 question (HL)

### Base PLC

Base PLC produces gym equipment for professional gyms and fitness centres. Their equipment is very high-quality

# 5.6

and uses the latest fitness technology. The business puts significant funds into R&D where it has a joint venture with a leading sports research department at a university. Part of their focus is adaptive creativity but they are also continuously trying to develop new gym products.

**a** Define the term 'adaptive creativity'. [2 marks]

**b** Outline how two types of innovation Base might use. [4 marks]

**c** Explain how innovation might increase Base's revenue. [4 marks]

**d** Discuss the benefits and costs to Base of significant investment in R&D. [10 marks]

[Total 20 marks]

## Key concept question

With reference to one or two organisation(s) that you have studied, examine how ethics and culture affect research and development. [20 marks]

### Exam tip

The 'discuss' command term in this question means offering a considered and balanced review that includes a range of arguments on Base's decision to invest in R&D.

# 5.7 | Crisis management and contingency planning (HL only)

**What you should know by the end of this chapter:**

- The difference between crisis management and contingency planning (AO2)

- The factors that affect effective crisis management: transparency, communication, speed and control (AO2)

- The advantages and disadvantages of contingency planning for a given organisation or situation: cost, time, risks and safety (AO2).

**Chapter illustrative example**
A low-cost airline

# Crisis management and contingency planning

**Key term**

**Contingency planning** is where an organisation has a written statement of policies and procedures it will put into place in a crisis situation.

The airline example has a **contingency plan** for the different crisis situations it might face including severe delays due to industrial disputes.

The airline has a step-by-step approach for all relevant employees and managers on how to act when a major incident occurs.

Contingency planning sets out the procedures for an emergency and **crisis management** is how the procedures will be put into practice.

**Key term**

**Crisis management** is the process an organisation uses to manage an emergency situation effectively.

# Factors that affect effective crisis management

## Transparency

It is important for managers to be honest and clear about a crisis situation so that:

- different stakeholder groups are aware of what the crisis is and how it might affect them

- rumours do not develop that mislead stakeholders

- after the event, a lack of transparency or dishonesty can be more damaging than the crisis.

The case example airline had to be transparent about excessive waiting times for passengers because of industrial action. By being clear about average six-hour waiting times, they could deny press reports of much longer waiting times.

## Communication

It is important to have lines of communication to reach different stakeholder groups effectively. This process involves:

- appointing a spokesperson who communicates effectively and calmly

- using a medium appropriate to the stakeholder group; the most relevant ones could be spoken to and others informed by email or website

- providing regular updates to make stakeholders feel supported and informed.

The airline example has an appointed person on duty to communicate a crisis situation at all times and it has a policy of always speaking personally to customers waiting in the terminal if there are excessive delays.

## Speed

It is important to communicate a crisis situation quickly to stakeholders so they receive accurate information and rumours are avoided. This is particularly important when social media can communicate a crisis so quickly. In the light of security threats, the example airline has a 30-minute response time for online communication through its website if there is an incident.

## Control

In crisis situations, it is important for the organisation to seem to be in control of events. This means the manner of managers and employees needs to be calm and composed so that stakeholders are not unnerved or panicked by an emergency situation. The airline, for example, trains all its cabin staff and pilots on how to act in an emergency situation during a flight.

## CASE STUDY

### BP

In April 2010, a BP-owned deep water oil drilling platform suffered a major incident when an explosion led to 11 deaths and 4.9 million barrels of oil spilled into the Gulf of Mexico, polluting the sea and the surrounding coastline. The resulting publicity and legal costs have adversely affected BP's profits for the past six years.

### Progress questions

1  Define the term 'contingency plan'. [2 marks]

2  Explain how transparency and communication would have been important in BP's management of this crisis situation. [4 marks]

3  Analyse two consequences to BP of not managing the oil spill crisis effectively. [6 marks]

**Exam tip**

The 'analyse' command term in this question means breaking down the two consequences of BP not managing the oil spill crisis effectively into its essential reasons.

# Contingency planning for a given organisation or situation

The low-cost airline example has a very well-defined and regulated set of procedures and policies. The nature of the industry, where air accidents can be very serious, has a significant impact on this. Safety consciousness is also a unique selling point of the organisation. Table 5.7.1 sets out details of the impact on cost, time, risks and safety of a contingency plan.

**Table 5.7.1**

| Impact of a contingency plan on: | Advantage | Disadvantage |
|---|---|---|
| Cost | An effective plan well implemented may reduce costs. A crisis well managed is less likely to lead to costly legal action. | A contingency plan may incur costs when staff have to be trained, equipment purchased and procedures developed. |
| Time | An effective plan means a crisis can be contained and time saved from lengthy investigations that follow. | Contingency plans mean putting into place policies that make everyday business operations more time-consuming. |
| Risks | Contingency plans allow a business to manage risks more effectively and reduce the probability of a crisis occurring. | A contingency plan may make employees and managers become more risk-averse, which reduces innovation in the organisation. |
| Safety | Contingency plans mean managers and employees think about health and safety and this improves the safety environment in the business. | If a business becomes too safety conscious, it can make an organisation a more bureaucratic place to work which increases costs and negatively affects staff morale. |

# Exam practice questions

## Paper 1 question (HL)

### Complete Cover Security

Complete Cover Security is a medium-sized security business based in Eastern Europe. It manufactures intruder alarm systems that use the most advanced electronic security solutions. The business operates a remote security software system that they use to cover the expensive residential market and commercial property. The software has been hacked and there has been a security breach that has had significant media coverage. The business has a contingency plan to deal with this type of situation.

**a** Outline two possible elements of a Complete Security Cover contingency plan. [4 marks]

**b** Analyse two benefits to Complete Cover Security of having a contingency plan. [6 marks]

[Total 10 marks]

## Paper 2 question (HL)

### Starlight Arena

Starlight Arena is a major event venue. It has seating capacity for 12 000 people and is used to hold concerts and sports events. It is a high-profile venue and it attracts plenty of media attention. Starlight's management understand the importance of contingency planning and crisis management.

**a** Define the term 'crisis management'. [2 marks]

**b** Outline two elements of effective crisis management. [4 marks]

**c** Explain two problems caused by ineffective crisis management. [4 marks]

**d** Evaluate the benefits to Starlight Arena of a contingency plan in case of a major incident. [10 marks]

[Total 20 marks]

**Exam tip**

The 'evaluate' command term in this question means weighing up the benefits and limitations of Starlight Arena using a contingency plan.

# Skills Practice

# Effective skills for the Business Management examination

# Good exam technique

An important part of the exam preparation process is developing good exam technique. You need to do the following to develop this effectively:

- understand the demands of the different examination papers

- manage your time effectively during each exam

- answer questions at a level appropriate to each assessment objective (AO).

## The demands of the different exam papers

Tables 6.1.1 and 6.1.2 summarise the breakdown in the two exam papers at Higher Level and Standard Level.

**Table 6.1.1** Higher level assessment

| | Paper 1 | Paper 2 | Internal assessment |
|---|---|---|---|
| Method | **Section A** | **Section A** | To write a report on a business decision facing an organisation or an analysis of a business decision taken by an organisation. |
| | Students must answer two from three structured questions. [20 marks] | Students must answer one structured question from two based on stimulus material with a quantitative element. [10 marks] | |
| | **Section B** | **Section B** | The report should include a separate action plan and research proposal on how the report is to be produced. |
| | Students must answer one compulsory structured question. [20 marks] | Students must answer two out of three structured questions based on stimulus material. [40 marks] | |
| | **Section C** | **Section C** | Maximum 2000 words. |
| | Students must answer one compulsory question based on strategic decision-making with the use of extension material. [20 marks]. | Students must answer one from three extended response questions based on two key concepts. [20 marks]. | |
| Total marks | 60 | 70 | 25 |
| Time | 135 minutes | 135 minutes | 30 hours |
| Weighting | 35% | 40% | 25% |

**Table 6.1.2** Standard level assessment

| | Paper 1 | Paper 2 | Internal assessment |
|---|---|---|---|
| Method | **Section A** | **Section A** | To write a written commentary based on three to five supporting documents on a real issue facing a business organisation. |
| | Students must answer two from three structured questions based on the case study. [20 marks.] | Students must answer one structured question from two based on stimulus material with a quantitative element. [10 marks] | Maximum 1500 words. |

**(continued)**

**Table 6.1.2 (continued)**

| | Paper 1 | Paper 2 | Internal assessment |
|---|---|---|---|
| | **Section B** | **Section B** | |
| | Students must answer one compulsory structured question. [20 marks] | Students must answer one out of three structured questions based on stimulus material. [20 marks] | |
| | | **Section C** | |
| | | Students must answer one from three extended response questions based on two key concepts. [20 marks]. | |
| Total marks | 40 | 50 | 25 |
| Time | 75 minutes | 105 minutes | 15 hours |
| Weighting | 30% | 45% | 25% |

# Approaching the exam

## Time management

It is important to get your time management right when you are approaching the Business Management examination.

- For Higher level Papers 1 and 2 you should allocate around 2 minutes per mark (20 minutes on a 10-mark question).

- For Standard level Paper 1 and 2 you should allocate 2 minutes per mark (20 minutes on a 10-mark question).

When you are answering questions in this book you can apply the timings to the questions to give you the opportunity to write answers under exam conditions.

## Planning in the exam

Once you are in the exam you will need to manage the ways you approach the questions and stimulus material.

- The five minutes' reading time for each of the papers will give you the opportunity to plan how to approach the questions on the paper.

- It is important to look through the questions and to decide which to choose based on the areas you feel most confident about.

- During the reading time in Papers 1 and 2 it is best to read the questions first and then the stimulus material.

## Using the stimulus material

Once you have finished your reading and you are approaching each question, it is very important in Paper 2 to read the stimulus material carefully before answering the questions. The case studies provide the foundation for your answers and should be used as a source of examples for all the points you make in your answers.

## Answering the questions

- **Reading the question** – Reading the question carefully and answering the question precisely are important. You should identify the key command terms in the question to determine how you should answer the question.

- **Setting out your answer** – Set out your answer in a way that clearly presents itself effectively to the examiner. An effective way to present written answers to a question is: make your point, use business theory to support it and use an example from the case study or stimulus material.

## Quantitative questions

Papers 1 and 2 for Higher and Standard Level have quantitative questions where you will be expected to carry out simple arithmetic operations. It is essential to clearly:

- show your working on calculation questions so that the examiner can see where the answer has been derived from

- set out layout of calculations, diagrams and charts

- draw your charts and diagrams using a pencil and ruler.

# Approaching the Paper 1 case study

Each of the five sections of this book have Paper 1 case studies with questions based on the case study. The case studies for each section are set out in Table 6.1.3.

Once you have received the pre-issued case study it is important for you to spend some time with your teacher and on your own preparing for it. Here are some important tips on how to approach it:

- Read through and annotate the case study carefully to understand fully the issues it raises.

- Draw up a timeline for the case study organisation that summarises the changes it has gone through in a chronological order.

- Consider the syllabus areas covered by the case study to focus your revision for the paper.

- Do some reading about the market the case study company is involved in to develop your understanding of the context of the market and the business.

**Table 6.1.3**

| Section | Case study |
| --- | --- |
| Business organisation and environment | The Fine Olive Company is a business that produces and markets its own high quality olives and olive oil. |
| Human resource management | The Juice Truck is a leading mobile beverage business. |
| Finance and accounts | Preciso is a watch manufacturer. |
| Marketing | Aderson Publishing is a worldwide publishing business. |
| Operations management | Complete Cover Security is a medium-sized security business. |

# Approaching the Key Concept question

Higher and Standard Level students have to do a compulsory Key Concept question in Paper 2. The Key Concept question is based on the following criteria:

- It is a 20-mark extended response (essay) question based on the key concept themes: change, culture, ethics, globalisation, innovation and strategy.

- You need to approach the Key Concept question using at least one real-world organisation that you have studied in the course.

- When you are applying case study examples to the Key Concept question you must focus on the perspectives of individuals and societies on which the real-world organisation impacts.

- You will need to demonstrate knowledge, reasoning, analysis and evaluation when you are writing your answer so the marking level goes up to assessment objective AO3.

# 6.1

## Example of a Key Concept question

This is an example of a Key Concept question:

With reference to one or two organisation(s) that you have studied, discuss how innovation and globalisation have affected their marketing strategy(s). [20 marks]

Table 6.1.4 sets out how you might approach this question to achieve to meet the demands of the marking criteria. The case study organisations chosen here as examples are Facebook and Nike.

**Table 6.1.4**

| | Marking criteria | Achievement required | Key question examples for the sample question using Facebook and Nike |
|---|---|---|---|
| A | Knowledge and understanding of tools, techniques and theories | Good knowledge and understanding of relevant tools, techniques and theories is demonstrated. | Marketing strategy, marketing mix, marketing models (Boston Matrix), market research. |
| B | Application | The relevant business management tools, techniques and theories are well applied to explain the situation and issues of the case study organisation. Examples are appropriate and illustrative. | The marketing mix and Boston Matrix have been effectively applied to Facebook and Nike. |
| C | Reasoned arguments | Relevant, balanced arguments are made and these are well justified. | The importance of innovation and globalisation in the way Facebook and Nike promote their products is developed. |
| D | Structure | An introduction, body, conclusion and fit-for-purpose paragraphs are present, and ideas are clearly organised. | How globalisation and innovation has affected the marketing strategies of Facebook and Nike is covered and there is a clear introduction, argument and conclusion. |
| E | Individual and societies | Balanced consideration is given to relevant individual and group perspectives. | The essay considers the impact of the question on the internal and external stakeholder groups affected by Facebook's and Nike's marketing strategies. |

# 6.2 | Internal assessment

# Higher Level internal assessment: research project

## Introduction

The Higher Level Business Management internal assessment (IA) is a 2 000-word research project. The project is based on a real business organisation and the research question should be a real issue the organisation faces. The IA gives you the chance to apply your business skills and knowledge to a real-world situation. You can focus your IA on one organisation or a number of organisations.

## Choice of topic

You should choose a topic that interests you and that you can tackle effectively within the word limit. You should also choose a syllabus area to cover that you are good at and interested in. Your teacher will be able to help you with this.

## Choice of organisation

It is important for you to have a clear understanding of the business and the market in which it operates. Local businesses are often a good choice because they give you plenty of access to primary research and you can access them easily, for example a local fast food restaurant, hairdressers, manufacturing firm or a cinema.

## Choosing a title

The title of your IA should be set out as a question. This will help you focus your research and analysis precisely and to come to an effective conclusion. It is very important that you choose a title that allows you to apply business techniques to solve a business problem. The title: 'How could the promotional mix of restaurant Z be improved to increase its sales?' allows you to apply, analyse and evaluate business techniques, come to a conclusion and make a recommendation to the business.

These are some examples of sample titles:

- How could XYZ leisure centre improve its cash flow?

- How could staff efficiency at supermarket ABC be improved?

- Should LNM Bank outsource its catering services?

- How can customer service at the ABC DIY store be improved?

- How can the stock-management system used by M and N building firm be improved?

## The research proposal

Part of the internal assessment involves writing a research proposal. This is a planning document that sets out how you are going to produce your project. The research proposal is part of the assessment criteria and it needs to be included as a separate document with your report.

The research proposal needs to be written as a plan and set out in the following way:

- the research question

- the rationale for study – why you have chosen this topic

- areas of the syllabus to be covered

- possible sources of information

- organisations and individuals to be approached

- methods to be used to collect and analyse data, and the reason for choosing them

- anticipated difficulties

- action plan that sets out the order of activities and timescale of the project.

## Setting out your report

Table 6.2.1 sets out how you can structure your report.

**Table 6.2.1**

| Section | Content | What it should include |
|---|---|---|
| Executive summary | This is a 200-word summary of your report. | Should set out the:<br>• Title<br>• Approach to the title<br>• Conclusions and recommendations. |
| Introduction | This includes a background to the business and the business issue. Try to keep this section fairly brief (around 200–300 words as a guideline) – avoid long descriptions of the company's history or its market(s). | Should set out:<br>• Who the business's customers are<br>• How big the business is<br>• Where it is located<br>• The business's basic legal structure (whether it is a partnership, private limited company, etc.)<br>• The market within which the business operates<br>• The context of the problem – how the decision you are looking at will affect the business. |
| Procedure or method | This is a short section that is structured around how you are going to research and then answer the question. | You should set out your research methods:<br>• Primary research – interviews, data collection<br>• Secondary research – books, articles, academic research. |
| Main results and findings | This section includes the results of your primary and secondary research. | You could use the following ways of displaying your data:<br>• Tables<br>• Pie charts<br>• Bar charts<br>• Graphs. |
| Analysis and discussion | This section means analysing the data and information you have collected using business techniques to answer the research question you have set. | Techniques you could use:<br>• Investment appraisal<br>• Decision trees<br>• Ratios<br>• Force field analysis<br>• SWOT analysis<br>• Management theorists<br>• Boston Matrix. |
| Conclusions and recommendations | This section should be based on the evidence and analysis included in your report and should answer the question set in the title. Your recommendation to the business should be based on the conclusions you have drawn. | Your conclusion should include:<br>• The title<br>• Research method<br>• Main findings<br>• Final conclusion. |

**(continued)**

**Table 6.2.1 (continued)**

| Section | Content | What it should include |
|---|---|---|
| Presentation | Your report is a formal document, so it must be meticulously presented. | The formal layout should be:<br>• Title page<br>• Acknowledgments<br>• Contents page<br>• Executive summary (abstract)<br>• Introduction<br>• Research question<br>• Procedure or method<br>• Main results and findings<br>• Analysis and discussion<br>• Conclusions and recommendations<br>• Bibliography and references<br>• Appendices. |

## The marking criteria

Table 6.2.2 sets out the marking criteria used to assess your research project and how to achieve the top mark for each of the criteria.

**Table 6.2.2**

| Criteria | Nature | Marks available | What is needed to achieve the top mark for each of the criteria |
|---|---|---|---|
| A | Research proposal and action plan | 3 | The research proposal must be appropriate, clear and focused. |
| B | Sources and data (written report) | 3 | The primary sources selected and the data collected must be appropriate, varied and sufficient. |
| C | Use of tools, techniques and theories (written report) | 3 | The tools, techniques and theories must:<br>• show a good understanding of relevant business management tools, techniques and theories<br>• be skilfully applied. |
| D | Analysis and evaluation (written report) | 6 | The analysis and evaluation must:<br>• be a skilful analysis of the results and findings<br>• have a coherent integration of ideas<br>• have consistent evidence of substantiated evaluation. |
| E | Conclusions (written report) | 2 | The conclusion must:<br>• be substantiated and consistent with the evidence presented in the main body of the written report<br>• suggest areas for further study that have been identified. |

**(continued)**

**Table 6.2.2 (continued)**

| Criteria | Nature | Marks available | What is needed to achieve the top mark for each of the criteria |
|---|---|---|---|
| F | Recommendations (written report) | 2 | The recommendation must:<br>• be substantiated and consistent with the conclusions<br>• answer the research question. |
| G | Structure (written report) | 2 | The structure must be organised into a structured argument that is appropriate for the research question and easy to follow. |
| H | Presentation (written report) | 2 | The report must include all of the required components in the correct order and format. |
| I | Reflective thinking (written report) | 2 | The report must include appropriate evidence of reflective thinking on the approach taken in this piece of research and its limitations. |
| | Total | 25 | |

# Standard Level internal assessment: written commentary

## Introduction

The Standard Level internal assessment requires you to write a 1500-word commentary on a real business issue or problem. It allows you the opportunity to show how you would apply business management tools, techniques and theories to a real-world situation.

## Choosing a topic

You have to choose a topic that interests you and allows you to tackle effectively within the word limit. It is helpful to select a business topic that enables you to score well on the marking criteria. Your teacher will be able to advise you on this.

## Setting a question

The title of the commentary needs to be in the form of a question facing a single business organisation, or a market/industry-wide issue that could affect an organisation. For example:

- Should XYZ gym introduce a new range of equipment?

- Could an improvement in non-income incentives improve the motivation at LNM coffee shop?

- Should company ABC purchase a new computer system to improve its efficiency?

- Should business X outsource its catering?

## Supporting documents and additional sources

Your commentary needs to be based on secondary data and it can also be supported by primary information you have collected. You will need to choose three to five supporting documents that will be attached to your commentary and will form part of your assessment. The best commentaries will use a range of different types of sources to support them.

These are some examples of the secondary sources you could use as supporting documents:

- final accounts

- market research reports

- newspaper articles

- market research surveys

- business plans

- extracts from web-based articles.

You could also use primary sources such as:

- responses to questionnaires

- transcripts of interviews you have conducted.

# Setting out your commentary

Table 6.2.3 sets out how you can structure your report.

**Table 6.2.3**

| Section | Content | What it should include |
|---|---|---|
| Introduction | Sets the scene to the commentary. | • Background to the organisation<br>• Context of the question being considered. |
| Use of business tools and techniques | A good commentary will use suitable business tools to answer the question in the title. | Examples of business techniques:<br>• PEST/SWOT analysis<br>• Ansoff Matrix<br>• Work of motivational theorists<br>• Financial ratios<br>• Marketing mix<br>• Methods of production. |
| Analysis | You will need to demonstrate that you can use appropriate analytical skills in your commentary. | You should use your business tools to develop the points you make in your commentary. In a marketing question this might mean analysing how the marketing mix affects a business's marketing strategy. |
| Evaluation of findings | To show effective evaluative and critical thinking you should question the evidence you have used in your commentary | You need to make judgements about the points you make in your commentary. In a marketing question using the marketing mix this might mean saying that price is the most important issue because consumers are so price-sensitive. |
| Conclusion | Your commentary should conclude the question that you have set. | • Summarise the evidence used to answer the research question<br>• Explicitly answer the question you have set<br>• Consider any unresolved question. |
| Presentation | Your report is a formal document, so it must be meticulously presented. | • Title<br>• Introduction<br>• Research using supporting documents<br>• Research findings<br>• Analysis and evaluation of the findings<br>• Conclusion<br>• Bibliography<br>• Appendices (the supporting documents). |

# Standard Level marking criteria

Your commentary is marked internally based on the
marking criteria set out in Table 6.2.4.

**Table 6.2.4**

| Criteria | Nature | Marks available | What is needed to achieve the top mark for each of the criteria |
|---|---|---|---|
| A | Supporting documents | 4 | The supporting documents must be:<br>• relevant<br>• sufficiently in depth<br>• provide a range of ideas and views. |
| B | Choice and application of business tools, techniques and theory | 5 | The business tools, techniques and theory used in the commentary must be:<br>• appropriate<br>• skilfully applied. |
| C | Choice and analysis of data and integration of ideas | 5 | The data selected from the supporting documents must be:<br>• appropriate<br>• skilfully analysed<br>• a coherent integration of ideas. |
| D | Conclusions | 3 | The conclusion to the commentary must:<br>• be consistent with the evidence presented<br>• answer the commentary question. |
| E | Evaluation | 4 | The commentary must:<br>• show evidence of thorough evaluation<br>• include judgements that are well substantiated |
| G | Structure | 2 | The work must be organised into a structured commentary that is appropriate for the research question and easy to follow. |
| H | Presentation | 2 | The commentary must include:<br>• a title page<br>• an accurate table of contents<br>• appropriate headings and sub-headings<br>• consistent referencing<br>• a complete bibliography<br>• numbered pages. |
|  | Total | 25 | |

# Unit
# 7

## Business Management and the Core

# 7.1 Extended essays in Business Management

# Nature of the extended essay

The extended essay in Business Management gives you the opportunity to do a major research project in the subject. It is a 4000-word essay that allows you to:

- develop your research skills

- understand how business theory, concepts and principles are applied in the real world

- collect business information from a wide range of sources

- critically analyse real business information

- evaluate evidence and arguments

- produce a clear, well structured, logical argument

- develop your report-writing skills

- manage your own piece of original academic work.

# Starting the extended essay process

## Choosing a research question (title)

Choosing the title is a very important part of the extended essay process. Your choice of research question is something you want to discuss at length with your supervisor. Make sure your research question is:

- a question

- easy to understand

- precise and focused

- accessible to analysis and evaluation using business techniques

- manageable within the 4000-word limit.

If you want to do a question on promotion at an organisation you could focus it in the following way:

To what extent has ABC cinema's rise in sales been increased by its change in promotion strategy?

## Possible titles

These are some titles that can work effectively for the extended essay:

- To what extent has the application of Dan Pink's motivation theory improved the productivity at XYZ Ltd?

- To what extent has just-in-time production improved efficiency at XYZ manufacturing?

- To what extent has the use of CSR been adopted more widely in country X than in country Y?

- Should manufacturer LNM adopt cell production to improve its efficiency?

- Has Italian restaurant X's market share been increased by changes in its product portfolio?

- To what extent has law firm X's investment in a new computer system increased its efficiency?

- Has the introduction of TQM at XYZ Ltd improved the quality of the firm's products?

- Why has the practice of publishing environmental audits been adopted more widely in industry X than in industry Y?

- Should FGH Ltd outsource its catering service?

## Planning the essay

Table 7.1.1 sets out a way of planning your extended essay to meet the marking criteria used to assess the essay. Effective planning is a crucial part of the process because it allows you to assess how manageable your research question is and what the important pieces of evidence are that you need to research to answer your research question.

The aim of the plan is to allow you to produce a well-structured, clearly presented essay that answers your research question.

**Table 7.1.1**

| Research question | To what extent has the application of Dan Pink's motivation theory improved the productivity at XYZ Ltd? |
|---|---|
| Research method | • Books on or containing motivation theory and human resource management <br> • Secondary survey on staff motivation in the retail industry <br> • Articles on the human resource management in the industry <br> • Research paper on staff motivation in the industry <br> • Interview with the managers and staff at XYZ Ltd. |
| Theory to be used | • Work of motivational theorists (Pink, Taylor, Maslow, Herzberg, Adams) <br> • Financial rewards <br> • Non-financial rewards <br> • Corporate culture <br> • Employee–employer relations. |

# Writing the essay

Once you have researched your essay you can start to write it. The extended essay is a formal academic document and it needs to be written and presented in that way. Figure 7.1.2 sets out an approach to writing your extended essay that meets the guidelines and marking criteria set by the IB.

**Table 7.1.2**

| Section | Approach |
|---|---|
| Introduction | Set out: <br> • the context of the essay <br> • why it is worthy of study <br> • some background about the organisation <br> • the research question <br> • the significance of the research question. |
| Research methodology | Show how you are going to research your essay through: <br> • secondary research: books, articles, government reports and academic articles <br> • primary research: Interviews and surveys. |
| Research analysis | Show your analytical and evaluative skills by: <br> • looking at cause and effect relationships <br> • using business theory to support arguments <br> • considering advantages and disadvantages of points made <br> • long- and short-term consequences <br> • impacts on different stakeholders <br> • prioritising the arguments by considering their significance. |

**(continued)**

**Table 7.1.2 (continued)**

| Section | Approach |
|---|---|
| Writing a conclusion | Your conclusion should include:<br>• the research question<br>• a summary of the main points of your argument<br>• the final answer to your research question<br>• an unanswered question you might have considered. |
| Presentation | Your essay must have:<br>• a title page<br>• a table of contents<br>• page numbers<br>• labels on all tables, charts and graphs<br>• clear sub-titles<br>• a very full bibliography of sources<br>• footnotes<br>• an abstract<br>Your essay must not exceed 4 000 words. |
| The abstract | A 300-word summary of your essay that sets out:<br>• the title of your essay<br>• how you researched the question you set and developed an argument.<br>• your final conclusion. |

# Using the marking criteria

Table 7.1.3 shows how you the extended essay will be assessed. It includes the marking criteria and 'descriptors' that set out what you will need to do in your essay to achieve the marks available for each criteria. When you are writing your essay, it is important that you consider descriptors you need in order to achieve the highest marks in the criteria.

**Table 7.1.3**

| Criteria | | Marks available | What is needed to achieve the top mark for each of the criteria |
|---|---|---|---|
| A | Research question | 2 | The research question should be:<br>• clearly stated in the introduction<br>• sharply focused<br>• effectively addressed within the word limit. |
| B | Introduction | 2 | The introduction should clearly:<br>• state the context of the research question<br>• explain the significance of the topic and why it is worthy of investigation. |
| C | Investigation | 4 | The data and sources should:<br>• be appropriate<br>• have an imaginative range<br>• be carefully selected<br>• be well planned. |

(continued)

**Table 7.1.3 (continued)**

| Criteria | | Marks available | What is needed to achieve the top mark for each of the criteria |
|---|---|---|---|
| D | Knowledge and understanding of the topic studied | 4 | The essay should show:<br>• a very good knowledge and understanding of the topic studied<br>• clearly and precisely the essay in an academic context. |
| E | Reasoned argument | 4 | The argument should be:<br>• presented in a clear, logical and coherent manner<br>• a reasoned and convincing argument to the research question. |
| F | Application of analytical and evaluative skills appropriate to the subject | 4 | The essay should show analytical and evaluative skills that are:<br>• appropriate<br>• effectively applied. |
| G | Use of language appropriate to the subject | 4 | The language used should:<br>• communicate information clearly and precisely<br>• use terminology appropriate to the subject accurately<br>• be used with skill and understanding. |
| H | Conclusion | 2 | The conclusion should:<br>• be clearly stated<br>• be relevant to the research question<br>• be consistent with the evidence presented in the essay<br>• include unresolved questions. |
| I | Formal presentation | 4 | Excellent presentation must achieve the highest standard of layout, organisation and appearance in terms of its:<br>• title page<br>• table of contents<br>• page numbers<br>• text<br>• illustrative material<br>• quotations<br>• references<br>• bibliography<br>• appendices. |
| J | Abstract | 2 | The abstract must clearly state:<br>• the research question<br>• how the investigation was undertaken<br>• the conclusion(s) of the essay. |
| K | Holistic judgement | 4 | This is a holistic judgement of the essay; an excellent essay should show:<br>• intellectual initiative<br>• deep understanding<br>• insight. |
| | **Total** | 36 | |

## Completing the process

Once you have finished your essay, your supervisor will conduct an interview with you called the Viva Voce. This is a short interview with you about your essay and the extended essay process. There are no marks for the Viva Voce but it can help your supervisor when they are reporting on your essay on the extended essay documentation and this can contribute to criteria K 'Holistic judgement'.

The essay is marked out of 36 and Table 7.1.4 shows the approximate grade boundaries.

It is very easy to be overly focused on the marking criteria and the final grade you get. This is important but the extended essay is also one of the most intellectually challenging, enjoyable and fulfilling parts of the IB programme. This is certainly worth bearing in mind when writing your essay.

**Table 7.1.4**

| Grade: | A | B | C | D | E |
|---|---|---|---|---|---|
| Assessment | Excellent | Good | Average | Mediocre | Poor |
| Mark range | 29–36 | 23–28 | 16–22 | 8–15 | 0–7 |

# 7.2 | Theory of Knowledge

Theory of Knowledge (TOK) is part of the IB's Core along with the community action and service and the extended essay. The principles of TOK are an essential part of the way you approach Business Management as a subject. Although TOK is not referred to specifically in the Business Management assessment, its approach to critical thinking and inquiry are certainly part of the way you should approach exam questions, the internal assessment and the extended essay.

made in an answer. These are Assessment Objective (AO3) questions that allow you to score the highest marks on a question. Evaluative answers have command terms such as: 'to what extent', 'discuss', 'evaluate', 'examine' and 'recommend'.

Table 7.2.1 sets out the way to approach evaluative questions using the TOK 'critical thinking' method.

# Exam questions

## Evaluative answers

Papers 1 and 2 at Higher Level and Standard Level have questions with a TOK theme that expect you to think critically when you are evaluating the points you have

# Internal assessment

The critical thinking skills you have developed doing TOK can help you with the IA at both Higher and Standard Level. When you are doing your IA you will need to use the following skills: analysis, discussion/evaluation, conclusions and recommendations.

**Table 7.2.1**

| Command term | Definition | Example question | Method of evaluation |
|---|---|---|---|
| Evaluate | Make an appraisal by weighing up the strengths and limitations. | Evaluate firm X's decision to use performance-related pay. | This means critically considering the advantages and disadvantages of performance-related pay to firm X. |
| To what extent | Consider the merits or otherwise of an argument or concept. | To what extent is the Boston Matrix a useful model to organisation Y as it develops its marketing strategy? | This would involve considering how the Boston Matrix might help organisation Y's marketing strategy and what factors might limit it. |
| Discuss | Offer a considered and balanced review that includes a range of arguments, factors or hypotheses. | Discuss the view that JIT will always improve business efficiency. | This question means considering how JIT might improve business efficiency and then questioning whether these improvements would actually take place. |
| Examine | Consider an argument or concept in a way that uncovers its assumptions. | Examine the view that leasing machinery will improve company Z's cash flow. | This means considering how leasing can improve cash flow based on assumption about the cost of leasing and other factors affecting cash flow. |
| Recommend | Present an advisable course of action with appropriate supporting evidence. | Recommend how business X can improve the quality of its product using TQM. | This questions means saying how TQM can be applied and considering the difficulties of the methods recommended. |

## Analysis

This means breaking down a point or argument into its essential elements or structure. If you are doing an IA that is answering a question about how a business can extension strategies to maintain the sales of a product, you might break down the elements of an extension strategy into its components. This might be how the business could change its approach to pricing.

## Discussion/evaluation

When you have developed your argument, to answer your question you will need to demonstrate critical thinking skills to make an appraisal of your argument by considering its strengths and limitations. If your question is about developing an extension strategy then you would consider the advantages and disadvantages of a business increasing its spending on promotion.

## Conclusions

This part of the IA means drawing points you have made together to produce a final answer to the question. A key critical thinking skill you will need to show is the ability to judge the significance of individual arguments you make and synthesise these into a final answer. This might be making a final judgement on the use of an extension strategy to maintain sales.

## Recommendation

Where your IA considers a course of action, you might conclude by recommending a particular course of action for the business you have chosen as part of your IA. The critical thinking approach here is showing your ability to use the evidence of your answer to support your theory of what a business might do, for example, to develop an extension strategy.

## Extended essay

The extended essay is a significant piece of academic writing that gets you to apply the critical thinking skills you have developed in TOK to answer a research question. The key skills of analysis, discussion/evaluation, conclusion and recommendation are applied in a Business Management extended essay in a similar way to a Business Management IA.

If your research question is: 'To what extent has the use of JIT at XZY manufacturing improved its efficiency?' then you would need to develop evidence about the how the introduction of JIT has affected business. You will then need to critically analyse, evaluate and conclude arguments based on that evidence.

## The Key Concepts

The Key Concepts that underpin the Business Management course: change, culture, ethics, globalisation, innovation and strategy are an important link with TOK. They provide you with the opportunity to think critically about the underlying principles of the subject and how different parts of the course relate to each other.

### Key Concept questions

Table 7.2.2 sets out how TOK relates to the Key Concept questions you might face in the Business Management examination.

**Table 7.2.2**

| Concept | TOK question | Key Concept question |
|---------|--------------|----------------------|
| Change | 'Businesses have to change to survive.' What effect does change in an organisation have on individuals? | With reference to one organisation that you have studied, examine how change and innovation have affected human resource management. [20 marks] |
| Culture | 'Globalisation has brought nothing but benefits to corporate culture'. To what extent do you think this is true? | With reference to one organisation that you have studied, evaluate the importance of culture and ethics on corporate culture. [20 marks] |
| Ethics | Are there always unethical consequences of businesses increasing their profit? | With reference to one organisation that you have studied, discuss the importance of strategy and ethics in finance. [20 marks] |
| Globalisation | Is collecting reliable information in a global business environment an impossible task? | With reference to one or two organisation(s) that you have studied, evaluate how innovation can support market research in a globalised business environment. [20 marks] |
| Innovation | Businesses normally know more about the products they sell than the consumers that buy them. Consider the ethical questions this poses for a business. | With reference to one or two organisation(s) that you have studied, evaluate how innovation and ethics might affect the way an organisation promotes its products. [20 marks] |
| Strategy | To what extent is business strategy affected by intuition ahead of reason and evidence? | With reference to one organisation that you have studied, examine how ethics and strategy have affected the organisation's growth. [20 marks] |

# Answers

## 1.1 Case study progress questions

### Apple

**1** Businesses are organisations that bring together resources to produce goods and services that are sold to customers.

**2** Two resources from: human, physical, financial.

**3** Two business functions from: human resources, finance, marketing, operations management.

### Gmail

**1** An intrapreneur is someone who works within a business in an entrepreneurial way to develop a firm's products to attract new consumers.

**2** Quaternary sector.

**3** Two roles from: initial business idea, providing finance, management of employees.

### CliniCloud

**1** Two reasons from: redundancy, independence, business opportunity, and greater income.

**2** Two problems from: competition, access to finance, regulation, lack of information, lack of management experience.

## Exam practice questions

### Paper 1

**a i** A business plan is a formal document that describes the business, sets out its objectives and strategy, identifies its market and provides its financial forecasts.

**b ii** An entrepreneur is an individual that sees a business opportunity in the form of consumer want and then brings together human, physical and financial resources to produce a product to satisfy that want.

**c** Two difficulties might include: competition, access to finance, regulation, lack of information and lack of management experience.

### Paper 2

**a** Two business functions from: human resources, finance, marketing, operations management

**b** Two reasons from: redundancy, independence, business opportunity and greater income.

**c** Two problems from: competition, access to finance, regulation, lack of information, lack of management experience.

**d** Usefulness in terms of: planning tool, information for stakeholders, direction for management. Evaluation, weaknesses: Cost and time to produce and difficult to be accurate.

## 1.2 Case study progress questions

### British Airways

**1** A private sector business is owned and controlled by individuals or groups of individuals that are not under state control.

**2** Two characteristics from: state-owned, objectives other than profit, subject to political control.

**3** Two benefits from: increased access to finance, profit can be made, not subject to political influence.

### Twitter

**1** A partnership is a business where two or more individuals jointly own and take responsibility for the enterprise.

**2** Two advantages from: increased access to finance, more expertise for decision-making, flexible decision-making.

**3** Benefits of being a plc: increased access to finance, economies of scale, limited liability. Evaluation, weaknesses: Loss of decision-making control, takeover threat, profits share among more shareholders

### Wikimedia

**1** Non-governmental organisations (NGOs) are legally constituted not-for-profit organisations that support issues in the public good.

**2** Two characteristics from: not-for-profit, support issues for the public good, can be supported by government.

**3** Benefits to a developing country: support to education, low cost, limited political influence. Evaluation, weaknesses: dependence, conflict with government and other organisations.

## Exam practice questions

### Paper 1

**a** Two characteristics from: single owners, small businesses, unlimited liability.

**b** Two benefits: increased access to finance, more expertise for decision-making.

### Paper 2

**a** Non-governmental organisations (NGOs) are legally constituted not-for-profit organisations that support issues in the public good.

**b** Two characteristics from: not-for-profit, support issues for the public good, can be supported by government.

**c** Any problem from: corporate impact on TED's aims/decision-making, puts off some investors/funders.

**d** Effective for global education because: low cost, expertise, trusted source, clear objective. Evaluation, weaknesses: access to finance, attracting best staff, political objectives.

## 1.3 Case study progress questions

### Nike

**1** Corporate aims are the long-term goals that a business wants to achieve in the future.

**2** Two differences: measurable outcomes, specific.

**3** Nike's objective is: specific, measurable, relevant, time specific. Evaluation: difficult to say objective is achievable.

### Netflix

**1** Business strategy is the long-term plan that sets out the ways a business is going to achieve its corporate aims.

**2** Two changes from: technological change, consumer behaviour, new competition.

**3** Two problems from: reluctant employees, financial cost, regulations, consumers do not want change.

### Virgin Galactic

**1** SWOT analysis is a planning tool used by organisations as a method for guiding business strategy by considering the strengths, weaknesses, opportunities and threats the business faces.

**2** Two ways: appraisal of current situation (strengths and weaknesses), future prospects (opportunities and threats).

**3** Two strengths from: sets out strategy, assessment of risk, good for presentation.

## Exam practice questions

### Paper 1

**a** Two reasons from: attracts consumers, brand image, attracts employees, avoid regulation.

**b** Two benefits from: better-quality product, government support, relations with local community, increased sales.

### Paper 2

**a** Business strategy is the long-term plan that sets out the ways a business is going to achieve its corporate aims.

**b** Two strengths from: customer service, experienced, specialist employees.

**c** Two threats from: economic recession, rise in costs, change in regulation, change in consumer tastes.

**d** Useful because: sets out strategy, assessment of risk, good for presentation, guide to decision-making. Evaluation: difficult with complex decisions, forecasting risk, changes in business environment

## 1.4 Case study progress questions

### Lidl

1  Stakeholders are any people, groups or organisations that have an interest in a particular organisation.

2  Two internal stakeholders from: shareholders, employees, trade unions.

3  Two reasons from: pay, job security, working conditions.

### Prada

1  Two stakeholders from: customers, suppliers, local community, government, competitors, lenders.

2  Two reasons from: tax, employment, contribution to the economy.

### American Airlines

1  Internal stakeholders are people or groups who are part of the organisation and external stakeholders are outside.

2  Benefits of the merger for shareholders: more finance, economies of scale. Evaluation: loss of control. Employees: more expertise, job opportunities, higher pay. Evaluation: redundancies, culture change.

## Exam practice questions

### Paper 1

a  Two reasons from: repayment, interest costs, cash flow, financial security.

b  Local community: pollution and environment. Government: regulation. Employees: job security.

### Paper 2

a  Two from: customers, suppliers, local community, government, competitors, lenders.

b  Two reasons from: dividends, share price, business security.

c  Two roles from protection of: pay, employment, working conditions.

d  Employee redundancies, less employment for local community, more profit for shareholders. Evaluation: increased profit might give greater job security for employees and lower pollution for the local community.

## 1.5 Case study progress questions

### Luxottica Group

1  Two factors from: ageing population, ethnic diversity, empowerment of women, health consciousness, sexual orientation.

2  Communication technology: advertising and promotion. Product innovation: new frame technology for frames.

3  Economic growth might lead to: rising sales, increasing prices.

### Bet365

1  Legal factors, one from regulations on: betting, employment, competition, contracts. Technology factors, one from: innovation, R&D, production, communication.

2  Two stakeholders who might not want to be involved with the ethics of gambling from: employees, lenders, local community, government, potential investors.

3  Social factors: growing acceptance of gambling. Technological factors: online gambling. Political factors: regulations on gambling. Evaluation: positive effects (technology), negative effects (regulations).

## Exam practice questions

### Paper 1

a  Two social changes: health consciousness, environmental awareness.

b  Two ways from: falling demand, lower costs, difficulty in getting finance, customers choose cheaper products.

Paper 2

**a** STEEPLE analysis is a strategic planning tool used by organisations to focus on the different aspects of the external environment that affect businesses when they are developing strategy and making decisions.

**b** Technological change: digital publications. Social change: fewer people reading published magazines.

**c** Possible strategy could be to increase digital publication: production, distribution, promotion.

**d** Strategy for young readers, youth orientated: online magazine, use of social media, promotion, pricing. Evaluation: problems of changing brand image.

## Key Concept question

Ways culture affects the business environment: social (tastes of consumers), political (aims of government), ethical (approach to ethical issues). Ways innovation affects the business environment: technological (new products), environment (sustainability), economic (competition), legal (regulations on use). Evaluation: other factors that might affect the business environment such as economic factors.

## 1.6 Case study progress questions

### Tesco

**1** Economies of scale are the cost advantages firms benefit from as their scale of production increases.

**2** Two types from: commercial, technical, financial, labour/managerial.

**3** Communication: complexity of the organisation. Motivation: worker identity in a large organisation.

### Jaguar Land Rover

**1** A joint venture is where two businesses enter into an agreement to create a separate entity to manage a particular project.

**2** A strategic alliance is an agreement between two businesses to manage a project but it is a less formal arrangement than a joint venture and does not involve creating a separate legal identity. A merger is where two firms agree to join together under a single legal identity.

**3** Two reasons: access to finance, shared expertise.

## Exam practice questions

### Paper 1

**a** Two types from: communication, motivation, administration.

**b** Two reasons from: flexibility, diseconomies of scale, niche market, image.

### Paper 2

**a** A multinational organisation is a business that has an operational base in more than one country.

**b** Two reasons from: growth, economies of scale, spread risk, lower costs.

**c** Two challenges: more competition, lower prices.

**d** Benefits of multinationals: employment, infrastructure, knowledge economy, linked suppliers, exports. Evaluation: exploitation of workers, repatriation of profits, loss of local culture.

## 1.7 Case study progress questions

### Instant Mug Company

**1** Causes of problems: capital (problems with machinery), employees (poor training).

**2** Any two ways from: use of scientific approach, 0 wide consideration of problems, effective visual aid.

# 2.1

## Espirit Camping

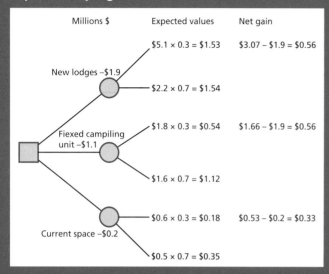

**1** and **2**

**3** Sets out: decision consequences, monetary consequences, risk, visual aid. Evaluation: problems of forecasting, assessing probabilities, complexity, static model.

## Solar Solutions

**1** Two ways from: sets out complex projects, efficient management of resources, sets a target, visual aid.

**2** See table on the next page

# Exam practice questions

## Paper 1

Fishbone strengths: scientific approach, innovative, visual aid. Evaluation: number of factors, irrelevant factors, opinions. Force field: sets out decision factors, objective values, qualitative and quantitative factors, visual aid. Evaluation: complexity, subjective values, accuracy of views.

## Paper 2

**a** Force field analysis is a model that assesses the relative importance of different environmental factors that impact on business strategy when managing change.

**b** Two driving forces: low set-up costs, export opportunity

**c** Cultural restraining forces: language, working practices, management methods.

**d** Force field: sets out decision factors, objective values, qualitative and quantitative factors, visual aid. Evaluation: complexity, subjective values, accuracy of views.

## 2.1 Case study progress questions

### Tamdown Group

**1** Annual labour turnover in an organisation measures the rate at which employees are leaving an organisation in one year.

**2** Number of employees leaving in one year / average number of people employed × 100.

**3** Two benefits from: lower recruitment and training costs, higher morale, better customer service.

### Accenture

**1** Two parts from: identify vacancy, write job description, person specification, advertise position, short list, interviews.

**2** Two factors from: demographic change, labour mobility, communication technology.

### Goldman Sachs

**1** Two reasons from: employee feedback, employee rewards, employee promotion, training.

**2** Two steps from: establish breach of contract, investigate the breach of contract, disciplinary hearing.

**3** Two ways from: develop the way employees think, improve the way people think, develops employee confidence.

## Exam practice questions

### Paper 1

**a i** Recruitment is the attraction, appraisal and selection of the right person to meet the employment needs of an organisation.

**a ii** Appraisal is an assessment of an employee's performance at work against an agreed set of targets between a worker and their line manager.

## Solar Solutions question 2 answer

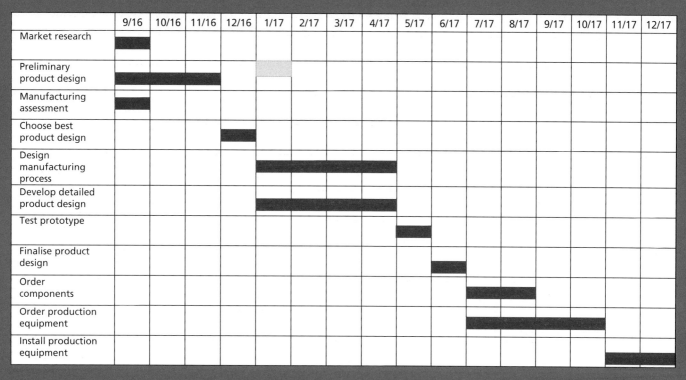

| | 9/16 | 10/16 | 11/16 | 12/16 | 1/17 | 2/17 | 3/17 | 4/17 | 5/17 | 6/17 | 7/17 | 8/17 | 9/17 | 10/17 | 11/17 | 12/17 |
|---|---|---|---|---|---|---|---|---|---|---|---|---|---|---|---|---|
| Market research | ■ | | | | | | | | | | | | | | | |
| Preliminary product design | ■ | ■ | ■ | | ░ | | | | | | | | | | | |
| Manufacturing assessment | ■ | | | | | | | | | | | | | | | |
| Choose best product design | | | | ■ | | | | | | | | | | | | |
| Design manufacturing process | | | | | | ■ | ■ | ■ | | | | | | | | |
| Develop detailed product design | | | | | | ■ | ■ | | | | | | | | | |
| Test prototype | | | | | | | | | ■ | | | | | | | |
| Finalise product design | | | | | | | | | | ■ | | | | | | |
| Order components | | | | | | | | | | | ■ | ■ | | | | |
| Order production equipment | | | | | | | | | | | ■ | ■ | ■ | | | |
| Install production equipment | | | | | | | | | | | | | | | ■ | ■ |

**b** Two benefits from: business controls the training, specific to the business, cost stays within the business.

### Paper 2

**a** A human resource plan is where a business sets out how many employees it needs with the appropriate skills to achieve the businesses corporate aims.

**b** Two elements from: establish corporate aims, human resource audit, forecast employees required, forecast skills required.

**c** Two reasons from: specialist employees, lower fixed costs, concentration on core functions.

**d** Benefits of international recruitment: more choice of workers, lower wages, access to more skilled workers, new ideas. Evaluation: cultural differences, language barriers, regulations.

## 2.2 Case study progress questions

### Qantas

**1** A hierarchical organisation structure is based on different levels of authority that exist in the organisation.

**2** The process: reducing the layers of hierarchy, fewer managers, wider span of control.

**3** Reduces costs: lower management salaries.

### Kentucky Fried Chicken

**1** Delegation is decision-making responsibility being passed down the chain of command to someone with a lower level of seniority.

**2** Two decisions from: hiring employees, employees' hours of work, ordering stock.

**3** Two benefits from: increased motivation of managers, managers know their business, greater decision-making flexibility.

## Exam practice questions

### Paper 1

a  Two factors from: ability of the manager, motivation of employees, business conditions.

b  Two consequences from: lower management costs, increased span of control, more delegation, shorter chain of command.

### Paper 2

a  Matrix organisation structures are used by businesses to manage projects they are working on by drawing on specialist employees from different parts of the business.

b  Two reasons from: slow decision-making, high management costs, reduces bureaucracy.

c  Two characteristics: structure based on different methods of employment, removes traditional hierarchy.

d  Benefits: lower management salaries, motivation of managers, reduced bureaucracy, more flexible decision-making. Evaluation: employee and management resistance, needs capable managers, increases management workload.

## 2.3 Case study progress questions

### Martha Stewart Living

1  Leadership style is the manner and approach a manager uses when carrying out their key management functions.

2  Two situations from: crisis/ difficult situations, quick problem solution, workers who want clear direction.

3  Leadership depends on: task, situation and the employees being managed.

### Gap

1  Two cultural factors from: language, customs, response to authority.

2  Ethical issues: treatment of employees, management systems, management methods, conduct of managers, management decisions. Evaluation: other factors that influence management issues - different management situations, corporate culture, market situation.

## Exam practice questions

### Paper 1

a  Two characteristics from: decentralised management, two-way communication, delegation.

b  Two factors from: increased employee motivation, employee contribution to decision making, improved communication with employees.

### Paper 2

a  Laissez-faire management is an approach that involves the full delegation of most of the day-to-day decision-making to employees.

b  Two reasons: delegation, personality factors.

c  Two reasons: skill of the employees, nature of the work.

d  Management challenges: conflict with employees, management of employees, impact on customers/ brand image, relationship with other managers. Evaluation: health and safety, nature of work, manager's personality.

## 2.4 Case study progress questions

### Google

1  Hygiene factors: good working conditions – childcare, free meals; competitive pay rates.

2  Two motivating factors from: responsibility, promotion, quality of the work, achievement at work.

3  Usefulness of human relations approach: understands complexity of employee motivation, what motivates different employees, guide to management.

Evaluation: cost of application, difficulty of application, validity of the research.

### Morgan Stanley

1 Profit-related pay is where employees receive a bonus payment on top of their basic pay related to the annual profit the business has made.

2 Two ways: financial reward, employee feels they have contributed to the organisation's success.

3 Benefits of financial incentives: financial reward (Taylor), Status (Maslow), fair reward (Adams). Evaluation: hygiene factor (Herzberg), autonomy/mastery (Pink).

## Exam practice questions

### Paper 1

a Two ways from: autonomy, purpose, mastery.

b Two non-financial factors from: empowerment through trust, autonomy, involved in decision-making.

### Paper 2

a Annual labour turnover in an organisation measures the rate at which employees are leaving an organisation in one year.

b Two factors from: low pay, boring work, poor conditions.

c Two reasons from: autocratic leadership, inconsistent management, employee favouritism.

d Employee motivation is increased by job enrichment (range and complexity of tasks), job enlargement (range of tasks), job rotation (movement between tasks). Evaluation: cost, ability of employees, corporate culture.

## 2.5 Case study progress questions

### SolarCity

1 Organisational/corporate culture is the values, philosophy and behaviour of the people who work in an organisation.

2 Two characteristics: military backgrounds, environmentally conscious, socially responsibility.

3 Two factors from: ownership, nature of employee, government influence.

### Gillette, and P&G

1 Two reasons for culture clashes: communication method, decision-making approach.

2 Two possible consequences: reduces productivity, negative corporate image, increased labour turnover.

## Exam practice questions

### Paper 1

a Two characteristics from: bureaucratic, formal hierarchy, precise roles, slow decision-making.

b Two consequences from: low productivity, slow decisions, poor corporate image, high labour turnover.

### Paper 2

a A power culture is decision-making centralised around the CEO or a few senior managers who have a great deal of control over the organisation.

b Two characteristics: autocratic CEO, high pressure working environment.

c Two ways: personality of the CEO, nature of the employees.

d Reasons for success: competitive workplace, financial incentives, fear of failure, direction and control of the CEO. Evaluation: market factors, could be more successful with a different culture, sustainability of success.

## Key Concept question

Ethics: management approach ethical decisions, ethical attitude of employees. Innovation: management attitude to product and production development, employees' reaction to innovation. Evaluation: relative importance of corporate culture in affecting ethics and innovation compared to other factors such as financial situation and government regulation.

# 3.1

## 2.6 Case study progress questions

### IG Metall

1 A trade union is an organisation set up by employees to represent the views and protect the rights of those employees.

2 Two roles from: representing employees, safety and security, organising industrial action, negotiating pay and conditions.

3 Useful for small employers who can negotiate collectively.

### French air traffic control unions SNCTA and UNSA

1 Strike action is where unions instruct their members to stop working for a certain period of time.

2 Two other methods from: slowdown/go slow, work to rule, overtime ban.

3 Two reasons: poor pay and conditions, passenger safety, threats to labour laws.

## Exam practice questions

### Paper 1

a Two ways: single union agreement, employees attending board meetings.

b Two reasons for operators: job losses, loss of independence.

### Paper 2

a Collective bargaining is where employer's negotiating team negotiate on behalf of the business with the representative trade union on the pay and conditions of employees.

b Two reasons from conflict: abrasive management style, poor communication, threat of change.

c Employees involved in decision-making, mechanism for conflict resolution.

d HR strategy: agreement and ownership through consultation, planning and timing through documentation, communicating changes through face to face meetings. Evaluation: negative reaction from the workforce, industrial action, slow decision-making process.

## 3.1 Case study progress questions

### AIROD

1 Two sources from: personal funds, retained profit, sale of assets.

2 Two reasons from: effective long-term finance, no interest costs, no repayment, outside expertise.

3 Possible implications: no repayment, no interest, political ties.

### Crowdmix

1 Short-term finance is funds a business raises for its normal operational activities that has a repayment period of less than 12 months.

2 Two types from: overdrafts, trade credit, debt factoring.

3 Long-term finance because the business raised funds for a period of more than five years to funds for a major project.

### Exam practice questions

#### Paper 1

a Two finance options from: secured bank loan, leasing, retained profit.

b Two reasons: no initial payment retains cash, access up to date capital.

#### Paper 2

a Trade credit is where a business receives goods or services on credit and agrees to pay for it at a point in the future (normally 30–90 days).

**b** Two problems: high interest rates, can be called in at any time.

**c** Two reasons: no initial payment for up to date capital.

**d** Factors from: length of finance needed, interest costs, nature of investment, need for control, cash flow position. Evaluation: impact the factors have on different stakeholders.

## 3.2 Case study progress questions

### Singapore Airline

**1** A business cost is the monetary value of resources used by a business to produce and sell a good or service.

**2** Cost per unit = total cost / units produced.

**3** Profit = revenue – cost: cost falls, profit rises.

### Taco Bell

**1** Direct costs can be clearly linked to each unit of output produced by a business or a cost centre of the business.

**2** Two examples from: rent, machinery, management salaries, insurance.

**3** Two examples from: administration, HR, marketing, rent.

**4** Fixed costs stay the same and variable costs rise.

## Exam practice questions

### Paper 1

**a** Export licences, shipping and insurance do not change with output.

**b** Two benefits: increased revenue and profit: spreads risk.

### Paper 2

**a** Indirect costs cannot be clearly linked to each unit of output produced by a business of a costs centre of the business.

**b** Two ways: redundancies, negotiate lower rent, better technology to improve efficiency.

**c** Two ways from: source new suppliers, negotiate lower buying price, buy cheaper paper.

**d** Benefits of selling online: lower production cost, increase revenue, spread risk, attract new customers, reaction to competition. Evaluation: reduces the sales of paper goods, high set-up costs.

## 3.3 Case study progress questions

### Frame it

**1** A breakeven chart is a graphical representation of the costs and revenues associated with producing a good or service.

**2** $35 000 / $12.5 - $3.5 = 4 375

**3**

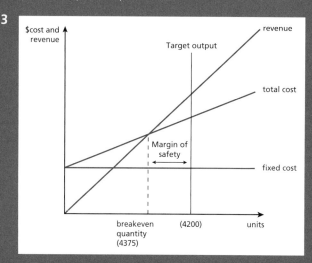

### Alp Dairy

**1** $58 000 / ($0.6 – $0.24) = 161 111

**2** Breakeven output rises, reduces profit.

## Exam practice questions

### Paper 1

**a** $210 000 / $500 – $360 = 1 500

**b** Two ways from: price increase, reduce material cost, reduce labour cost.

### Paper 2

**a** Hotel charges change with output.

**b** $945\,000 - (\$29\,700 + \$486\,000 + \$255\,000) =$
$174\,300$ (profit)

$255\,000 / (\$3\,500 - \$1910) = \$160$ (breakeven)

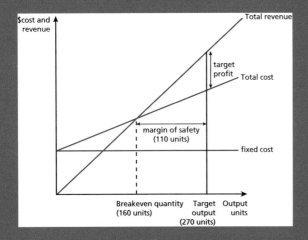

**c** Strengths: decision-making, simplicity, pictorial, flexibility. Evaluation: linear variable costs, linear costs, semi-variable cost, forecasted data.

## 3.4 Case study progress questions

### ARP Mowers

**1** Gross profit is sales revenue less cost of goods sold.

**2**

| Profit and loss account | $m |
|---|---|
| Sales revenue | 75 |
| Direct cost | 32.9 |
| Gross profit | 42.1 |
| Overhead | 16.1 |
| Net profit | 26 |
| Interest | 6.6 |
| Net profit before tax | 19.4 |
| Profit before tax | 4.85 |
| Profit after tax | 14.55 |

### Seetha Cosmetics

**1** The balance sheet is a statement of the value of a business at a particular point in time in terms of its assets, liabilities and equity.

**2** Appear as assets because they are owned by the business.

**3**

| | $000s |
|---|---|
| Fixed assets | |
| Buildings | 140000 |
| Machinery | 110000 |
| | 250000 |
| Current assets | |
| Stock | 25000 |
| Cash | 11000 |
| Debtors | 21000 |
| | 57000 |
| Creditors less than 12 months | 35000 |
| Net current assets | 22000 |
| Loans more than 12 months | 80000 |
| Net assets | 192000 |
| Share capital | 145000 |
| Retained profit | 47000 |
| Total equity | 192000 |

### Delhi Express Coach Travel

**1** $180\,000 - \$70\,000 / 5 = \$22\,000$

**2** Two reasons: simple method, effective for forecasting

## Exam practice questions

Paper 1

**a**

| Profit and loss account | $000s |
|---|---|
| Sales revenue | 830 |
| Direct cost | 390 |
| Gross profit | 440 |
| Overhead | 200 |
| Net profit | 240 |
| Interest | 30 |
| Net profit before tax | 210 |
| Profit before tax | 31.5 |
| Profit after tax | 178.5 |

**b** Dividends to shareholders or retained profit.

**c** Accounting principles: integrity, objectivity, professional competence, confidentiality. Evaluation: problems of applying the principles.

## Paper 2

**a** Fixed assets are the permanent assets of the business used to facilitate its operations.

**b**

|  | $000s |
|---|---|
| Fixed assets |  |
| Buildings | 220 |
| Vehicles | 540 |
|  | 760 |
| Current assets |  |
| Stock | 9 |
| Debtors | 34 |
| Cash | 25 |
|  | 68 |
| Creditors less than 12 months | 14 |
| Net current assets | 54 |
| Loans more than 12 months | 76 |
| Net assets | 738 |
| Share capital | 693 |
| Retained profit | 45 |
| Total equity | 738 |

**c** Funds put into business by the owners.

**d** Usefulness to: shareholders (dividends), workers (job security), banks (repayment), government (tax), suppliers (payment). Evaluation: reliability of figures, non-financial factors, accounting methods.

## 3.5 Case study progress questions

### Clear Site

**1** Gross profit / sales revenue × 100 = gross profit margin;
net profit / sales revenue × 100 = net profit margin.

**2** Gross profit margin is the percentage of gross profit (sales revenue – cost of goods sold) a firm earns on each dollar of sales it makes. Net profit margin is the percentage of net profit (gross profit – expenses) a firm earns on each dollar of sales it makes.

**3** Gross profit margin: 42%; net profit margin: 17.2%; return on capital employed: 5.81%.

### Col Cycles

**1** Net profit margin is the percentage of net profit (gross profit – expenses) a firm earns on each dollar of sales it makes.

**2** Two reasons from: lower sales revenue, higher direct cost, lower selling price.

**3** Methods to increase gross and net profit margin from: increase prices, cut direct costs, cut indirect costs, promotion to increase sales. Evaluation: increasing price reduces sales, cutting costs reduces the quality of the product, cost of promotion.

## Exam practice questions

### Paper 1

**a** Falling acid test and current ratios means Preciso has a deteriorating liquidity position with less current assets to cover its current liabilities.

**b** Two ways from: leasing fixed assets, taking a loan, selling new shares.

### Paper 2

**a** Liquidity is the ease with which a business can turn its assets into cash.

**b** Current ratio: 1.03; acid test 0.20

**c** The ratios are low, which suggests the business is in a weak liquidity position.

**d** Strategies from: leasing fixed assets, taking a loan, selling new shares. Evaluation: cost of leasing assets, interest on a loan, loss of control from selling new shares.

## 3.6 Case study progress questions

### Norton and Teller

**1**

|  | 2014 | 2015 | 2016 |
|---|---|---|---|
| Stock turnover days | 68 days | 76 days | 85 days |

**2** debtor / sales × 365 = debtor days

**3** Creditors demand quicker payment because the business looks riskier.

### Gamer

**1** Cost of goods sold / stock = stock turnover; creditors / cost of goods sold × 365 = creditor days.

**3** Strategies: reduce the stock levels, reduce the credit period, Increase the time it takes to pay. Evaluation: stock out costs, lost credit sales, interest costs.

## Exam practice questions

### Paper 1

**a** Debtor days is the average amount of time it takes customers who have bought goods on credit to pay a business during the accounting year. Creditor days is the average amount of time it takes a business to pay for the goods it has bought on credit from its suppliers during the accounting year.

**b** Debtor days: debtors paying more slowly because they have liquidity problems. Creditor days: Preciso pays more quickly because of tighter credit restrictions from suppliers.

### Paper 2

**a** Creditors is where a business buys stock or services from a supplier and agrees to pay for the stock or services at some point in the future.

**b** Stock turnover: 4.875; debtor days: 13 days; creditor days: 105 days; gearing 33.94%.

**c** Benefits: injections of funds, no interest, no repayment. Evaluation: loss of control, dividend payments.

## 3.7 Case study progress questions

### Davos Dairy Farm

**1** Cash flow is the continuous movement of money in and out of a business resulting from its operations.

**2** Two reasons from: fall in revenue, increase in costs, late payment by debtors.

**3** Two reasons from: funds for investment, security against bankruptcy, funds for payments.

### Angelino's Coffee Shop

**1** Working capital is the short-term liquidity a business has to fund its everyday operations.

**2** Angelino's working capital cycle is the changes in current assets and current liabilities as it buys stock of coffee, produces its product and sells it to consumers.

**3**

| $000s | Jan | Feb | Mar | Apr | May | Jun |
|---|---|---|---|---|---|---|
| Inflow | | | | | | |
| Revenue | 23 | 23 | 23 | 23 | 23 | 23 |
| Outflow | | | | | | |
| Stock buying | 4.3 | 4.3 | 4.3 | 4.3 | 4.3 | 4.3 |
| Wages | 6.2 | 6.2 | 6.2 | 6.2 | 6.2 | 6.2 |
| Indirect expenses | 5.5 | 5.5 | 5.5 | 5.5 | 5.5 | 5.5 |
| Interest | 1 | 1 | 1 | 1 | 1 | 1 |
| New machine | | 9 | | | | |
| Tax | | | | 3 | | |
| Total outflow | 17 | 26 | 17 | 20 | 17 | 17 |
| **Net cash flow** | **6** | **(3)** | **6** | **3** | **6** | **6** |
| Opening balance | 3 | 9 | 6 | 12 | 15 | 21 |
| **Closing balance** | **9** | **6** | **12** | **15** | **21** | **27** |

## Exam practice questions

### Paper 1

**a** Two things from: cash inflows, cash outflows, net cash flows, opening and closing cash balances.

**b** Two strategies from: cutting labour and raw material costs, advertising spending to increase sales, short and long term borrowing.

Paper 2

a The working capital cycle is the constant change in current assets and current liabilities as a business goes through its normal course of trading.

b

| $000s | Jan | Feb | Mar | Apr | May | Jun |
|---|---|---|---|---|---|---|
| Inflow | | | | | | |
| Revenue | 220 | 220 | 220 | 220 | 220 | 220 |
| Outflow | | | | | | |
| Stock buying | 105.3 | 105.3 | 105.3 | 105.3 | 105.3 | 105.3 |
| Wages | 35.2 | 35.2 | 35.2 | 35.2 | 35.2 | 35.2 |
| Indirect expenses | 46.6 | 46.6 | 46.6 | 46.6 | 46.6 | 46.6 |
| Interest | 12 | 12 | 12 | 12 | 12 | 12 |
| New machine | | | | | | 85 |
| Tax | | | | 30 | | |
| Total outflow | 199.1 | 199.1 | 199.1 | 229.1 | 199.1 | 284.1 |
| **Net cash flow** | **20.9** | **20.9** | **20.9** | **(9.1)** | **20.9** | **(64.1)** |
| Opening balance | 20 | 40.9 | 61.8 | 82.7 | 73.6 | 94.5 |
| **Closing balance** | **40.9** | **61.8** | **82.7** | **73.6** | **94.5** | **30.4** |

c A new assets purchase is a significant cash outflow.

d Strategies to improve cash flow problems: cutting labour and raw material costs, advertising spending to increase sales, borrowing, sale and lease machinery. Evaluation: fall in product quality, worker morale falls, cost of advertising, interest payments, cost of leasing.

## 3.8 Case study progress questions

### The Boot Maker

1 Investment is when a business uses funds to buy new capital.

2 Payback: 2 years and 228 days; ARR 18%.

3 Two advantages: simple calculation, useful for comparing projects, for small firms with constrained cash flow.

### Metro Stop

1 The net present value of an investment is the sum of discounted net cash flows of a project less the initial outlay of the investment.

2 NPV: $486 000; 4 years and 9 days.

3 Two advantages from: time value of money, covers the entire project, project comparison.

## Exam practice questions

### Paper 1

a 15% ARR is the average annual net cash flow or profit of an investment project expressed as a percentage of the initial investment. Payback within four years is the time it takes an investment project's net cash inflows to cover the initial outlay of the investment.

b Benefits: covers the entire life of the project, used for comparing projects of different sizes.

### Paper 2

a Two things from: purchase of system, training staff, installation cost.

b ARR: 14.6%; two years 247 days.

c 14.6% ARR is the average annual net cash flow or profit of an investment project expressed as a percentage of the initial investment.

d Strengths of ARR: covers the entire life of the project, used for comparing projects of different sizes. Strengths of payback: simple calculation, useful for comparing projects, for small firms with constrained cash flow. Evaluation: forecasted cash flows, time value of money, non-monetary factors.

## Key Concept question

Globalisation: competition, access to funding, new market opportunities, joint ventures. Innovation: more advanced capital, more advanced products, competition, new market opportunities. Evaluation: significance of different changes, impact on stakeholders, long- and short-term factors.

## 3.9 Case study progress questions

### Carlton Cards

1 A budget is a plan for the future costs, revenues and use of resources by a business.

2 A cost centre is a department within an organisation that does not generate any revenues but is only associated with costs. A profit centre is a department within an organisation that is responsible for generating costs and revenues.

3 Two reasons from: controlling revenue and cost, managing resources effectively, setting targets, measuring performance.

### Ezpectcy Sandwich Shop

1 A variance is where a business has a difference between an actual figure achieved in its operations in an accounting year and a budgeted figure.

**2 and 3**

|  | Budget | Actual | Variance | Favourable or adverse |
|---|---|---|---|---|
| Sales revenue | 65600 | 69430 | 3830 | Favourable |
| Direct materials | 15560 | 19540 | 3980 | Adverse |
| Direct labour | 14870 | 16410 | 1540 | Adverse |
| Gross profit | 35170 | 33480 | 1690 | **Adverse** |
| Indirect expenses | 13150 | 14200 | 1050 | Adverse |
| Net profit | 22020 | 19280 | 2740 | **Adverse** |

4 Revenues are a positive aspect but costs increase by more than the rise in revenue which is a negative aspect.

## Exam practice questions

### Paper 1

a Two ways from: controlling revenue and cost, managing resources effectively, setting targets, measuring performance.

b Two ways from: budgetary control, measuring performance, management of employees against budget.

### Paper 2

a A variance is where a business has a difference between an actual figure achieved in its operations in an accounting year and a budgeted figure.

b

|  | Budget | Actual | Variance | Favourable or adverse |
|---|---|---|---|---|
| Sales revenue | 124600 | 119450 | 5150 | Adverse |
| Direct materials | 38450 | 37560 | 890 | Favourable |
| Direct labour | 42130 | 43230 | 1100 | Adverse |
| Gross profit | 44020 | 38660 | 5360 | **Adverse** |
| Indirect expenses | 26780 | 27970 | 1190 | Adverse |
| Net profit | 17240 | 10690 | 6550 | **Adverse** |

c Two reasons: lower selling price, lower units sold

d Two ways: set targets for corporate aims, provide information to access performance.

## 4.1 Case study progress questions

### Spotify

1 Market orientation is where an organisation uses an outward-looking approach to marketing by focusing on what the consumer wants and producing a product that satisfies this.

2 Two ways: use of market research, responding to changes in consumer tastes.

3 Two differences: importance of customer service, intangible nature of the product.

### Nike

1 Market share is the proportion of total market sales revenue one business's sales revenue accounts for.

2 Total annual sales revenue / market total annual sales revenue × 100.

3 Two benefits from: brand image, economies of scale, bargaining position.

# Exam practice questions

## Paper 1

a Two differences from: tangible nature of books, where books and online content can be accessed, price differences.

b Two consequences: development of a USP, attracts politically minded consumers.

## Paper 2

a Marketing is where a business produces a good or service that satisfies the needs and wants of the customer.

b Two aims from: raise awareness of conflict issues, raise funds, attract support.

c Two differences: broader scope of objectives, non-financial objectives

d Ethical: raising awareness of issues, honesty of presentation, nature of promotion. Cultural: nature of promotion, sensitivity of presentation. Evaluation: conflict between cultural and ethical marketing objectives, conflict between wider marketing objectives and cultural and ethical objectives.

### Key Concept question

Innovation: new products, changes in price, promotional methods, changes in distribution. Ethics: types of product sold, prices charged, nature of promotion, where the product is sold. Evaluation: other factors that affect strategy, market share, sales and profits.

## 4.2 Case study progress questions

### Rolex

1 A marketing plan is where a business sets out the marketing strategies and tactics it is going to use to achieve its marketing objectives.

2 Two aspects from: PESTLE analysis, SWOT analysis, market research, marketing objectives.

3 Analysis of premium price and high-quality product.

### R.L. Bhatia & Co

1 A target market is the group of consumers a business is looking to sell its good or service to.

2 Two characteristics from: cricketers, male, domestic and export market.

3 Two profiles from: young school cricketer, professional cricketer, leisure cricketer.

## Exam practice questions

### Mast Chocolate

1 A unique selling point (USP) is the key factor that differentiates a good or service from the competing products in the market.

2 Two ways from: high quality of the product, promotion, high price.

3 Two changes: desire for a high quality product, want to buy a product from a specialist business.

### Paper 1

a Two segments: non-fiction reader, fiction reader.

b Two ways: development of marketing mix, setting target segment, understanding of the product relative to the competition.

### Paper 2

a A unique selling point (USP) is the key factor that differentiates a good or service from the competing products in the market.

# 4.3

**b** Two reasons from: narrower target market, less competition, growing market.

**c** Promotion: adverting targeted at parents of children under five, selling through retailers that sell to parents of children under five.

**d** For parents of children under five and people who care about recycling. Similarities and differences between the product, pricing, promotion and distribution methods used.

## 4.3 Case study progress questions

### Chill-out

**1** Sales forecasting is where business uses data and other information to predict future sales.

**2**

| Year | Sales revenue $000s | 3 year moving average |
|---|---|---|
| 2011 | 45 | |
| 2012 | 56 | 55 |
| 2013 | 64 | 59 |
| 2014 | 58 | 62 |
| 2015 | 65 | 62 |
| 2016 | 64 | |

**3**

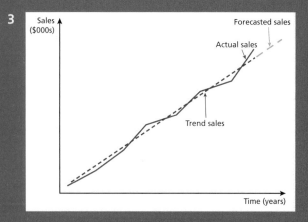

**4** Trend: increasing sales.

## Genius Gift Cards

### 1, 3

| Year | Quarter | Sales revenue ($000000s) | 4 Quarter moving total | 8 Quarter moving total | Quarterly moving average | Seasonal variation |
|---|---|---|---|---|---|---|
| 2014 | 4 | 27 | | | | |
| 2015 | 1 | 16 | | | | |
| | 2 | 19 | | | 21.13 | −2.13 |
| | 3 | 22 | 84 | | 21.13 | 0.87 |
| | 4 | 28 | 85 | 169 | 20.88 | 7.12 |
| 2016 | 1 | 15 | 84 | 169 | 20.5 | −5.5 |
| | 2 | 18 | 83 | 167 | 20.38 | −2.38 |
| | 3 | 20 | 81 | 164 | | |
| | 4 | 29 | 82 | 163 | | |

**2**

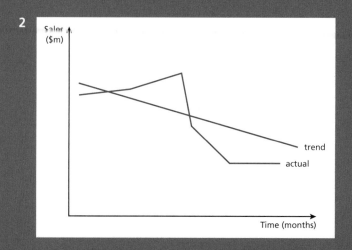

**3** The trend in sales is downwards.

## Exam practice questions

### Paper 1

**a** Two reasons from: forecast future resource needs, forecast profits, set budgets.

**b** Two limitations from: accuracy of forecasts, changes in price, non-monetary factors.

## Paper 2

**a** A four-part moving average means calculating a mean average over a four period time in a series of data.

**b, c**

| Year | Quarter | Sales revenue $000s | 4 Quarter moving total | 8 Quarter moving total | Quarterly moving average | Seasonal variation |
|------|---------|---------------------|------------------------|------------------------|--------------------------|--------------------|
| **2015** | 1 | 36 | | | | |
| | 2 | 18 | | | | |
| | 3 | 16 | | | 22.5 | −6.5 |
| | 4 | 22 | 92 | | 21.88 | 0.12 |
| **2016** | 1 | 32 | 88 | 180 | 21.63 | 10.37 |
| | 2 | 17 | 87 | 175 | 21.38 | −4.38 |
| | 3 | 15 | 86 | 173 | | |
| | 4 | 21 | 85 | 171 | | |

**d** Benefits of sales forecasting: forecast future resource needs, forecast profits, set budgets. Evaluation: accuracy of forecasts, changes in price, non-monetary factors.

## 4.4 Case study progress questions

### Twitter

**1a** Market research is a process where organisations collect information about the consumers and the market they are selling their product to.

**1b** Secondary market research is where a business uses data and material prepared by an outside source to generate market research information.

**2** Two methods from: market analyses, academic journals, government publications, media articles.

**3** Two benefits from: specific to the marketing objective, control over data collection, better for qualitative information.

### Fujitsu

**1** A focus group is where a business selects a group of people to obtain qualitative market research information.

**2** Two reasons from: specific information to the business, generates new ideas, source of qualitative information.

**3** Quota sampling: gathering information from a chosen group based on certain criteria. Snowballing: People chosen to be part of a sample are used to recruit other people to form a larger sampled group.

**4** Two difficulties from: cost, time consuming, needs a relatively large sample.

## Exam practice questions

### Paper 1

**a** Two reasons from: useful for statistical analysis, used for comparison over time, objective results.

**b** Two limitations from: sampling problems, cost, honesty of respondents, interpreting results.

### Paper 2

**a** Secondary market research is where a business uses data and material prepared by an outside source to generate market research information.

**b** Two reasons: specialist information, up-to-date.

**c** Two methods from: academic journals, government publications, media articles.

**d** Strengths of secondary research: wide coverage of the market, relatively low cost, provided by specialist sources, quick information. Evaluation: not specific to the research objective, reliability of sources, no control over data collection.

## 4.5 Case study progress questions

### Colgate-Palmolive Company

**1** The product life cycle is the change in the sales revenue of a product as it moves through different phases in its life.

# 4.6

2 Two elements from: introduction, growth, maturity, decline.

3 Two ways from: managing the marketing mix, extension strategies, cash flow management.

## Walt Disney Company

1 A brand is where a business creates an identity for its good or service through its marketing characteristics.

2 Brand loyalty: long-term sales. Brand value: higher selling price.

3 Benefits of branding: attracts consumers, develops consumer loyalty, can be used for new products, creates a USP, achieve a higher selling price. Evaluation: other factors that make Walt Disney successful such as product quality and effective promotion.

## Sony PlayStation

1 Skimming is where a business sets an initially high price to attract consumers who like to buy products when they are first launched.

2 Two reasons: profit to cover development costs, consumers willing to pay a high price.

3 Two pricing strategies from: cost plus pricing, penetration pricing, psychological pricing.

## VTM

1 Guerrilla marketing is promotion that uses unconventional methods to raise consumer awareness.

2 Two advantages: wide audience, low cost.

3 Two other methods: viral marketing, social media marketing.

## Exam practice questions

### Paper 1

a Two methods from: costs plus pricing, market skimming, psychological pricing, price discrimination.

b Two problems from: low profit margins, makes the product look poor-quality.

### Paper 2

a The marketing mix is the way organisations use, product, price, promotion and place as part of their marketing plan.

b Above-the-line promotion is where businesses use mass media to promote brands to their target market. Below-the-line promotion is where an organisation uses techniques that allow it to reach its target market more directly than using mass media.

c Two reasons from: opportunity to sell in bulk, knowledge of the market.

d Strengths of Boston Matrix: assesses the market position of products, strategy for all products a business sells, long-term planning, cash flow management. Evaluation: based on average changes in products sales, problems of forecasting, changes in external factors.

## 4.6 Case study progress questions

### Costco

1 The people element of the marketing mix is the way employees and managers of an organisation interact with its customers.

2 Two reasons from: direct service, after-sales service, complaints.

3 Two benefits from: improves brand image, USP, better service attracts customers, customer loyalty.

### McDonald's

1 Processes are the procedures, methods and policies a business puts into place when a good or service is being provided to the consumer.

2 Two elements from: taking orders, preparing food, serving meals, taking payment.

3 Two benefits from: quality of the product, meeting consumer expectations, brand image.

## Exam practice questions

### Paper 1

a Two reasons from: improves brand image, USP, better service attracts customers, customer loyalty.

b Two ways from: training, effective management, use of incentives.

### Paper 2

a Physical evidence is the physical environment in service-based organisations where the service is delivered to the customer.

b Two ways from: 24 opening hours, equipment, software, trainers.

c Two possible elements from: organising membership, taking payment, changing facilities, servicing equipment, use of trainers.

d Importance of extended marking mix: attracts customers, customer experience/satisfaction, USP, brand image, brand loyalty. Evaluation: importance of price, promotion and place.

## 4.7 Case study progress questions

### Coca-Cola and Endomondo

1 A joint venture is where two businesses enter into an agreement to create a separate entity to manage a particular project.

2 Two benefits from the joint venture – Coca-Cola's: brand name, network, global experience.

3 Two benefits from the joint venture – Endomondo's: health image, social media network, access to fitness market.

### Cath Kidston

1 Two opportunities: sales growth, brand awareness, spreading risk, economies of scale.

2 Two threats: different consumer tastes, regulations, exchange rates, competition.

3 Two elements from: product, price, promotion, place.

## Exam practice questions

### Paper 1

a Two reasons from: sales growth, brand awareness, spreading risk, economies of scale.

b Two cultural factors from: language, manner and custom, beliefs and value.

### Paper 2

a International marketing is where a business develops a marketing plan to sell its goods and services in different countries.

b Two methods from: exporting, producing abroad, joint venture, licensing, franchising.

c Promotion: language/culture. Pricing: competition/incomes.

d Benefits of expanding into international markets: sales growth, brand awareness, spreading risk, economies of scale. Evaluation: different consumer tastes, regulations, exchange rates, competition.

## Key Concept question

How cultures (language, manner and custom, beliefs and value) affect the international marketing strategy (objectives, market research, marketing mix). Evaluation: relative importance of cultural factors compared to factors such competition, corporate culture, brand image.

## 4.8 Case study progress questions

### HSBC

1 E-commerce is where a business uses the internet and electronic media as part of its marketing of its goods and services.

# 5.1

**2** Two ways from: international exposure, interaction with customer, personalisation, information gathering.

**3** Promotion: use of social media. Product: range of online services.

## eBay

**1** Business-to-consumer (B2C) is where goods and services are directly market by businesses to final consumers.

**2** Two characteristics: consumers trade with each other, use of online marketing.

**3** Benefits include access to consumers, reduced cost of selling, new promotional opportunities.

## Exam practice questions

### Paper 1

**a** Two aspects: business-to-consumer marketing, online books, online promotion.

**b** Two costs from: falling sales of books, falling prices and profit margins, more competition.

### Paper 2

**a** Business-to-business (B2B) is where businesses directly market goods and services to other businesses using the internet.

**b** Product: efficiency of booking. Place: shows broadcast through cinemas.

**c** Online adverting, use of social media, opportunity to show clips of shows.

**d** Benefits of e-commerce: increased access to consumers, knowledge of consumers, promotional opportunities, new products, internet booking. Evaluation: set up costs, internet security, online shows reduce demand for live shows.

## 5.1 Case study progress questions

### Costa Coffee

**1** Operations management is the way a business plans, organises and coordinates its use of resources to produce its good or service.

**2** Human resources: interaction between employees and customers. Marketing: importance of the 'process'/ product aspect of the marketing mix.

**3** Two ways from: ordering and delivering stock, service provision, customer service.

### Samsung

**1** Ecological sustainability is business activity that does not disrupt the physical environment's ability to meet the needs of people in the future.

**2** Social sustainability is business activity that satisfies the needs of individuals in society in the short term and the long term. Economic sustainability is business activity that enables a business to maintain production in the future and contribute to the economic activity of a country in the long term.

**3** Importance of sustainability: positive publicity, attracts employees, meets government regulations, attractive to consumers, relationships with local community. Evaluation: increased production cost, loss of competitive advantage, limits products that can be produced.

## Exam practice questions

### Paper 1

**a** Two functions: to ensure production efficiency, product quality.

**b** Two ways: investment costs, production costs, need to raise finance.

## Paper 2

a Economic sustainability is business activity that enables a business to maintain production in the future and contribute to the economic activity of a country in the long term.

b Two reasons: increase efficiency, ensure product quality.

c Two ways from: pollution from their plants, environment effects of building plants.

d Ecological: reduced pollution. Social: loss of benefits to the local community. Economics: loss of jobs. Evaluation: significance of positive and negative consequences.

## 5.2 Case study progress questions

### Church Shoes

1 A production method is the processes an organisation uses to turn resource inputs into a final good or service.

2 Batch production is where a business produces a set number of units of a good where the units move through each stage of the production process at the same time.

3 Two characteristics: short production runs, flexible, small/medium-sized manufacturing.

### Woods Bagot

1 Job production is where a business produces a specific unit to meet the wants and needs of a particular customer.

2 Two characteristics from: individual customer jobs, skilled labour, higher prices, smaller businesses.

3 Two reasons: nature of architecture work, skilled labour needed.

## Exam practice questions

### Paper 1

a Two characteristics from: modular capital organisation, team working, job enrichment.

b Two reasons: increased efficiency, motivation of employees.

### Paper 2

a Flow production is used in mass production when very large numbers of the same product pass continuously through each stage of production.

b Two characteristics: large-scale manufacturing, continuous production, low unit costs, capital intensive.

c Two reasons: to be price competitive, to increase profit margins.

d Advantages of the move to cell production: increased efficiency, motivation of employees, improve product quality. Evaluation: investment costs, disruption to production, higher operating costs.

## 5.3 Case study progress questions

### Toyota

1 Lean production is an approach to production that focuses on eliminating waste from all aspects of the production process.

2 Two aspects from: waste reduction, continuous improvement, JIT.

3 Kanban is a stock control system based on coloured cards that signal to production line workers when more stock is needed to maintain production. Andon is a manufacturing system used to identify and signal when there is quality or process problem on the production line.

# 5.5

### Boeing

**1** Quality control is continuously monitoring the goods and services produced by a business to ensure they meet a set standard.

**2** Two aspects from: setting quality standard, set production policies, continuous quality checking.

**3** Two ways from: small teams of employees, regular meetings, aim to improve quality, training in quality assurance.

**4** Two reasons from: importance of safety in the industry, competition, customer satisfaction.

## Exam practice questions

### Paper 1

**a** Two characteristics from: continuous improvements to production, data analysis of production, managers and employees work together.

**b** Two ways from: appraisal of current quality standards, research into industry standards, strategy to raise standards to industry level.

### Paper 2

**a** Quality circles are groups or teams of workers organised by a business to identify and offer solutions to quality issues.

**b** Two characteristics from: focusing on the consumer, continuous work to improve quality, setting quality standards.

**c** Group work and responsibility empowers workers.

**d** Benefits: greater efficiency, lower costs, empowered workers, improved product quality. Evaluation: costs of implementation, pressure on employees, cost of hiring and training quality staff.

## 5.4 Case study progress questions

### BASF

**1** Two factors from: in an expanding market, low production costs, access to raw materials.

**2** Two reasons: rise in sales from new market, lower production costs in Bangladesh.

### Thomas Cook

**1** Outsourcing is a where a business subcontracts areas of production to an outside producer.

**2** Two reasons from: specialist business is more efficient, reduced indirect costs, reduced fixed costs.

**3** Two ways: increased efficiency raise numbers booking, sales connections of outsource firm.

## Exam practice questions

### Paper 1

**a** Two ways from: specialist business is more efficient, reduced indirect costs, reduced fixed costs.

**b** Two disadvantages from: loss of control, cost of the outsource firm, fall in quality of outsourced transport.

### Paper 2

**a** Offshoring is when a business moves a business activity to another country.

**b** Two reasons from: lower production costs, lower taxes, fewer rules and regulations, access to overseas markets.

**c** Two problems from: loss of control, cost of outsourcing, quality of outsourced output.

**d** Benefits of insourcing: regain control, cost saved on outsourced activity, control over security. Evaluation: fixed cost of insource activity, indirect cost, employees spend less time on core activities.

## 5.5 Case study progress questions

### Dell

**1** The supply chain is the series of links between a business and its suppliers that allow the production of a product and its distribution to consumers.

**2** Two aspects from: buy components, manufacture computers, sell computers to customers.

3 Two benefits from: reduce storage costs, reduces insurance costs, reduces management costs.

## Nissan

1 Productivity rate is a measure of business efficiency that is expressed as output per unit of resource input.

2 It measured annual output per worker.

3 Use the equation: actual output per year / maximum capacity output per year $\times$ 100 = capacity utilisation rate.

## Exam practice questions

### Paper 1

a Direct labour costs are labour costs that can be clearly linked to each unit of output produced by a business

b i $1150000

b ii $1100000

c Financial: the buy decision is lower cost. Non-financial: supplier expertise, no fixed cost of machinery, lacks capacity to produce.

### Paper 2

a A stock control chart is a model that shows a business how the stock level of an organisation changes overtime.

b i 9 units

b ii 4 weeks

b iii 15 weeks

c Buffer stock is the minimum level of stock a business holds.

d Benefits of JIT: reduce storage costs, reduces insurance costs, reduces management costs, improves productive efficiency. Evaluation: loss sales from running out of stock, increased pressure on employees.

## 5.6 Case study progress questions

### Ford

1 Research and development (R&D) is where an organisation uses resources to explore ways to innovate new products and methods of production.

2 Two reasons from: meet changes in consumer taste, to be competitive, reaction to advances in technology, develop new production system.

### Fitbit

1 Innovative creativity is innovation where a business develops a new product to meet consumer needs or unmet needs.

2 Two types from: production, process, positioning, paradigm.

3 Cost of innovation, risk of failure.

## Exam practice questions

### Paper 1

a Two types from: production, process, positioning, paradigm.

b Two ways from: increased competition, technological advances in the industry, changes in consumer tastes.

### Paper 2

a Adaptive creativity is innovation is where an organisation develops existing products in response to changes in market conditions.

b Two types from: production, process, positioning, paradigm.

c Two ways from: new products, better products, lower costs allow for lower prices.

d Benefits: meet changes in consumer taste, to be competitive, reaction to advances in technology, develop new production system. Evaluation: cost, risk of failure, need for skilled employees.

# 5.7

## 5.7 Case study progress questions

### BP

1 A contingency plan is a written statement of policies and procedures an organisation will put into place in a crisis situation.

2 Transparency: clear information for stakeholders. Communication: clear statement of the management's reaction to the crisis to the stakeholders.

3 Two consequences from: bad publicity, government penalties, higher costs.

## Exam practice questions

### Paper 1

a Two elements from: write policies, write procedures, communicate with stakeholders, staff training.

b Two benefits from: reduces cost of a crisis, contains a crisis, manage risk, assessment of risk.

### Paper 2

a Crisis management is the process an organisation uses to manage an emergency situation effectively.

b Two elements from: write policies, write procedures, communicate with stakeholders, staff training.

c Two problems from: higher costs, bad publicity, government penalties.

d Benefits: reduces cost of a crisis, contains a crisis, manage risk, assessment of risk. Evaluation: cost of the plan, creates bureaucracy, risk aversion.

# Glossary

**Ansoff's** Matrix a business strategy tool used by management to develop a marketing plan.

**Appraisal** The assessment of an employee's performance at work against an agreed set of targets between the worker and their line manager.

**Arbitration** Here a third party court is called into an industrial dispute to make a judgement on the dispute that has to be followed by both parties.

**Autocratic leadership** Where a leader keeps strict centralised control over decision making, communication, information and the workers they manage.

**Bureaucracy** The rules, policies and procedures that exist in an organisation.

**Business plan** A formal document that describes the business, sets out its objectives and strategy, identifies its market and provides its financial forecasts.

**Business** An organisation that brings together resources to produce goods and services that are sold to customers.

**Business angels** These are wealthy individual investors who use their own funds to invest in small and medium sized companies.

**Business cost** A monetary value of resources used by a business to produce and sell a good or service.

**Business function organisation structure** An organisation structure based on the different functions of a business.

**Business functions** Different aspects of business operations that can be put into four different areas: human resources, finance, marketing and operations.

**Business product organisation structure** An organisation structure based on the different products produced by a business.

**Capital expenditure** Spending by businesses on assets that can be used by the business to support its operation in the long term.

**Centralisation** Where the senior management of an organisation maintains a high level of control over decision making in the organisation.

**Chain of command** The link between the manager who has overall responsibility for making a decision and the employees who are responsible for carrying out the decision.

**Changes of contract** An employer changes the contract of employment of an employee, such as making workers go on one-year contract.

**Charity** A not-for-profit organization set up to provide money and support to people in need.

**Collective bargaining** Unions negotiate on behalf of their members with employer's representatives on pay and conditions of employees.

**Commission** Payment to sales people made on the value or volume of sales they make.

**Conciliation** Where a third party is called into conflict situation where there is an industrial dispute to help the employer and the trade union to provide a compromise solution that both parties agree to.

**Cooperative** An organisation jointly owned by a group of people (members) who democratically run the organisation to meet the needs and aspirations of its members.

**Corporate aims** the long-term goals that a business wants to achieve in the future.

**Corporate culture** The values, philosophy and behaviour of the people who work in an organisation.

**Corporate social responsibility CSR** where the organisation considers the interests of society by taking responsibility for the effects their decisions and activities on customers, employees, communities and the environment.

**Cost centre** An area of the business which is responsible for generating expenses.

**Debentures** Unit loans sold by the business to lenders to raise long term loan funding.

301

**Debt factoring** A business can sell the debts that are owed to it by customers to a debt factoring agency.

**Decentralisation** Where the CEO and senior management delegate decision making responsibility to managers in different areas of the business.

**Decision tree** A tool used by organisations to assess the different possible financial outcomes of a particular decision.

**Delayering** Where the senior managers of the organisation remove layers from the organisational hierarchy to make it 'flatter'.

**Delegation** Involves decision making responsibility being passed down the chain of command to someone with a lower level of seniority.

**Democratic leadership** Involves decentralised management where employees are given some role in decision making through delegation.

**Direct costs** Costs that can be clearly linked to each unit of output produced by a business or a cost centre of the business.

**Diseconomies of scale** The cost disadvantages that result from the increase in the size of an organisation.

**Economic factor** Relates to resource allocation in individual markets and in the wider country.

**Economic growth** Rise in output of goods and services produced by a country in a given time period.

**Economies of scale** The cost advantages firms benefit from as their scale of production increase

**Effective communication** When information is transmitted by the sender and received and understood by the receiver.

**Employee share ownership schemes** Employees receive a financial reward above their normal pay in the form of shares in the business.

**Empowerment** Workers are delegated a greater role in decision making which gives more autonomy and control over their work.

**Entrepreneur** An individual that sees a business opportunity in the form of consumer want and then brings together human, physical and financial resources to produce a product to satisfy that want.

**Environmental factor** Based on the land and living things that society exists in.

**Ethical factor** Based on the values held by people in society

**Exchange rate** The price of one country's currency in terms of another.

**Expected values** Used in a decision tree model to assess a decision's financial outcome by multiplying its probability and forecasted financial outcome

**External growth** When a business grows by joining together with other organisations through mergers, takeovers, joint ventures and strategic alliances.

**External stakeholders** Are people, groups and organisations that are outside the organization that are affected by an organisation's decisions such as suppliers.

**Fishbone diagram** A diagram method used to set out the cause and effect of a business issue or problem.

**Fixed** Cost that do not change as a business changes output.

**Flat/horizontal organisation structures** An organisation structure that has few levels in its hierarchy.

**Force field analysis** A model that attempts to assess the relative importance of different environmental factors that impact on business strategy when managing change.

**Franchise** where a business (a franchiser) sells the rights to produce a good or service under its brand name to another business (a franchisee).

**Fringe payments (perks)** Sometimes called 'perks' they involve non-money payments such as company cars, private healthcare, pension and discounts on the firm's products.

**Gantt chart** A planning tool used to make the management of activities during business projects as effective as possible.

**Globalisation** The increasing international influence in the business environment in terms of growth in international trade, movement of labour and influence of multinational organisations.

**Grants** This is an amount of money given to a business that does not have to be repaid which is used fund a particular project or activity.

**Hierarchical organisation structure** An organisation structure based on different levels of authority that exist in the organisation.

**Human resource plan** When an organisation sets the objective of having the right number of employees with the appropriate skills to achieve the businesses corporate aims.

**Indirect cost/overheads** Costs that cannot be clearly linked to each unit of output produced by a business of a costs centre of the business.

**Industrial action** When employees are in dispute with their employers, trade unions negotiate with the employers to try and resolve the dispute.

**Inflation** Rise in the overall price level of an economy in a given time period.

**Interest rate** Cost of borrowing and the reward for lending money over time.

**Internal growth** Sometimes called organic growth and is where an organisation increases in scale using its own resources.

**Internal stakeholders** Are stakeholders who are part of the organization such as employees.

**Intrapreneur** Someone who works within a business in an 'entrepreneurial' way to develop the firm's product to attract new consumers.

**Job enlargement** The work of an employee remains basically the same but the number and variety of tasks is increased so that the worker does not have to do the same task over and over again.

**Job enrichment** Changes an employee's job to increase the range and complexity of tasks they have along with giving them greater responsibility and autonomy.

**Job rotation** Where there are a number of similar tasks in a particular area of a business, workers are periodically moved between those tasks.

**Joint venture** Where two businesses enter into an agreement to create a separate entity to manage a particular project.

**Labour turnover** Measures the rate at which employees are leaving an organisation in one year.

**Laissez-faire leadership** An approach which involved the full delegation of most of the day-to-day decision making to employees.

**Leader** Someone in an organisation who employees choose to follow.

**Leasing** This is used by a firm to acquire assets like vehicles without having to purchase them but make a series of payments over the lease period.

**Legal factor** Are the laws, rules and regulations that organisations have to follow.

**Loan capital** These are long term loans businesses receive that have a set repayment period (more than one year), have interest costs and are often secured against an asset.

**Lock-outs** An employer can prevent employees from entering the premises to do their work.

**Long term finance** Where a business raise funds for a period of more than 5 years to funds major projects and growth of the business.

**Manager** Someone appointed by an organisation to be in charge of a group of employees to achieve a particular objective.

**Matrix organisation structures** Organisation structures that are developed to deal with particular projects an organisation is working on.

**Medium term finance** Where a business raises funds for a period of 3 to 5 years to fund particular projects.

**Merger** This is where two firms agree to join together under a single legal identity.

**Microfinance** Providing financial services for poor and low-income customers who do not have access to normal banking services.

**Mission statement** where an organisation formally sets out and publicises its core objectives.

**Multinational** a business that has an operational base in more than one country.

**Non-governmental organisations** Are legally constituted not-for-profit organisations that support issues in the public good.

**No-strike agreement** This is where a trade union agrees not to strike in return for greater involvement is a business' decision making process.

**Objectives** the step-by-step targets a business needs to achieve from different parts of the business to achieve its corporate aims.

**Offshoring** Where a business relocates a human resource activity done in one country to another country.

**Organisational structure** The formal human resource framework of a business which sets out how managers and employees are linked together and the way authority is passed through an organisation.

**Outsourcing** A human resource strategy where a business contracts out an activity to another business.

**Overdrafts** A short term bank loan where a business is allowed to draw more money from it account than there is in the account.

**Overtime ban** Unions stop workers completing extra work outside their contracted hours of work.

**Partnership** A business where two or more individuals jointly own and take responsibility for the enterprise.

**Paternalistic leadership** An autocratic leader who has a controlling presence who 'cares' and looks after their employees.

**Performance related pay** A payment system where employees receive extra payment on top of their salary to reward them for good performance in their job.

**Personal funds** When a sole trader uses their own money to put finance into a business.

**Person culture** Decision making is focused on specific individual and exists to benefit those individual rather than wider business objectives.

**Political factor** How governments influence organisations at local, national and international level.

**Power culture** Decision making is centralised around the CEO or a few senior managers who have a great deal of control over the organisation.

**Private company** A business that has shareholders who are invited to buy shares in the business by the existing owners.

**Private sector** Made up of business and organisations owned and controlled by individuals or groups of individuals.

**Profit-related pay** Where employees receive a bonus payment on top of their basic pay related to the annual profit the business has made.

**Public limited company** Private sector businesses that sell their shares on a stock exchange.

**Public-private partnerships** Where a public sector organisation has a contract with a private sector business to support the provision of a public service.

**Public sector** Made up of organisations that are primarily financed and controlled by a country's government.

**Recruitment** The attraction, appraisal and selection of the right person to meet the employment needs of an organisation

**Redundancy** Where a worker leaves a business because their job is no longer required by the business.

**Regional organisation structure** An organisation structure based on the different regions a business operates in.

**Re-shoring** Where the human resource activities of a business are brought back to the country of origin

**Retained profit** Profit made by a firm after tax and payments have been made to shareholders

**Revenue** The income a business receives from selling its products.

**Revenue expenditure** Spending by businesses on the costs incurred by the business to generate its revenue.

**Revenue stream** The different ways a business generates income from its activities.

**Role culture** Decision making is based on a small number of senior management positions where the position rather than the person has control.

**Salary** Fixed amount of pay made to permanent employees on a monthly or annual basis.

**Sale of assets** Finance generated by selling things like equipment, land and buildings.

**Secured loan** Where the value of the loan is covered by the value of a borrower's asset and if the loan is not repaid the lender takes the asset in place of the outstanding debt.

**Semi-variable** Costs that can change with output but the but not in a direct way because there is a fixed and variable element.

**Share capital** A business sells shares in itself to raise funds.

**Shareholders** Are the individuals who own the shares in a business which makes them part owners in the organization.

**Short term finance** Funds a business raises for its normal operational activities that has a repayment period of less than 12 months.

**Single-union agreement** This is when an organisations and its employees agree that one union should represent all the employees of the business.

**Situational leadership** Where there the leadership depends on the task, situation and the employees being managed.

**Slowdown/go slow** Where employees work at the minimum pace required by their contract.

**Social factor** Culture, demography and attitudes of the people.

**Sole trader** An organisation owned and controlled by a single person.

**Span of control** This is the number of subordinates (workers) a manager is directly responsible for.

**Stakeholders** Any people, groups or organisations that have an interest in a particular organisation.

**STEEPLE analysis** A strategic planning tool used by organisations to focus on the different aspects of the external environment.

**Strategic alliance** An agreement between two businesses to manage a project but it is a less formal arrangement than a joint venture and does not involve creating a separate legal identity.

**Strategy** the long term plan that sets out the ways a business is going to achieve its corporate aims.

**Strike action** Unions instruct their members to stop working for a certain period of time.

**Subsidy** Funds governments provide to businesses to contribute to paying their operating costs over a given time period.

**SWOT analysis** a planning tool used by organisations as a method for guiding business strategy.

**Tactics** the specific techniques used by a business to achieve its objectives.

**Takeover** When one firm acquires more than a certain of number shares in another firm and effectively takes control of that business.

**Tall/vertical organisation structures** An organisation structure that has many levels in its hierarchy.

**Task culture** Decision making is focused on specific job or projects where workers are organised in teams.

**Team working** Where employees are organised into groups to work together to complete a particular job.

**Technological factor** How advances in equipment, machinery, communications and IT impact on organisations.

**Threat of redundancies** The employer say they will be forced make a number of workers redundant if an agreement is not reached because some employees jobs will no longer exist without an agreement.

**Trade credit** Where a business receives good or service on credit and agrees to pay for then at a point in the future (normally 30 – 90 days).

**Trade union** An organisation set up by employees to represent the views and protect the rights of those employees.

**Training** The process of improving the knowledge and skills of its employees to give them the ability to do their work more effectively.

**Unemployment** Number of people in the economy who are in the labour market actively seeking work but who do not have a job.

**Variable** Costs that do change as output changes.

**Venture capital** This is share capital finance that is provided by specialist investment organisations looking to take some ownership in a small or medium sized company.

**Vision statement** where an organisation sets out where the it would like to be in the long term based on its values.

**Wage piece rates** Worker are paid for each unit they produce.

**Wage time based** Payment to workers on a fixed time basis: hourly, daily and weekly.

**Work to rule** Employees refuse to do any work that is outside their employment contact.

# Index